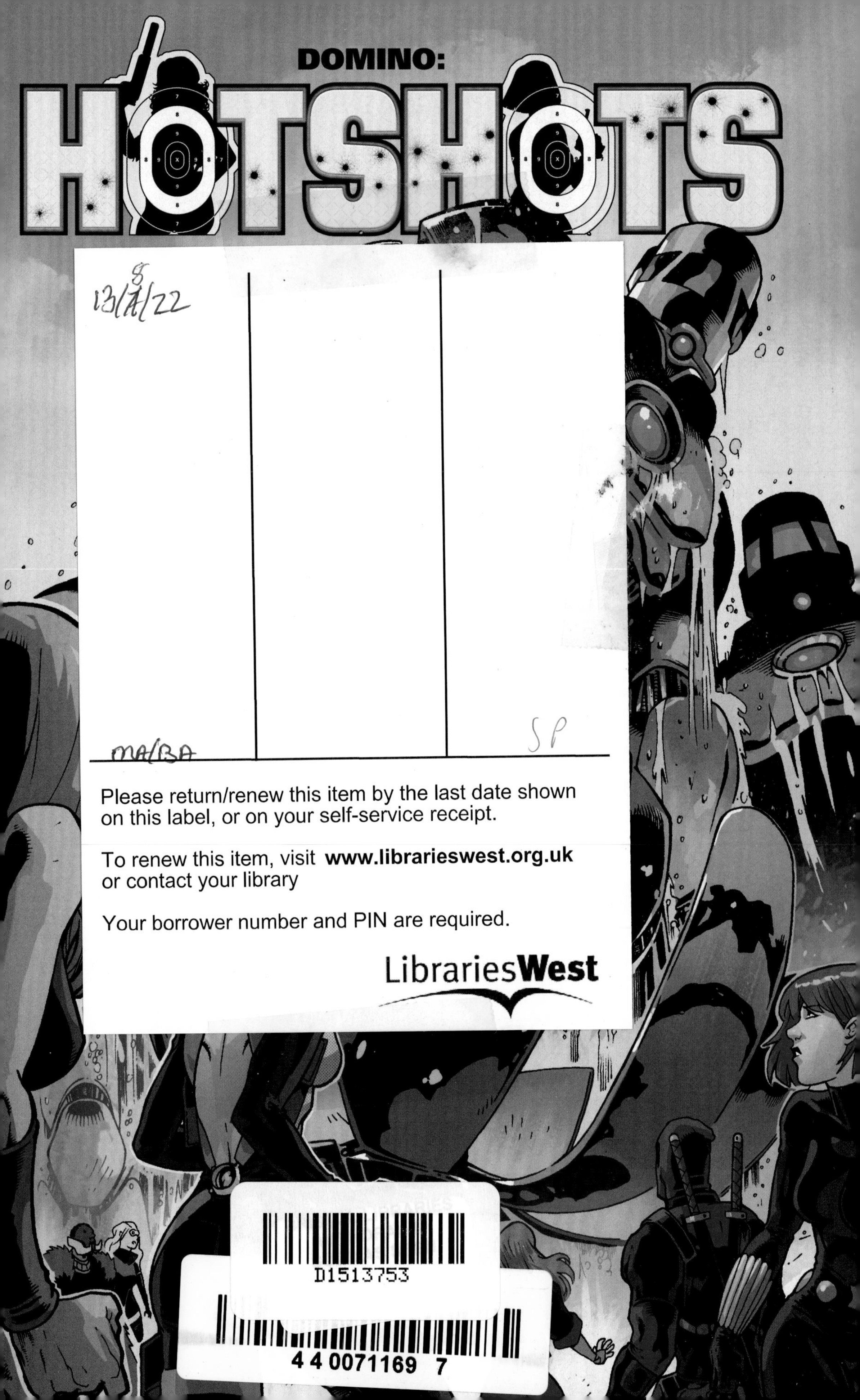
DOMINO:
HOTSHOTS

ALWAYS OUTMANNED
BUT NEVER OUTGUNNED

DOMINO: HOT

DOMINO. OUTLAW. DIAMONDBACK. ATLAS BEAR. WHITE FOX. BLACK WIDOW. SIX HIGHLY TRAINED WOMEN WITH UNIQUE SKILLS AND A HABIT OF GETTING INTO TIGHT SITUATIONS AND EVEN TIGHTER GETUPS. ALWAYS OUTMANNED BUT NEVER OUTGUNNED... UNDERESTIMATE THEM FOR THEIR LOOKS AT YOUR OWN RISK: THEY TAKE THE SHOTS NO ONE ELSE WILL!

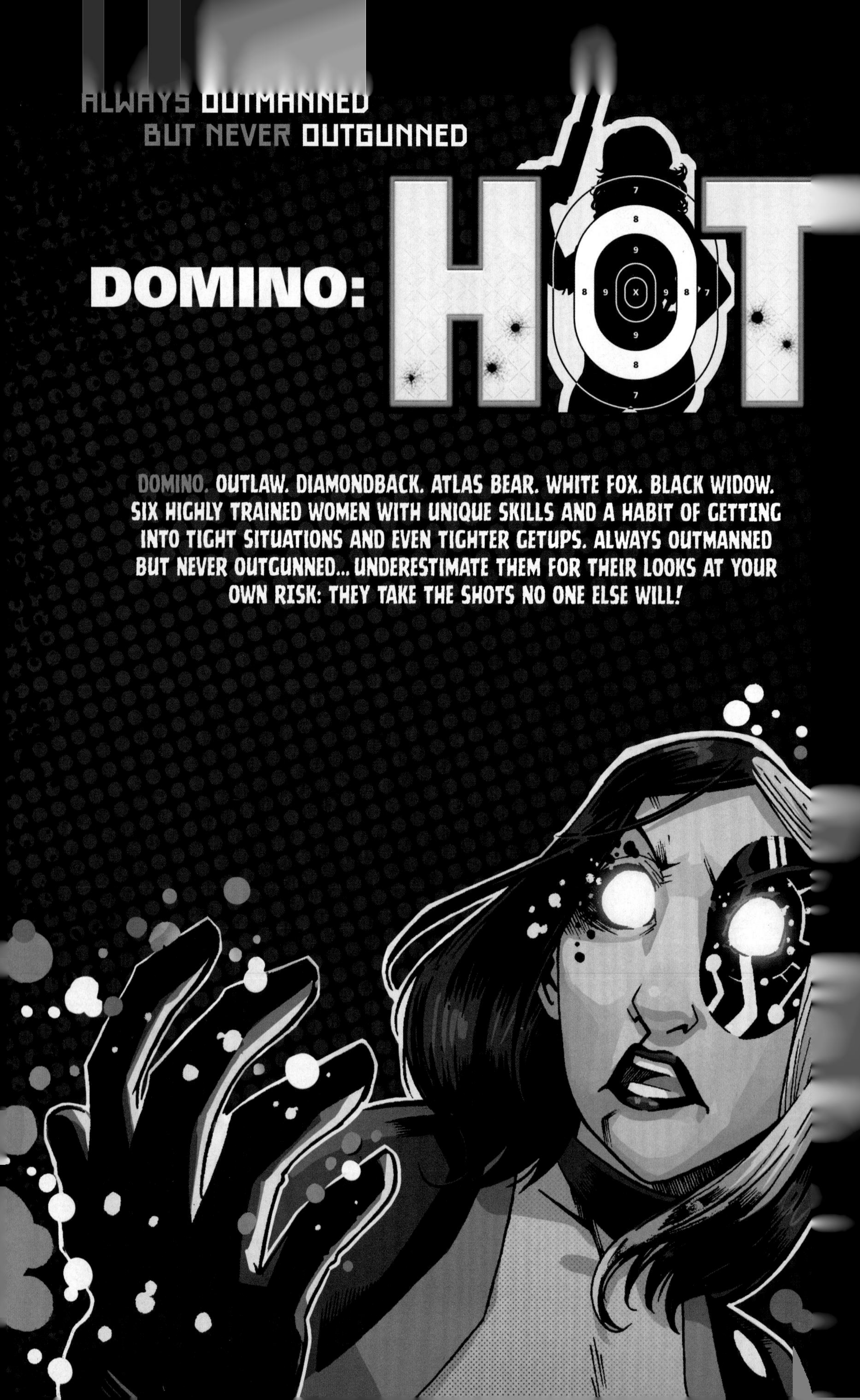

SHOTS

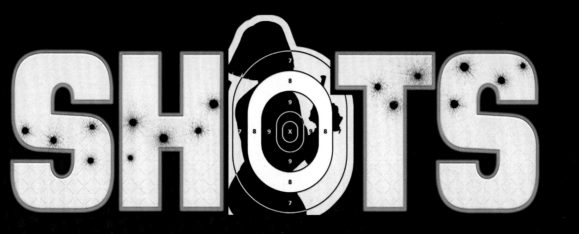

GAIL SIMONE
WRITER

DAVID BALDEÓN & MICHAEL SHELFER (#3-5)
ARTISTS

JIM CHARALAMPIDIS
COLOR ARTIST

CRAIG YEUNG
ADDITIONAL INKS, #4

VC's CLAYTON COWLES
LETTERER

R.B. SILVA WITH NOLAN WOODARD (#1), FRANK D'ARMATA (#2-3), DIEGO RODRIGUEZ (#4) & FEDERICO BLEE (#5)
COVER ARTISTS

CHRIS ROBINSON
EDITOR

JORDAN D. WHITE
X-MEN GROUP EDITOR

COLLECTION EDITOR **JENNIFER GRÜNWALD** • ASSISTANT EDITOR **CAITLIN O'CONNELL**
ASSOCIATE MANAGING EDITOR **KATERI WOODY** • EDITOR, SPECIAL PROJECTS **MARK D. BEAZLEY**
VP PRODUCTION & SPECIAL PROJECTS **JEFF YOUNGQUIST** • BOOK DESIGNER **JAY BOWEN**

SVP PRINT, SALES & MARKETING **DAVID GABRIEL** • DIRECTOR, LICENSED PUBLISHING **SVEN LARSEN**
EDITOR IN CHIEF **C.B. CEBULSKI** • CHIEF CREATIVE OFFICER **JOE QUESADA**
PRESIDENT **DAN BUCKLEY** • EXECUTIVE PRODUCER **ALAN FINE**

DOMINO: HOTSHOTS. Contains material originally published in magazine form as DOMINO: HOTSHOTS #1-5. First printing 2019. ISBN 978-1-302-91833-0. Published by MARVEL WORLDWIDE, INC., a subsidiary of MARVEL ENTERTAINMENT, LLC. OFFICE OF PUBLICATION: 135 West 50th Street, New York, NY 10020. © 2019 MARVEL No similarity between any of the names, characters, persons, and/or institutions in this magazine with those of any living or dead person or institution is intended, and any such similarity which may exist is purely coincidental. **Printed in Canada.** DAN BUCKLEY, President, Marvel Entertainment; JOHN NEE, Publisher; JOE QUESADA, Chief Creative Officer; TOM BREVOORT, SVP of Publishing; DAVID BOGART, Associate Publisher & SVP of Talent Affairs; DAVID GABRIEL, SVP of Sales & Marketing, Publishing; JEFF YOUNGQUIST, VP of Production & Special Projects; DAN CARR, Executive

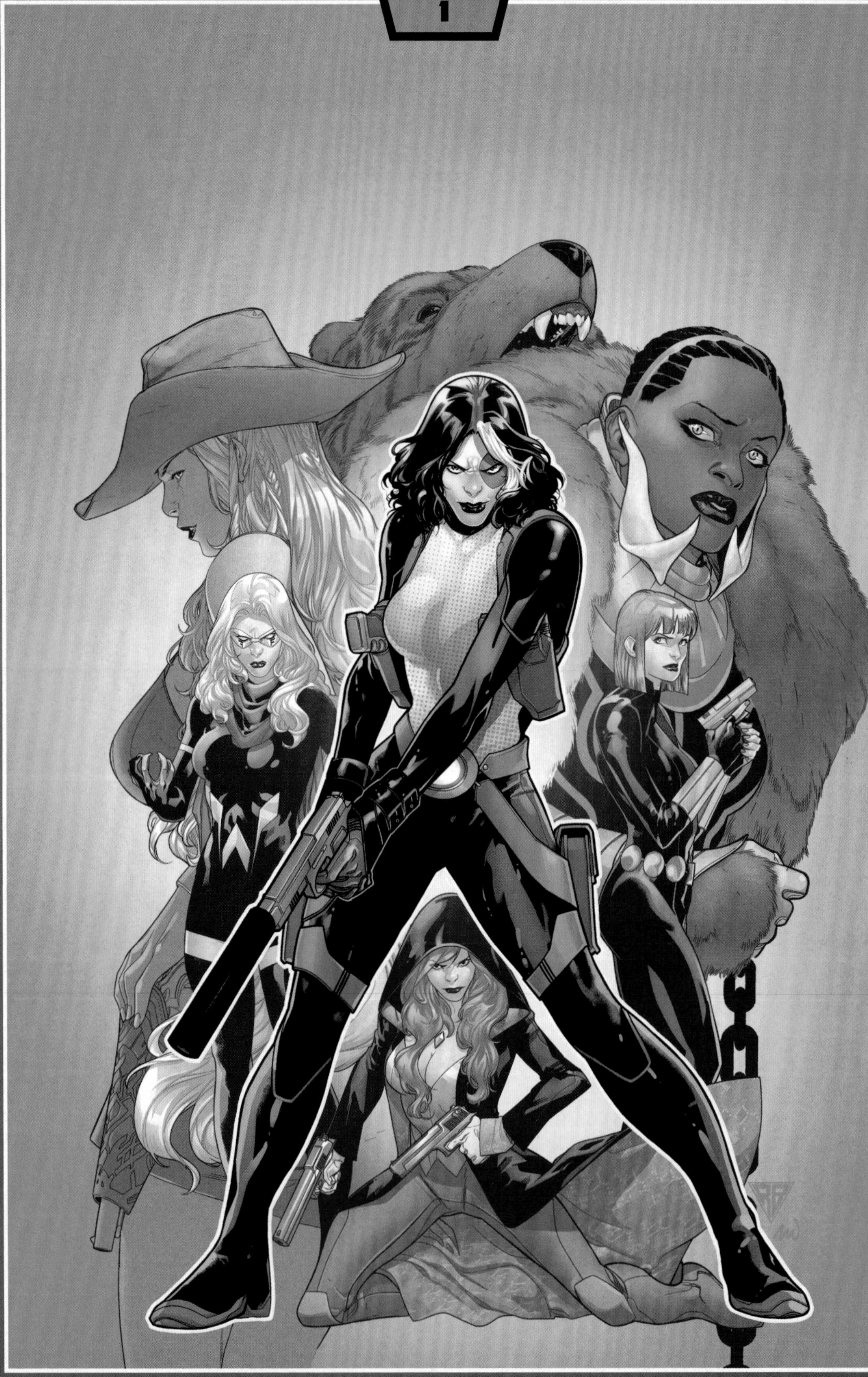

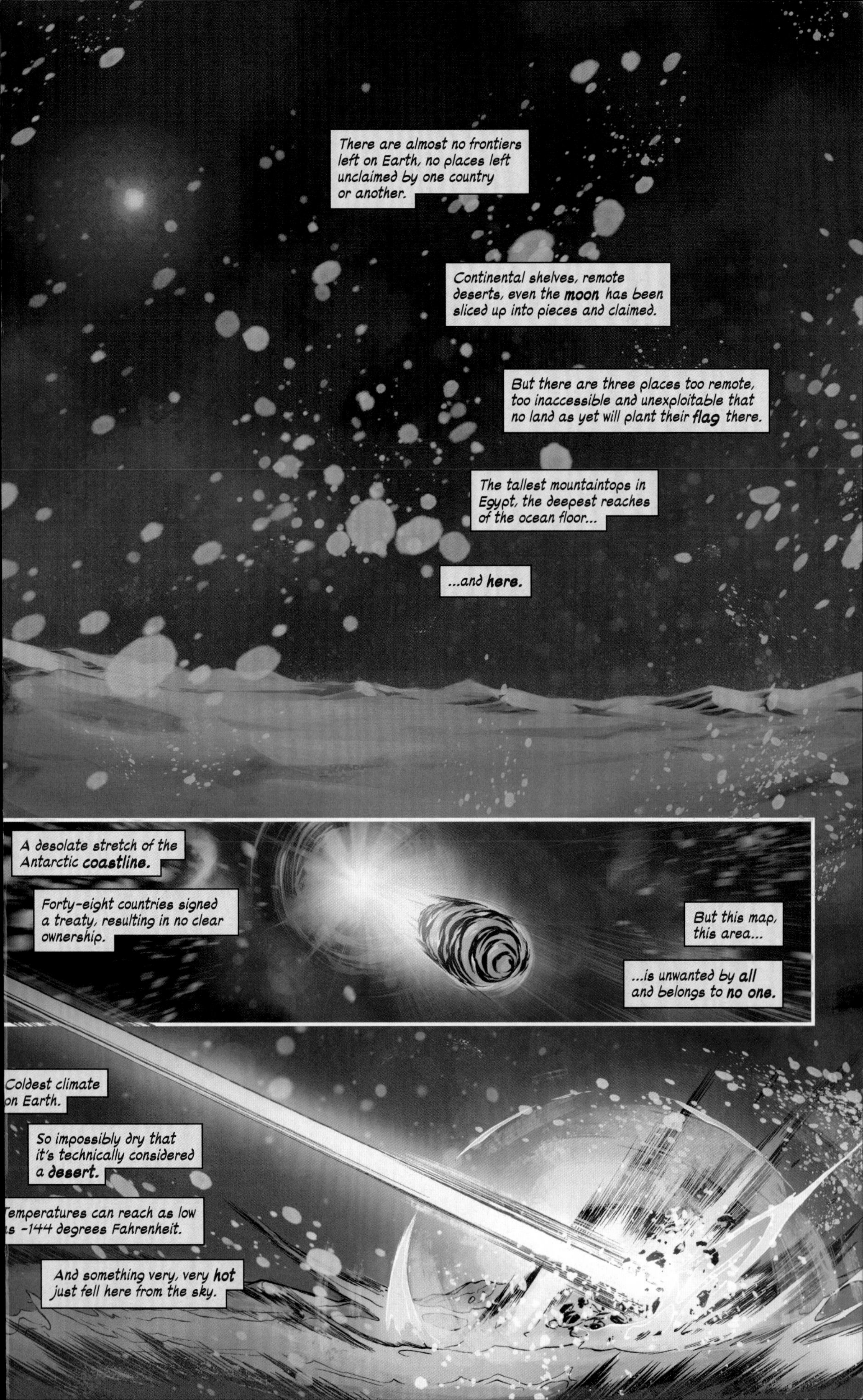
There are almost no frontiers left on Earth, no places left unclaimed by one country or another.
Continental shelves, remote deserts, even the moon has been sliced up into pieces and claimed.
But there are three places too remote, too inaccessible and unexploitable that no land as yet will plant their flag there.
The tallest mountaintops in Egypt, the deepest reaches of the ocean floor...
...and here.
A desolate stretch of the Antarctic coastline.
Forty-eight countries signed a treaty, resulting in no clear ownership.
But this map, this area...
...is unwanted by all and belongs to no one.
Coldest climate on Earth.
So impossibly dry that it's technically considered a desert.
Temperatures can reach as low as -144 degrees Fahrenheit.
And something very, very hot just fell here from the sky.

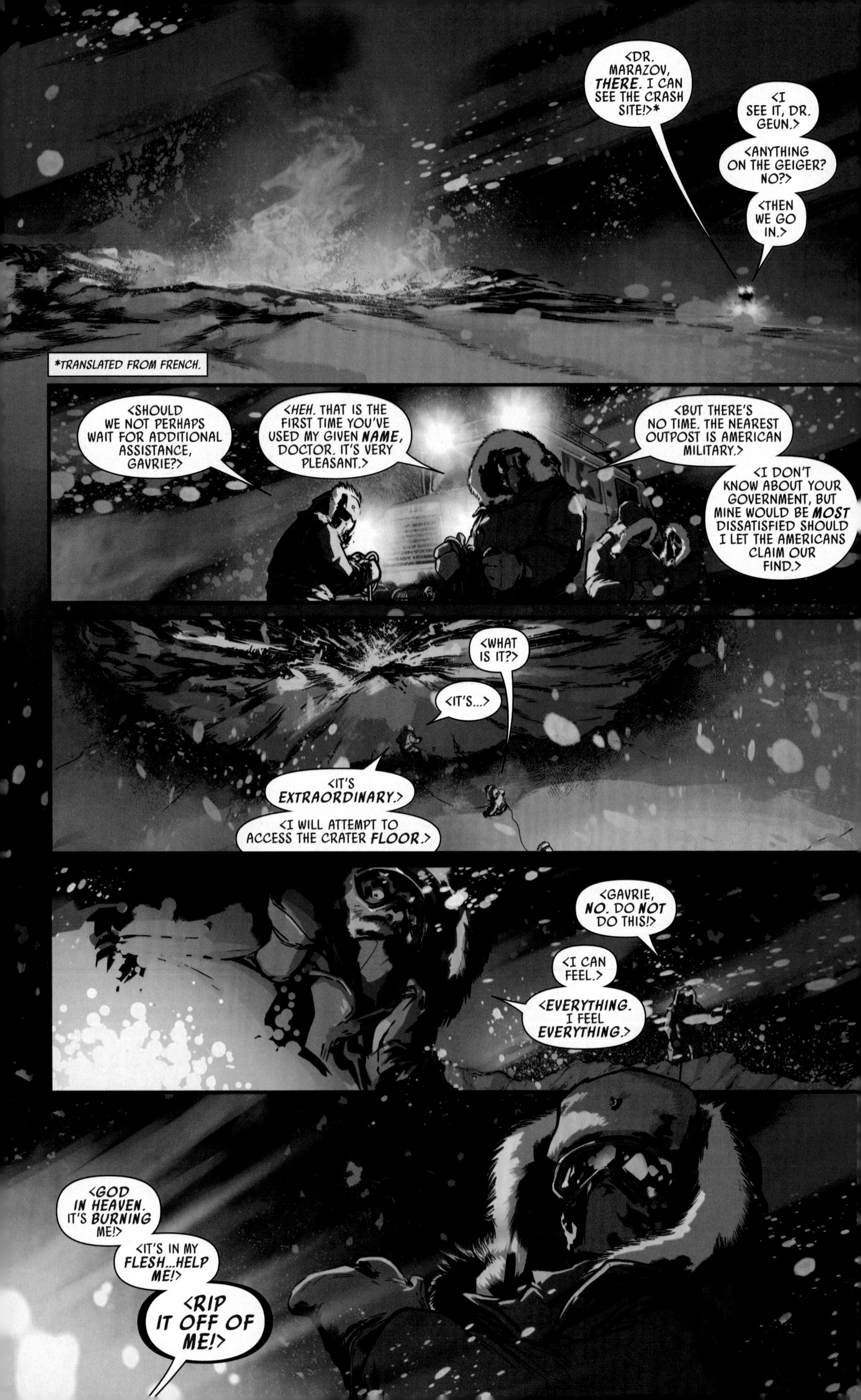

<DR. MARAZOV, THERE. I CAN SEE THE CRASH SITE!>*
<I SEE IT, DR. GEUN.>
<ANYTHING ON THE GEIGER? NO?>
<THEN WE GO IN.>
*TRANSLATED FROM FRENCH.
<SHOULD WE NOT PERHAPS WAIT FOR ADDITIONAL ASSISTANCE, GAVRIE?>
<HEH. THAT IS THE FIRST TIME YOU'VE USED MY GIVEN NAME, DOCTOR. IT'S VERY PLEASANT.>
<BUT THERE'S NO TIME. THE NEAREST OUTPOST IS AMERICAN MILITARY.>
<I DON'T KNOW ABOUT YOUR GOVERNMENT, BUT MINE WOULD BE MOST DISSATISFIED SHOULD I LET THE AMERICANS CLAIM OUR FIND.>
<WHAT IS IT?>
<IT'S...>
<IT'S EXTRAORDINARY.>
<I WILL ATTEMPT TO ACCESS THE CRATER FLOOR.>
<GAVRIE, NO. DO NOT DO THIS!>
<I CAN FEEL.>
<EVERYTHING. I FEEL EVERYTHING.>
<GOD IN HEAVEN. IT'S BURNING ME!>
<IT'S IN MY FLESH...HELP ME!>
<RIP IT OFF OF ME!>

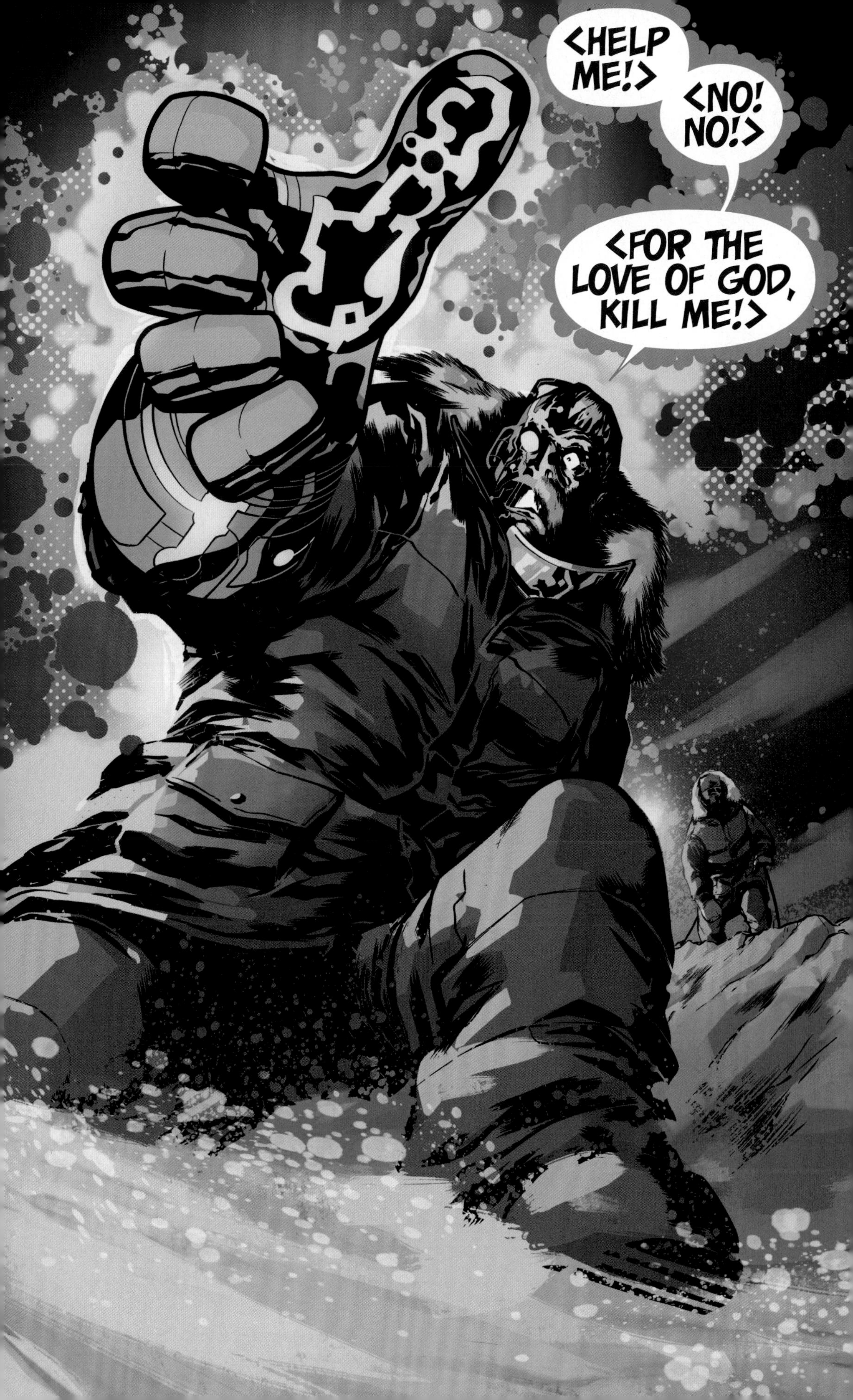
<HELP ME!>
<NO! NO!>
<FOR THE LOVE OF GOD, KILL ME!>

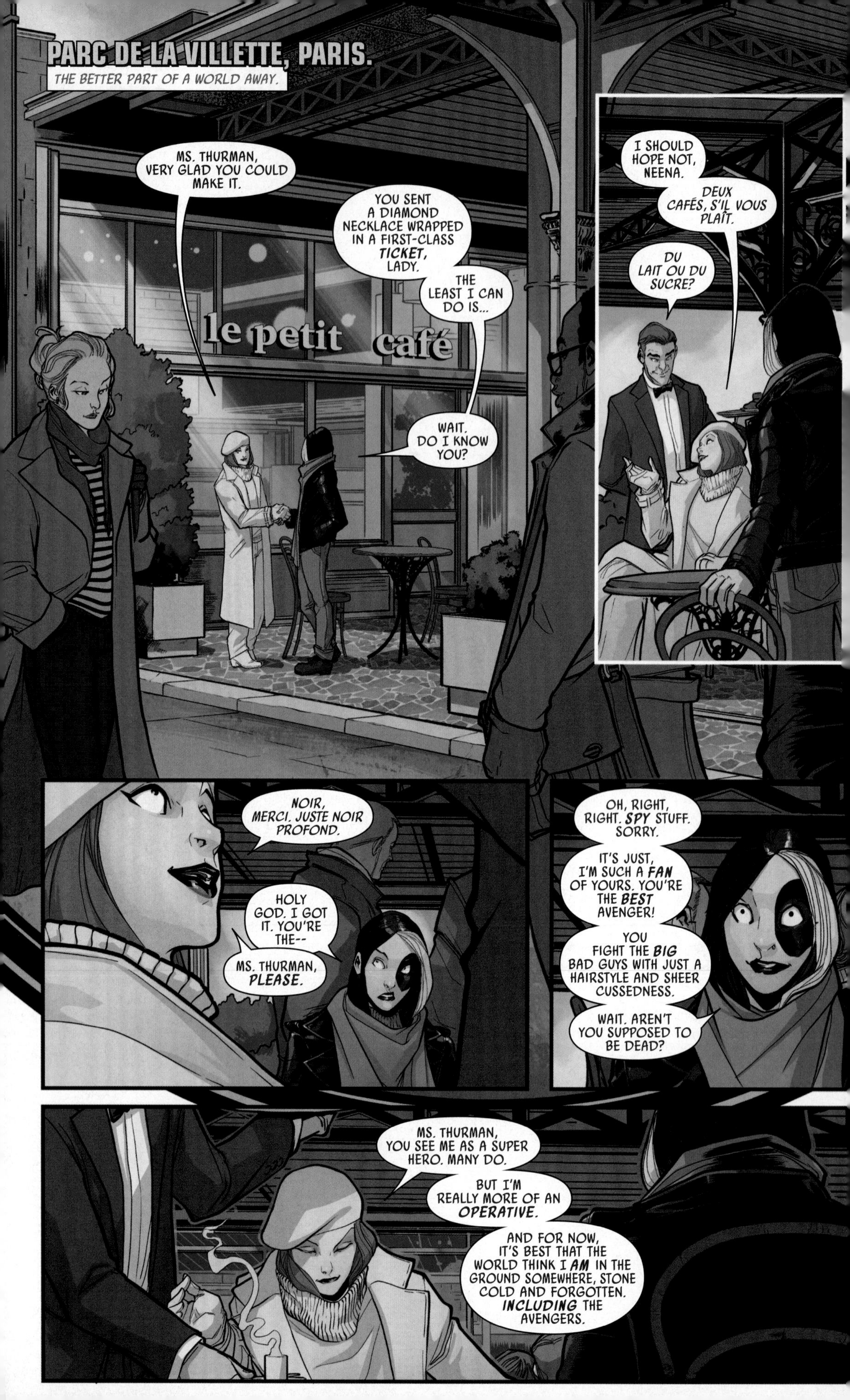
PARC DE LA VILLETTE, PARIS.
THE BETTER PART OF A WORLD AWAY.
MS. THURMAN, VERY GLAD YOU COULD MAKE IT.
YOU SENT A DIAMOND NECKLACE WRAPPED IN A FIRST-CLASS TICKET, LADY.
THE LEAST I CAN DO IS...
le petit café
WAIT. DO I KNOW YOU?
I SHOULD HOPE NOT, NEENA.
DEUX CAFÉS, S'IL VOUS PLAÎT.
DU LAIT OU DU SUCRE?
NOIR, MERCI. JUSTE NOIR PROFOND.
HOLY GOD. I GOT IT. YOU'RE THE--
MS. THURMAN, PLEASE.
OH, RIGHT, RIGHT. SPY STUFF. SORRY.
IT'S JUST, I'M SUCH A FAN OF YOURS. YOU'RE THE BEST AVENGER!
YOU FIGHT THE BIG BAD GUYS WITH JUST A HAIRSTYLE AND SHEER CUSSEDNESS.
WAIT. AREN'T YOU SUPPOSED TO BE DEAD?
MS. THURMAN, YOU SEE ME AS A SUPER HERO. MANY DO.
BUT I'M REALLY MORE OF AN OPERATIVE.
AND FOR NOW, IT'S BEST THAT THE WORLD THINK I AM IN THE GROUND SOMEWHERE, STONE COLD AND FORGOTTEN. INCLUDING THE AVENGERS.

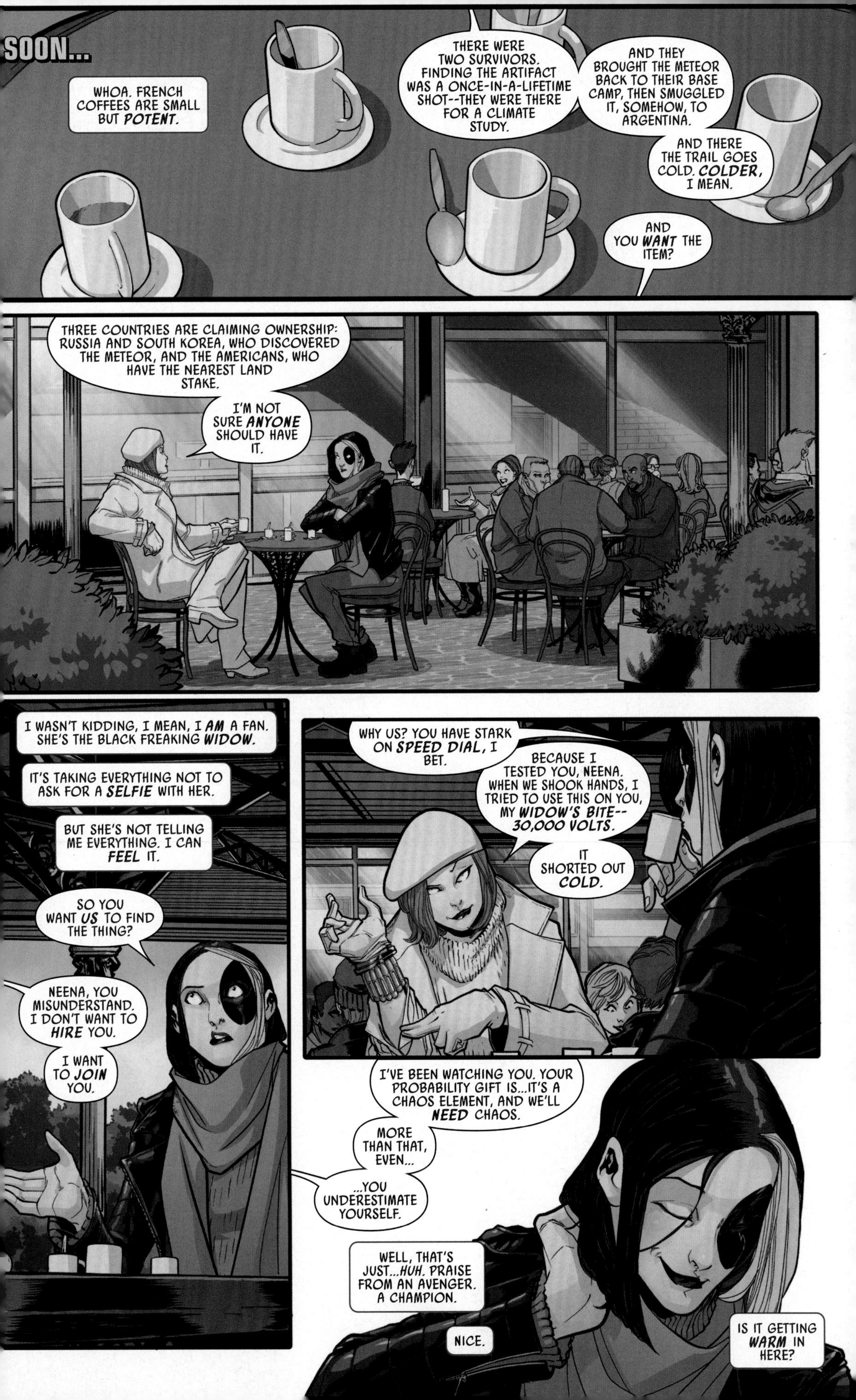
SOON...
WHOA. FRENCH COFFEES ARE SMALL BUT POTENT.
THERE WERE TWO SURVIVORS. FINDING THE ARTIFACT WAS A ONCE-IN-A-LIFETIME SHOT--THEY WERE THERE FOR A CLIMATE STUDY.
AND THEY BROUGHT THE METEOR BACK TO THEIR BASE CAMP, THEN SMUGGLED IT, SOMEHOW, TO ARGENTINA.
AND THERE THE TRAIL GOES COLD. COLDER, I MEAN.
AND YOU WANT THE ITEM?
THREE COUNTRIES ARE CLAIMING OWNERSHIP: RUSSIA AND SOUTH KOREA, WHO DISCOVERED THE METEOR, AND THE AMERICANS, WHO HAVE THE NEAREST LAND STAKE.
I'M NOT SURE ANYONE SHOULD HAVE IT.
I WASN'T KIDDING, I MEAN, I AM A FAN. SHE'S THE BLACK FREAKING WIDOW.
IT'S TAKING EVERYTHING NOT TO ASK FOR A SELFIE WITH HER.
BUT SHE'S NOT TELLING ME EVERYTHING. I CAN FEEL IT.
SO YOU WANT US TO FIND THE THING?
NEENA, YOU MISUNDERSTAND. I DON'T WANT TO HIRE YOU.
I WANT TO JOIN YOU.
WHY US? YOU HAVE STARK ON SPEED DIAL, I BET.
BECAUSE I TESTED YOU, NEENA. WHEN WE SHOOK HANDS, I TRIED TO USE THIS ON YOU, MY WIDOW'S BITE-- 30,000 VOLTS.
IT SHORTED OUT COLD.
I'VE BEEN WATCHING YOU. YOUR PROBABILITY GIFT IS...IT'S A CHAOS ELEMENT, AND WE'LL NEED CHAOS.
MORE THAN THAT, EVEN...
...YOU UNDERESTIMATE YOURSELF.
WELL, THAT'S JUST...HUH. PRAISE FROM AN AVENGER. A CHAMPION.
NICE.
IS IT GETTING WARM IN HERE?

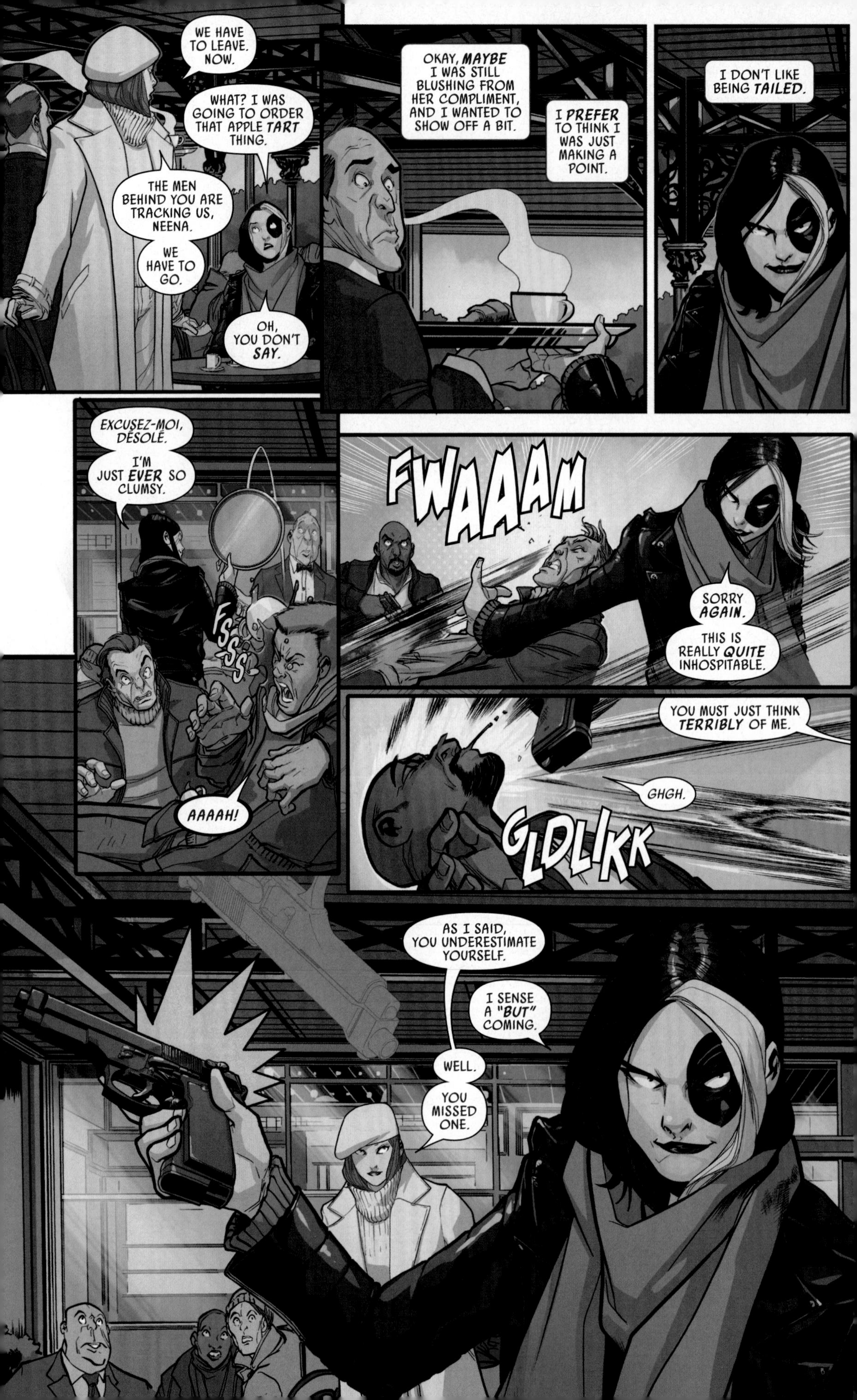
WE HAVE TO LEAVE. NOW.
WHAT? I WAS GOING TO ORDER THAT APPLE TART THING.
THE MEN BEHIND YOU ARE TRACKING US, NEENA.
WE HAVE TO GO.
OH, YOU DON'T SAY.
OKAY, MAYBE I WAS STILL BLUSHING FROM HER COMPLIMENT, AND I WANTED TO SHOW OFF A BIT.
I PREFER TO THINK I WAS JUST MAKING A POINT.
I DON'T LIKE BEING TAILED.
EXCUSEZ-MOI, DÉSOLÉ.
I'M JUST EVER SO CLUMSY.
FSSSS
AAAAH!
FWAAAAM
SORRY AGAIN.
THIS IS REALLY QUITE INHOSPITABLE.
YOU MUST JUST THINK TERRIBLY OF ME.
GHGH.
GLDLIKK
AS I SAID, YOU UNDERESTIMATE YOURSELF.
I SENSE A "BUT" COMING.
WELL.
YOU MISSED ONE.

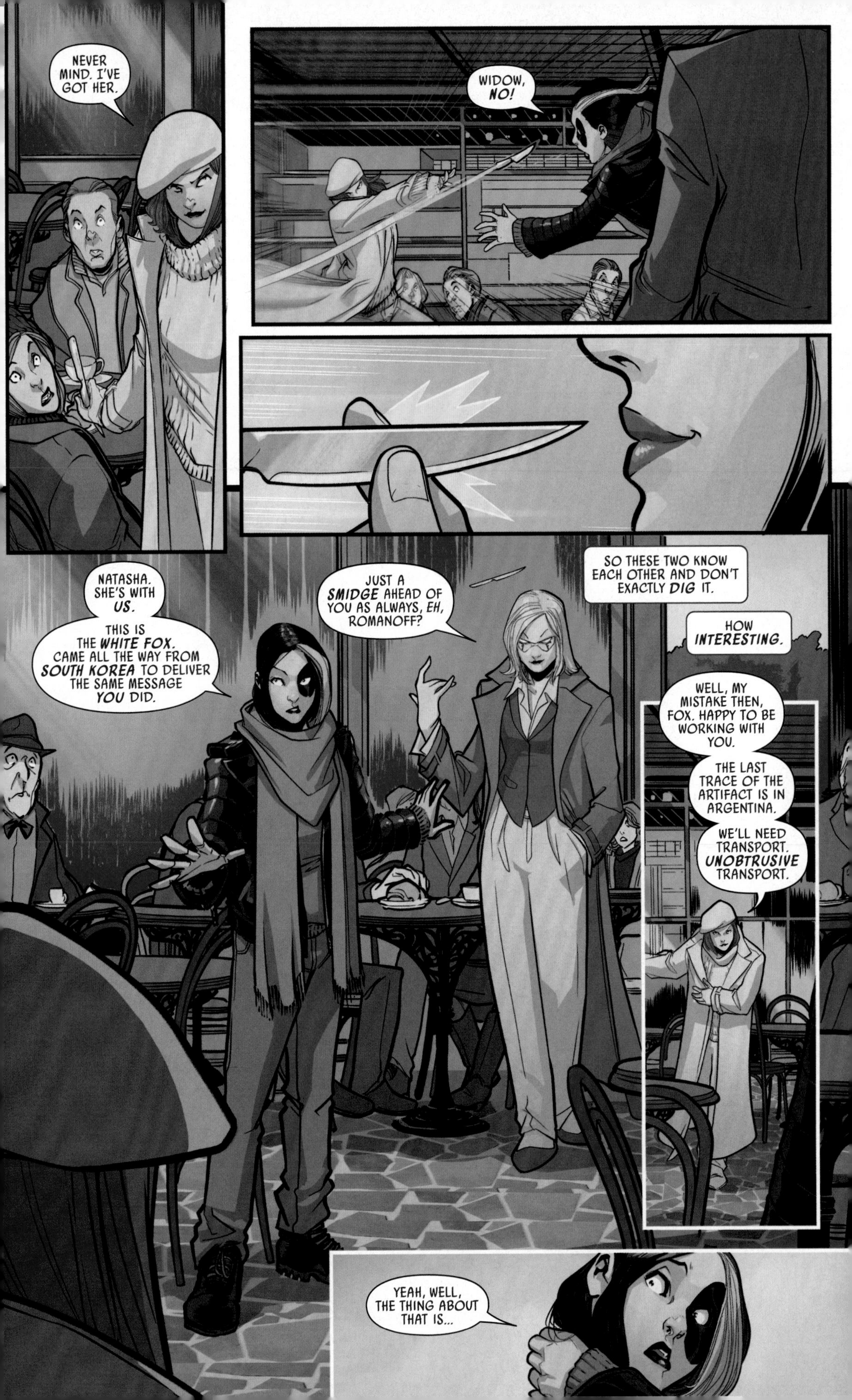
NEVER MIND. I'VE GOT HER.
WIDOW, NO!
NATASHA. SHE'S WITH US.
THIS IS THE WHITE FOX. CAME ALL THE WAY FROM SOUTH KOREA TO DELIVER THE SAME MESSAGE YOU DID.
JUST A SMIDGE AHEAD OF YOU AS ALWAYS, EH, ROMANOFF?
SO THESE TWO KNOW EACH OTHER AND DON'T EXACTLY DIG IT.
HOW INTERESTING.
WELL, MY MISTAKE THEN, FOX. HAPPY TO BE WORKING WITH YOU.
THE LAST TRACE OF THE ARTIFACT IS IN ARGENTINA.
WE'LL NEED TRANSPORT. UNOBTRUSIVE TRANSPORT.
YEAH, WELL, THE THING ABOUT THAT IS...

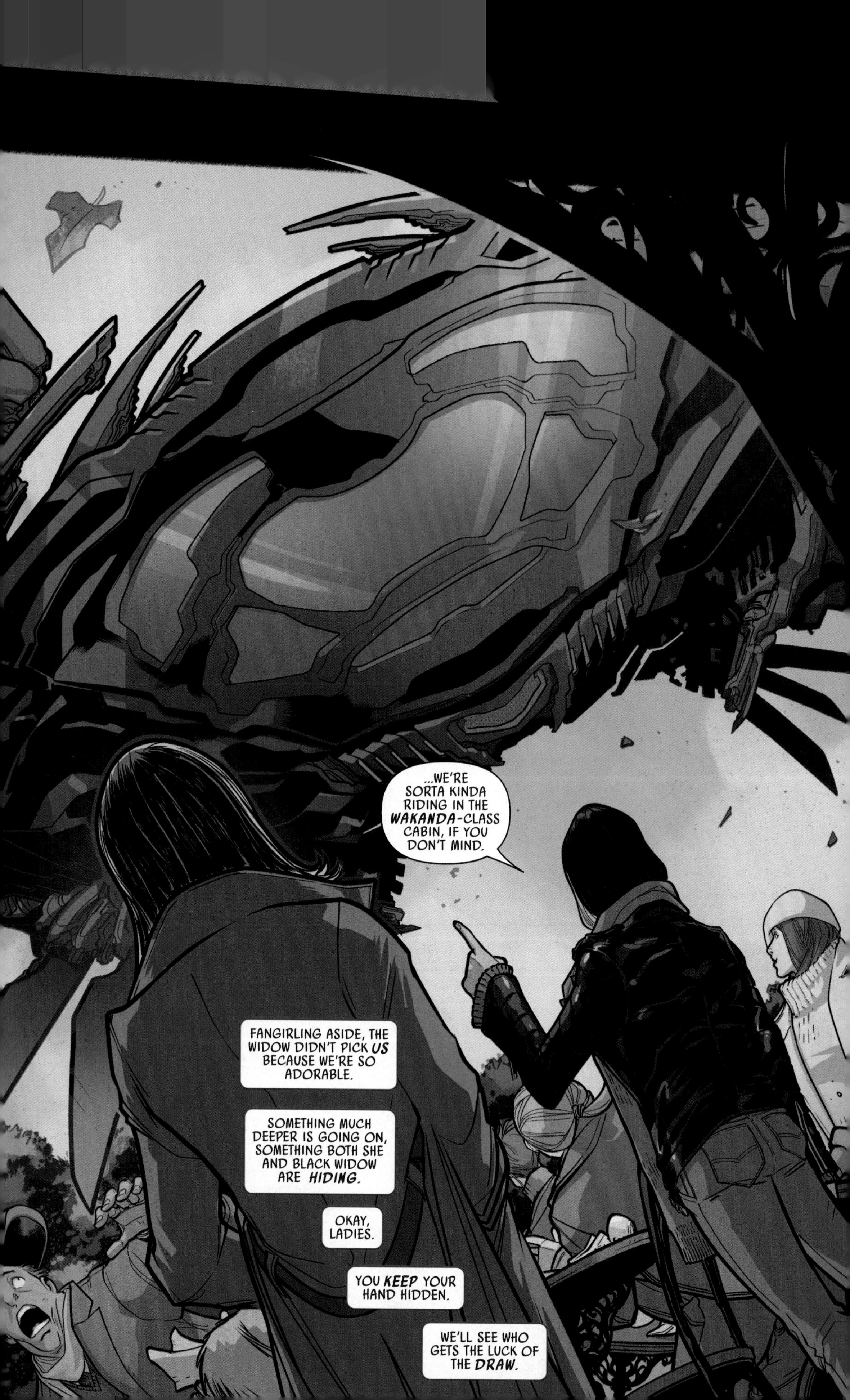
...WE'RE SORTA KINDA RIDING IN THE WAKANDA-CLASS CABIN, IF YOU DON'T MIND.
FANGIRLING ASIDE, THE WIDOW DIDN'T PICK US BECAUSE WE'RE SO ADORABLE.
SOMETHING MUCH DEEPER IS GOING ON, SOMETHING BOTH SHE AND BLACK WIDOW ARE HIDING.
OKAY, LADIES.
YOU KEEP YOUR HAND HIDDEN.
WE'LL SEE WHO GETS THE LUCK OF THE DRAW.

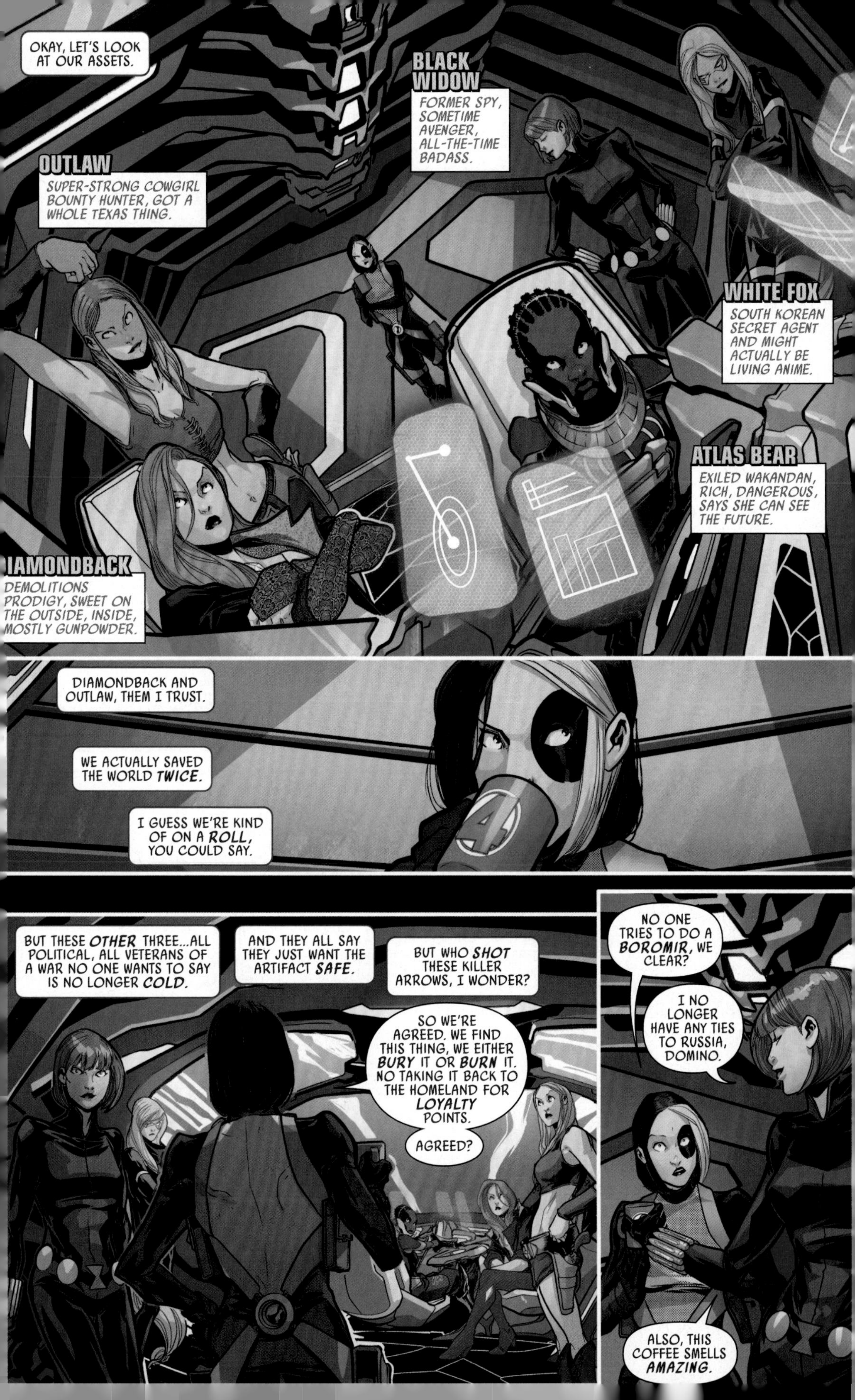
OKAY, LET'S LOOK AT OUR ASSETS.
BLACK WIDOW
FORMER SPY, SOMETIME AVENGER, ALL-THE-TIME BADASS.
OUTLAW
SUPER-STRONG COWGIRL BOUNTY HUNTER, GOT A WHOLE TEXAS THING.
WHITE FOX
SOUTH KOREAN SECRET AGENT AND MIGHT ACTUALLY BE LIVING ANIME.
ATLAS BEAR
EXILED WAKANDAN, RICH, DANGEROUS, SAYS SHE CAN SEE THE FUTURE.
IAMONDBACK
DEMOLITIONS PRODIGY, SWEET ON THE OUTSIDE, INSIDE, MOSTLY GUNPOWDER.
DIAMONDBACK AND OUTLAW, THEM I TRUST.
WE ACTUALLY SAVED THE WORLD TWICE.
I GUESS WE'RE KIND OF ON A ROLL, YOU COULD SAY.
BUT THESE OTHER THREE...ALL POLITICAL, ALL VETERANS OF A WAR NO ONE WANTS TO SAY IS NO LONGER COLD.
AND THEY ALL SAY THEY JUST WANT THE ARTIFACT SAFE.
BUT WHO SHOT THESE KILLER ARROWS, I WONDER?
SO WE'RE AGREED. WE FIND THIS THING, WE EITHER BURY IT OR BURN IT. NO TAKING IT BACK TO THE HOMELAND FOR LOYALTY POINTS.
AGREED?
NO ONE TRIES TO DO A BOROMIR, WE CLEAR?
I NO LONGER HAVE ANY TIES TO RUSSIA, DOMINO.
ALSO, THIS COFFEE SMELLS AMAZING.

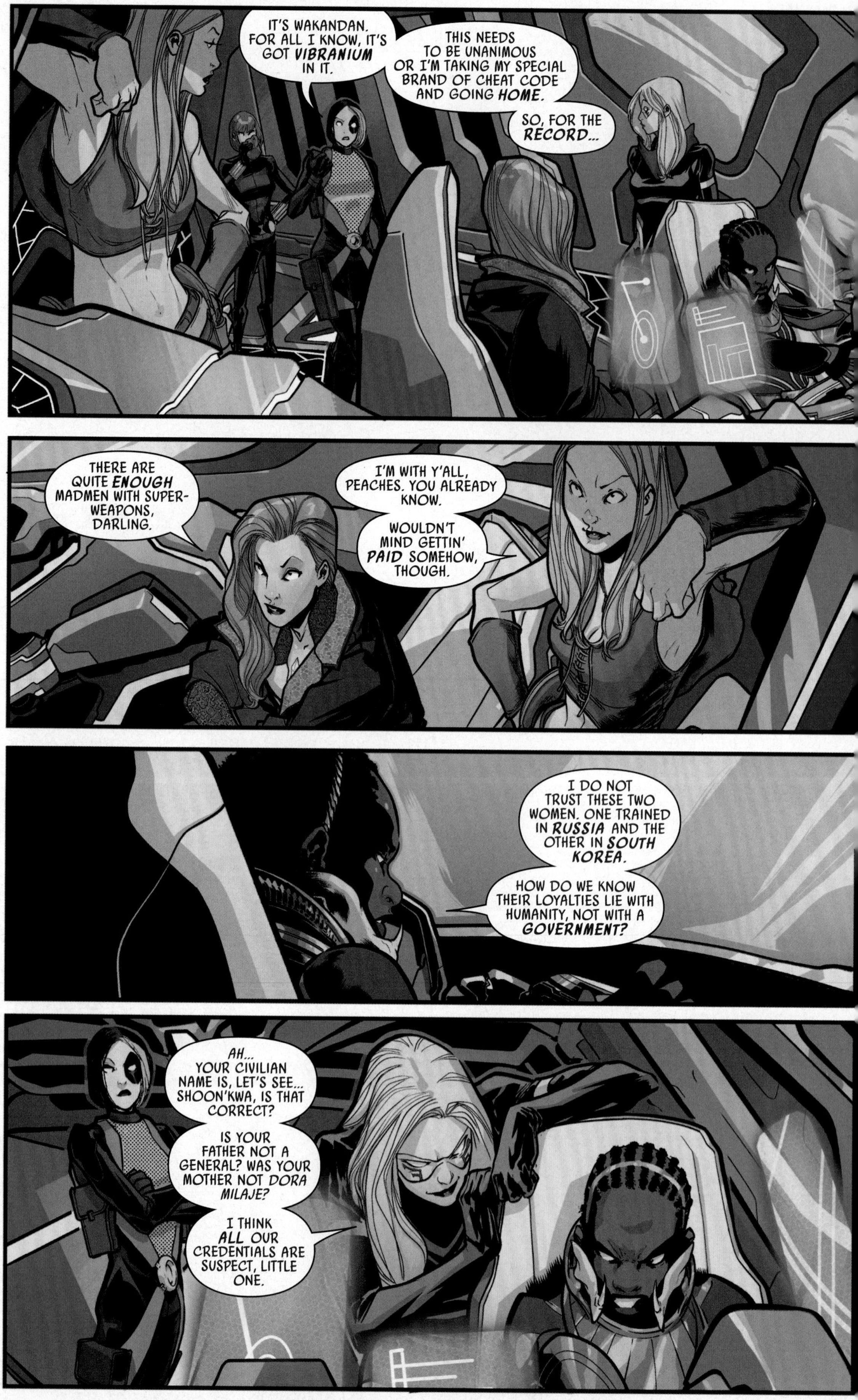
IT'S WAKANDAN. FOR ALL I KNOW, IT'S GOT VIBRANIUM IN IT.
THIS NEEDS TO BE UNANIMOUS OR I'M TAKING MY SPECIAL BRAND OF CHEAT CODE AND GOING HOME.
SO, FOR THE RECORD...
THERE ARE QUITE ENOUGH MADMEN WITH SUPER-WEAPONS, DARLING.
I'M WITH Y'ALL, PEACHES. YOU ALREADY KNOW.
WOULDN'T MIND GETTIN' PAID SOMEHOW, THOUGH.
I DO NOT TRUST THESE TWO WOMEN. ONE TRAINED IN RUSSIA AND THE OTHER IN SOUTH KOREA.
HOW DO WE KNOW THEIR LOYALTIES LIE WITH HUMANITY, NOT WITH A GOVERNMENT?
AH... YOUR CIVILIAN NAME IS, LET'S SEE... SHOON'KWA, IS THAT CORRECT?
IS YOUR FATHER NOT A GENERAL? WAS YOUR MOTHER NOT DORA MILAJE?
I THINK ALL OUR CREDENTIALS ARE SUSPECT, LITTLE ONE.

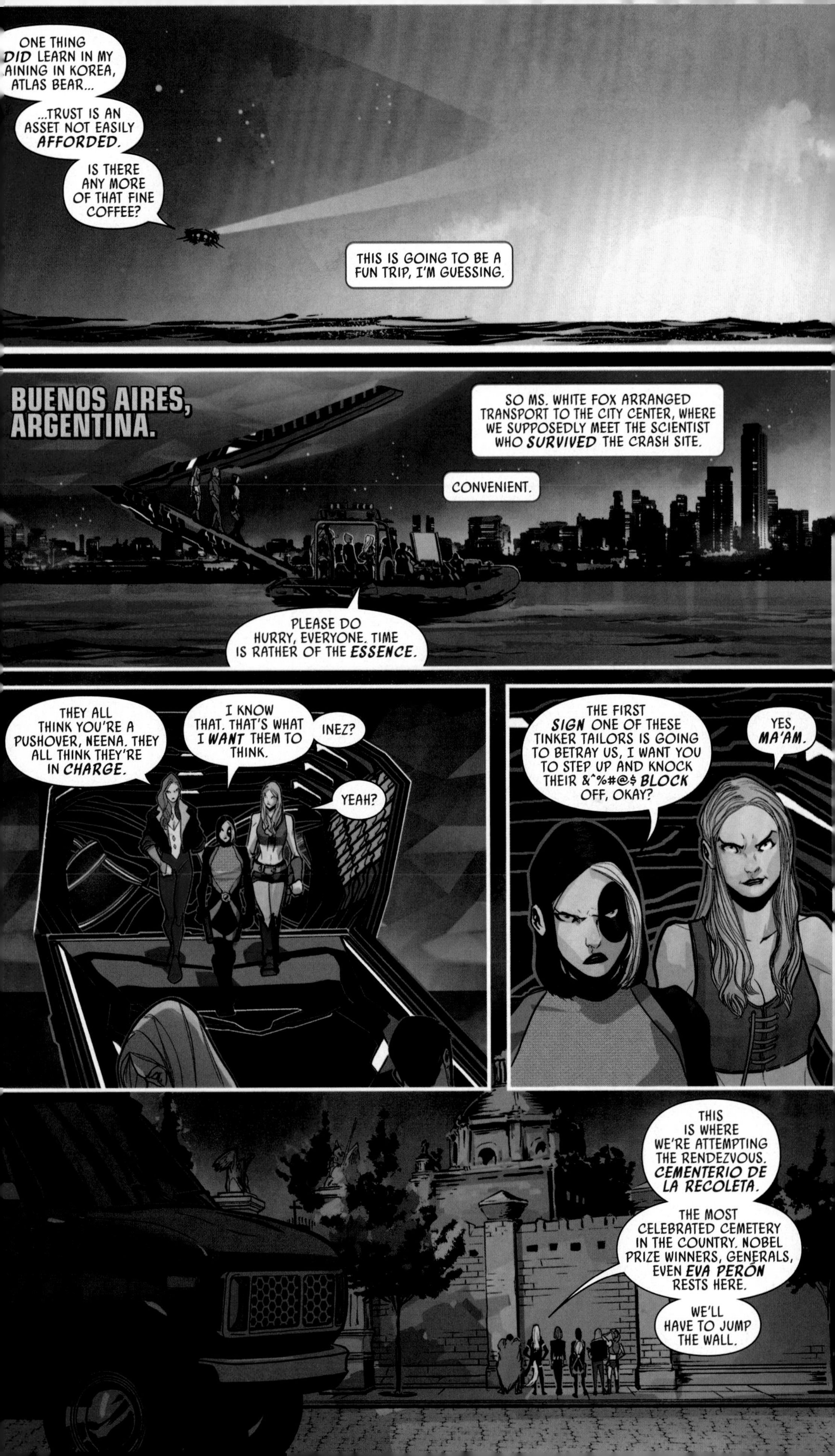
ONE THING DID LEARN IN MY AINING IN KOREA, ATLAS BEAR...
...TRUST IS AN ASSET NOT EASILY AFFORDED.
IS THERE ANY MORE OF THAT FINE COFFEE?
THIS IS GOING TO BE A FUN TRIP, I'M GUESSING.
BUENOS AIRES, ARGENTINA.
SO MS. WHITE FOX ARRANGED TRANSPORT TO THE CITY CENTER, WHERE WE SUPPOSEDLY MEET THE SCIENTIST WHO SURVIVED THE CRASH SITE.
CONVENIENT.
PLEASE DO HURRY, EVERYONE. TIME IS RATHER OF THE ESSENCE.
THEY ALL THINK YOU'RE A PUSHOVER, NEENA. THEY ALL THINK THEY'RE IN CHARGE.
I KNOW THAT. THAT'S WHAT I WANT THEM TO THINK.
INEZ?
YEAH?
THE FIRST SIGN ONE OF THESE TINKER TAILORS IS GOING TO BETRAY US, I WANT YOU TO STEP UP AND KNOCK THEIR &^%#@$ BLOCK OFF, OKAY?
YES, MA'AM.
THIS IS WHERE WE'RE ATTEMPTING THE RENDEZVOUS. CEMENTERIO DE LA RECOLETA.
THE MOST CELEBRATED CEMETERY IN THE COUNTRY. NOBEL PRIZE WINNERS, GENERALS, EVEN EVA PERÓN RESTS HERE.
WE'LL HAVE TO JUMP THE WALL.

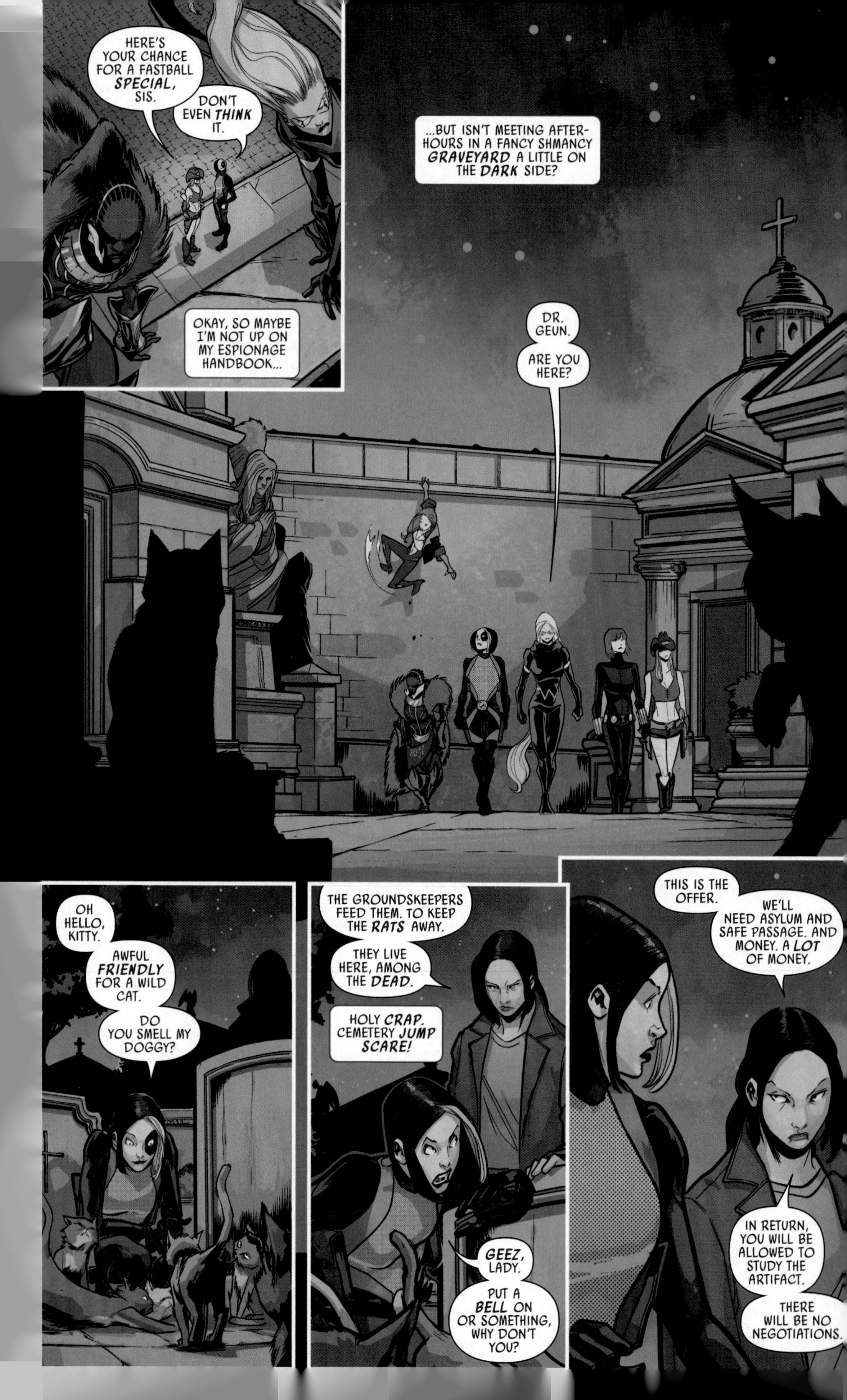
HERE'S YOUR CHANCE FOR A FASTBALL SPECIAL, SIS.
DON'T EVEN THINK IT.
OKAY, SO MAYBE I'M NOT UP ON MY ESPIONAGE HANDBOOK...
...BUT ISN'T MEETING AFTER-HOURS IN A FANCY SHMANCY GRAVEYARD A LITTLE ON THE DARK SIDE?
DR. GEUN.
ARE YOU HERE?
OH HELLO, KITTY.
AWFUL FRIENDLY FOR A WILD CAT.
DO YOU SMELL MY DOGGY?
THE GROUNDSKEEPERS FEED THEM. TO KEEP THE RATS AWAY.
THEY LIVE HERE, AMONG THE DEAD.
HOLY CRAP. CEMETERY JUMP SCARE!
GEEZ, LADY.
PUT A BELL ON OR SOMETHING, WHY DON'T YOU?
THIS IS THE OFFER.
WE'LL NEED ASYLUM AND SAFE PASSAGE. AND MONEY. A LOT OF MONEY.
IN RETURN, YOU WILL BE ALLOWED TO STUDY THE ARTIFACT.
THERE WILL BE NO NEGOTIATIONS.

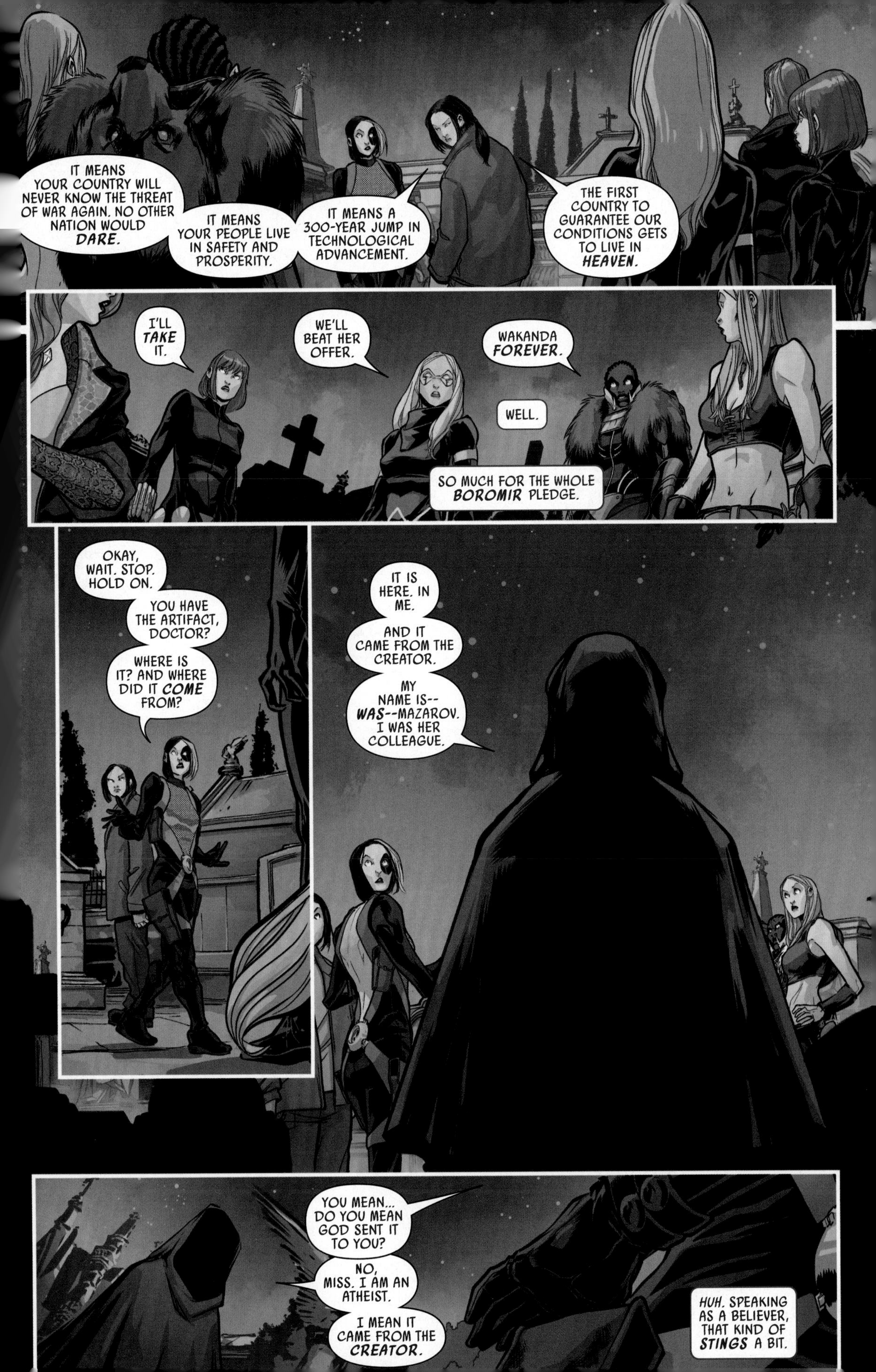
IT MEANS YOUR COUNTRY WILL NEVER KNOW THE THREAT OF WAR AGAIN. NO OTHER NATION WOULD DARE.
IT MEANS YOUR PEOPLE LIVE IN SAFETY AND PROSPERITY.
IT MEANS A 300-YEAR JUMP IN TECHNOLOGICAL ADVANCEMENT.
THE FIRST COUNTRY TO GUARANTEE OUR CONDITIONS GETS TO LIVE IN HEAVEN.
I'LL TAKE IT.
WE'LL BEAT HER OFFER.
WAKANDA FOREVER.
WELL.
SO MUCH FOR THE WHOLE BOROMIR PLEDGE.
OKAY, WAIT. STOP. HOLD ON.
YOU HAVE THE ARTIFACT, DOCTOR?
WHERE IS IT? AND WHERE DID IT COME FROM?
IT IS HERE. IN ME.
AND IT CAME FROM THE CREATOR.
MY NAME IS--WAS--MAZAROV. I WAS HER COLLEAGUE.
YOU MEAN... DO YOU MEAN GOD SENT IT TO YOU?
NO, MISS. I AM AN ATHEIST.
I MEAN IT CAME FROM THE CREATOR.
HUH. SPEAKING AS A BELIEVER, THAT KIND OF STINGS A BIT.

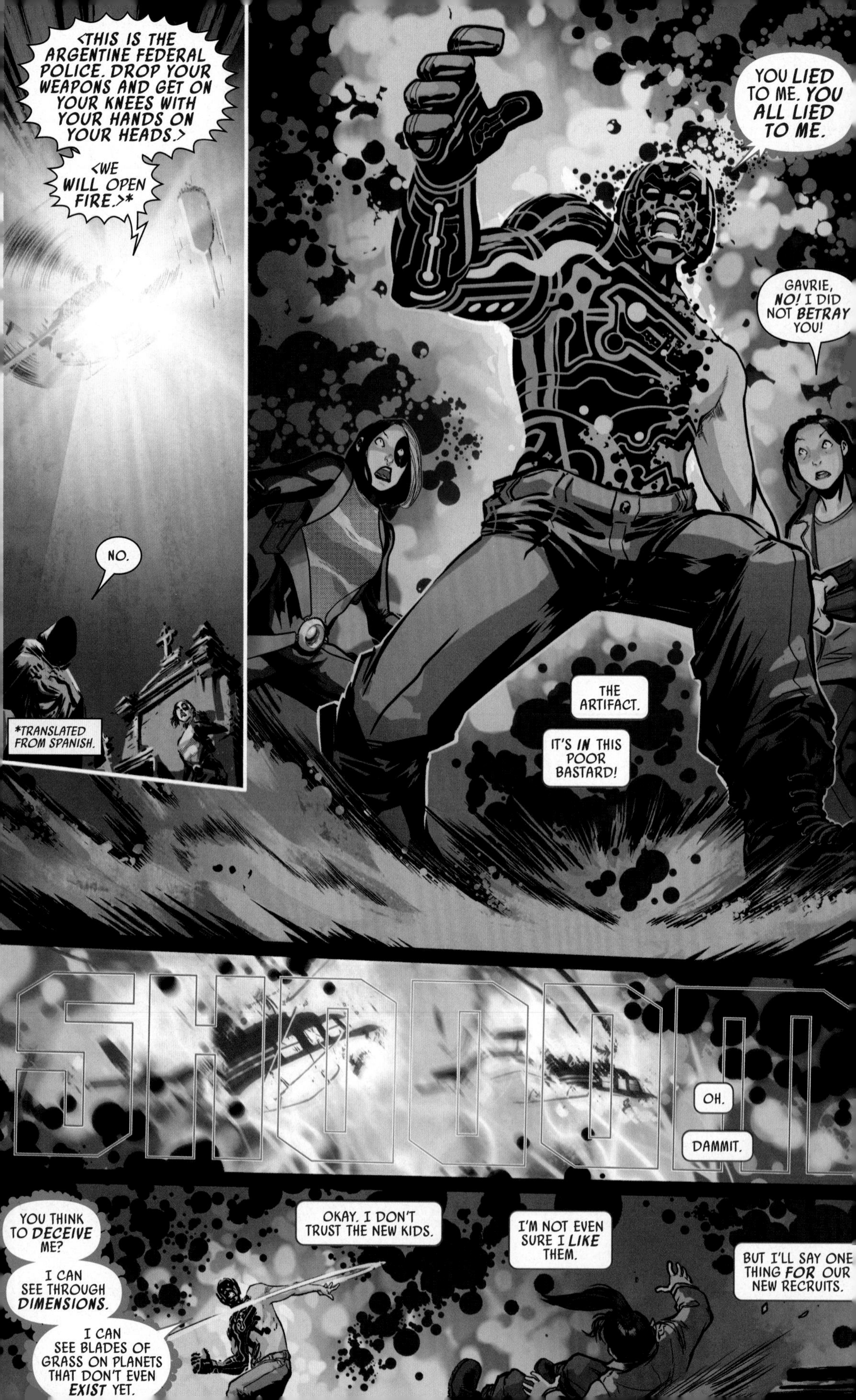

<THIS IS THE ARGENTINE FEDERAL POLICE. DROP YOUR WEAPONS AND GET ON YOUR KNEES WITH YOUR HANDS ON YOUR HEADS.>
<WE WILL OPEN FIRE.>*
NO.
*TRANSLATED FROM SPANISH.
YOU LIED TO ME. YOU ALL LIED TO ME.
GAVRIE, NO! I DID NOT BETRAY YOU!
THE ARTIFACT.
IT'S IN THIS POOR BASTARD!
OH.
DAMMIT.
YOU THINK TO DECEIVE ME?
I CAN SEE THROUGH DIMENSIONS.
I CAN SEE BLADES OF GRASS ON PLANETS THAT DON'T EVEN EXIST YET.
OKAY. I DON'T TRUST THE NEW KIDS.
I'M NOT EVEN SURE I LIKE THEM.
BUT I'LL SAY ONE THING FOR OUR NEW RECRUITS.

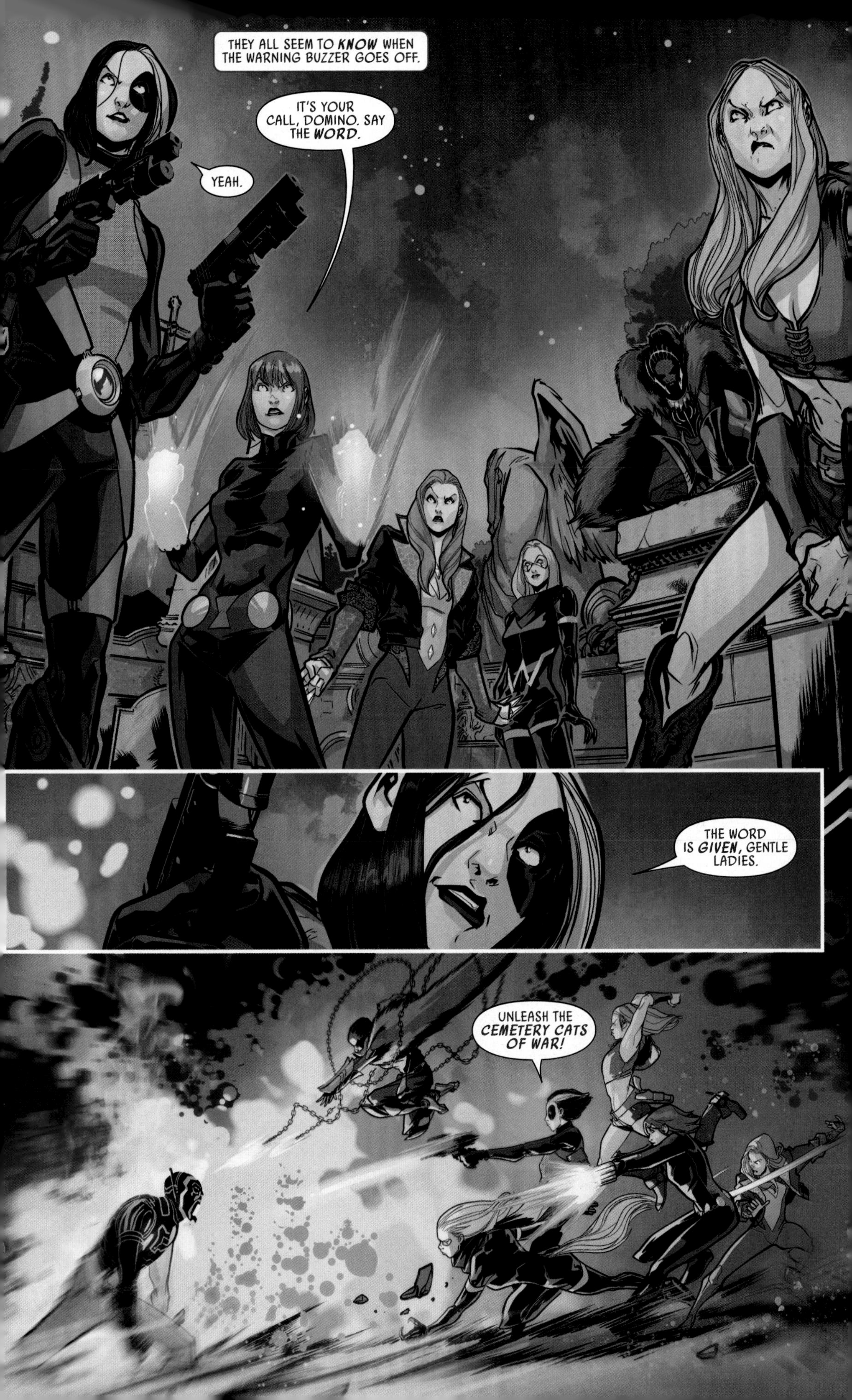
THEY ALL SEEM TO KNOW WHEN THE WARNING BUZZER GOES OFF.
IT'S YOUR CALL, DOMINO. SAY THE WORD.
YEAH.
THE WORD IS GIVEN, GENTLE LADIES.
UNLEASH THE CEMETERY CATS OF WAR!

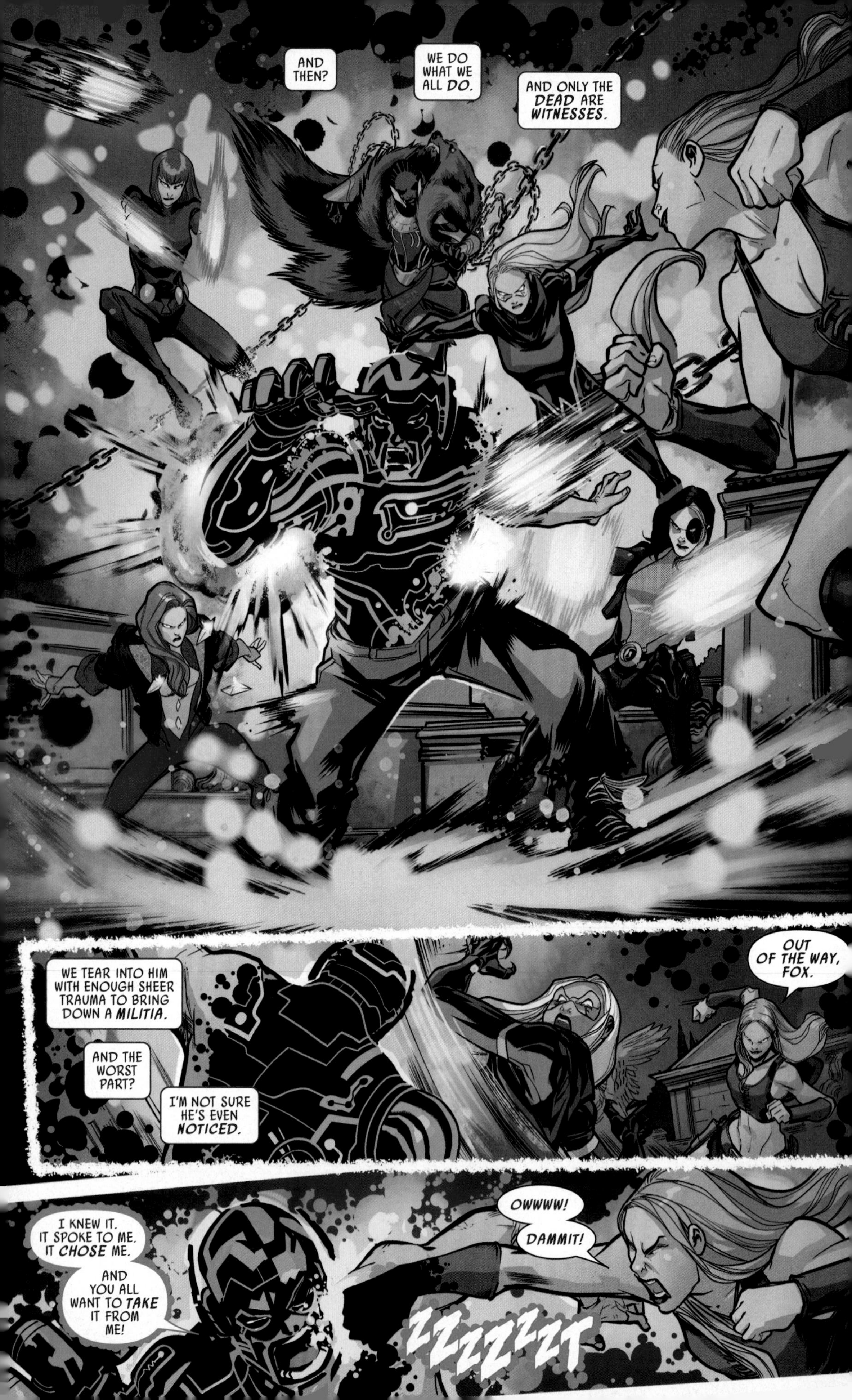
AND THEN?
WE DO WHAT WE ALL DO.
AND ONLY THE DEAD ARE WITNESSES.
WE TEAR INTO HIM WITH ENOUGH SHEER TRAUMA TO BRING DOWN A MILITIA.
AND THE WORST PART?
I'M NOT SURE HE'S EVEN NOTICED.
OUT OF THE WAY, FOX.
I KNEW IT. IT SPOKE TO ME. IT CHOSE ME.
AND YOU ALL WANT TO TAKE IT FROM ME!
OWWWW!
DAMMIT!
ZZZZZZZT

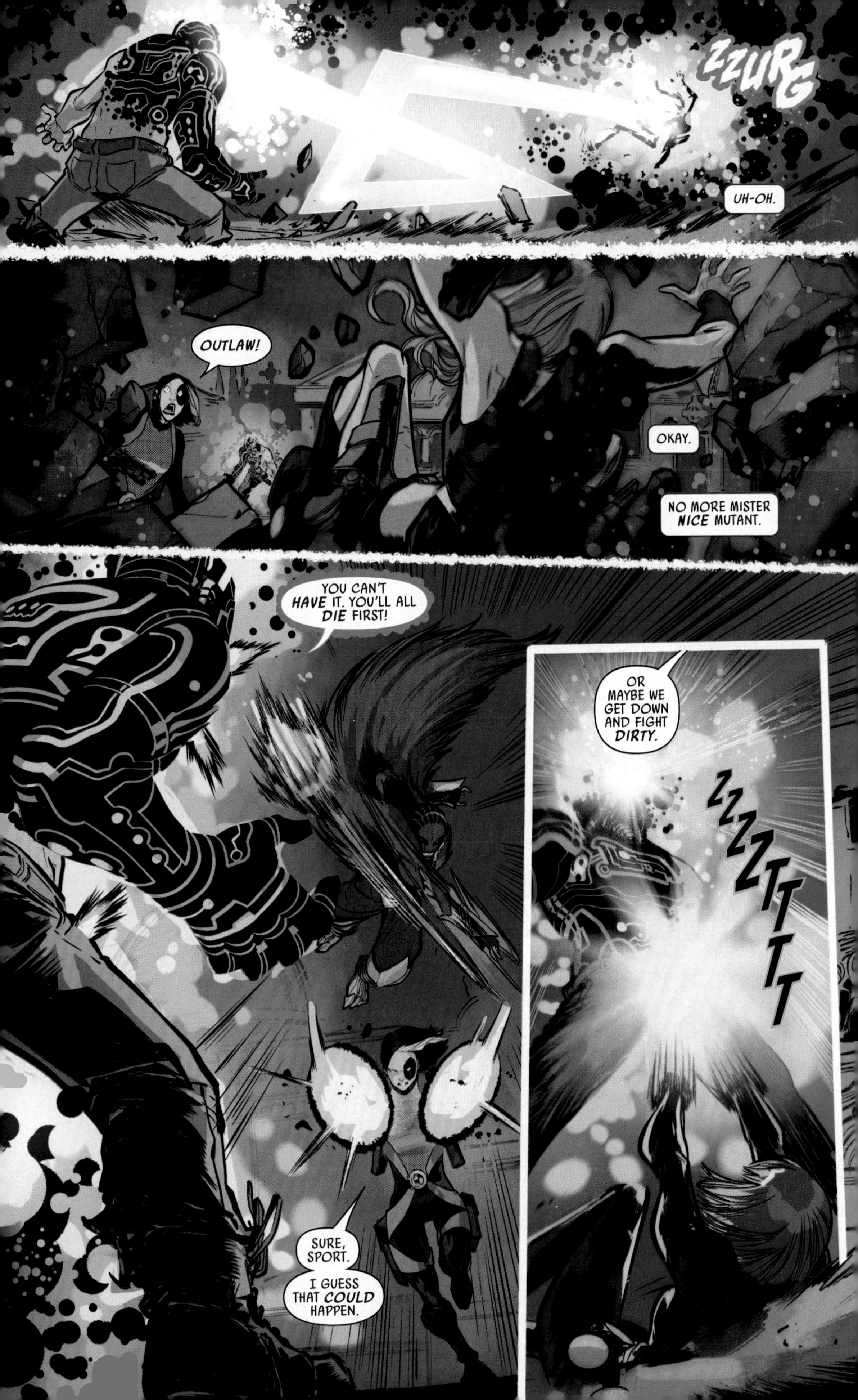

ZZURG
UH-OH.
OUTLAW!
OKAY.
NO MORE MISTER NICE MUTANT.
YOU CAN'T HAVE IT. YOU'LL ALL DIE FIRST!
SURE, SPORT.
I GUESS THAT COULD HAPPEN.
OR MAYBE WE GET DOWN AND FIGHT DIRTY.
ZZZZTTTT

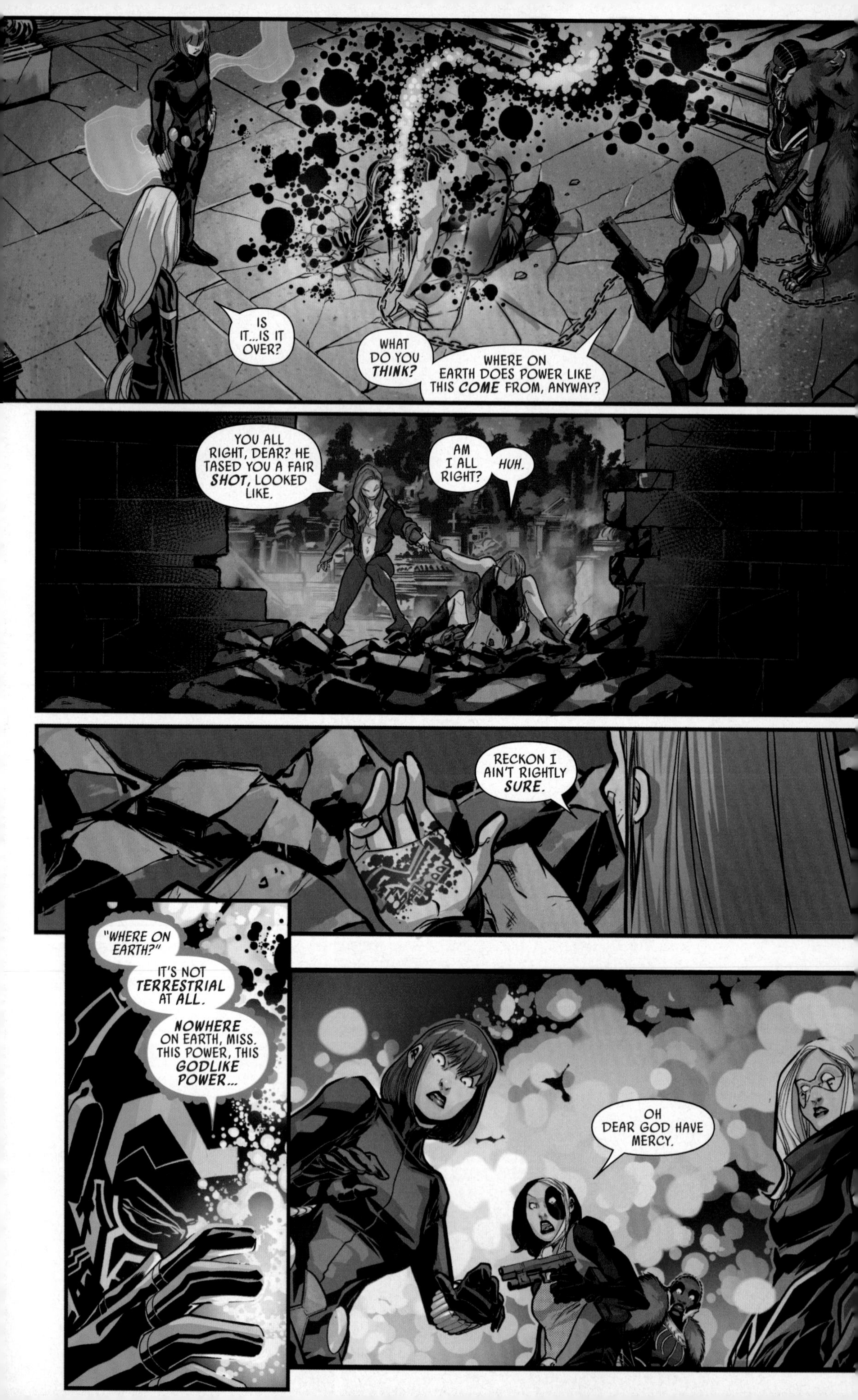

IS IT...IS IT OVER?
WHAT DO YOU THINK?
WHERE ON EARTH DOES POWER LIKE THIS COME FROM, ANYWAY?
YOU ALL RIGHT, DEAR? HE TASED YOU A FAIR SHOT, LOOKED LIKE.
AM I ALL RIGHT?
HUH.
RECKON I AIN'T RIGHTLY SURE.
"WHERE ON EARTH?"
IT'S NOT TERRESTRIAL AT ALL.
NOWHERE ON EARTH, MISS. THIS POWER, THIS GODLIKE POWER...
OH DEAR GOD HAVE MERCY.

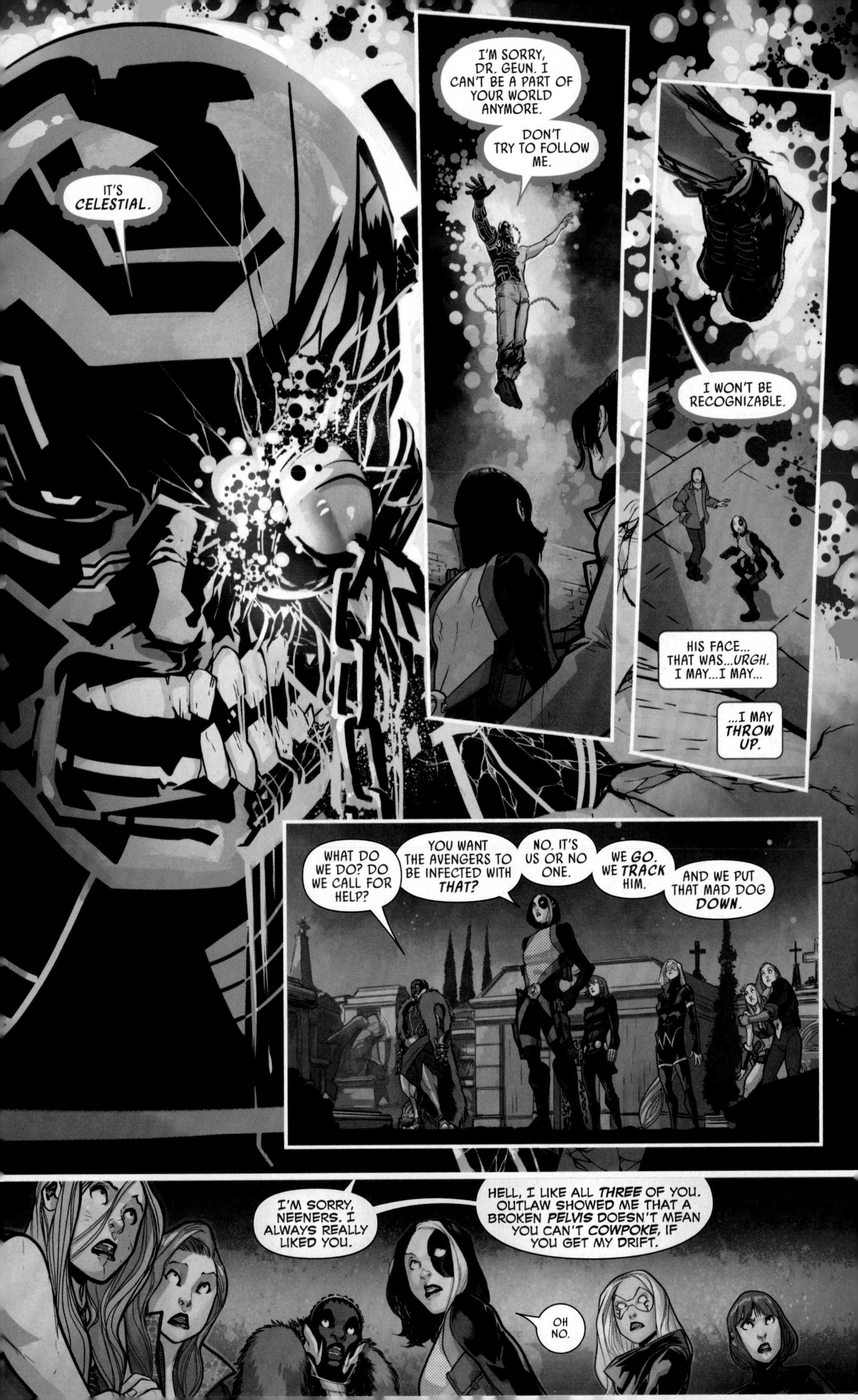
IT'S CELESTIAL.
I'M SORRY, DR. GEUN. I CAN'T BE A PART OF YOUR WORLD ANYMORE.
DON'T TRY TO FOLLOW ME.
I WON'T BE RECOGNIZABLE.
HIS FACE... THAT WAS...URGH. I MAY...I MAY...
...I MAY THROW UP.
WHAT DO WE DO? DO WE CALL FOR HELP?
YOU WANT THE AVENGERS TO BE INFECTED WITH THAT?
NO. IT'S US OR NO ONE.
WE GO. WE TRACK HIM.
AND WE PUT THAT MAD DOG DOWN.
I'M SORRY, NEENERS. I ALWAYS REALLY LIKED YOU.
HELL, I LIKE ALL THREE OF YOU. OUTLAW SHOWED ME THAT A BROKEN PELVIS DOESN'T MEAN YOU CAN'T COWPOKE, IF YOU GET MY DRIFT.
OH NO.

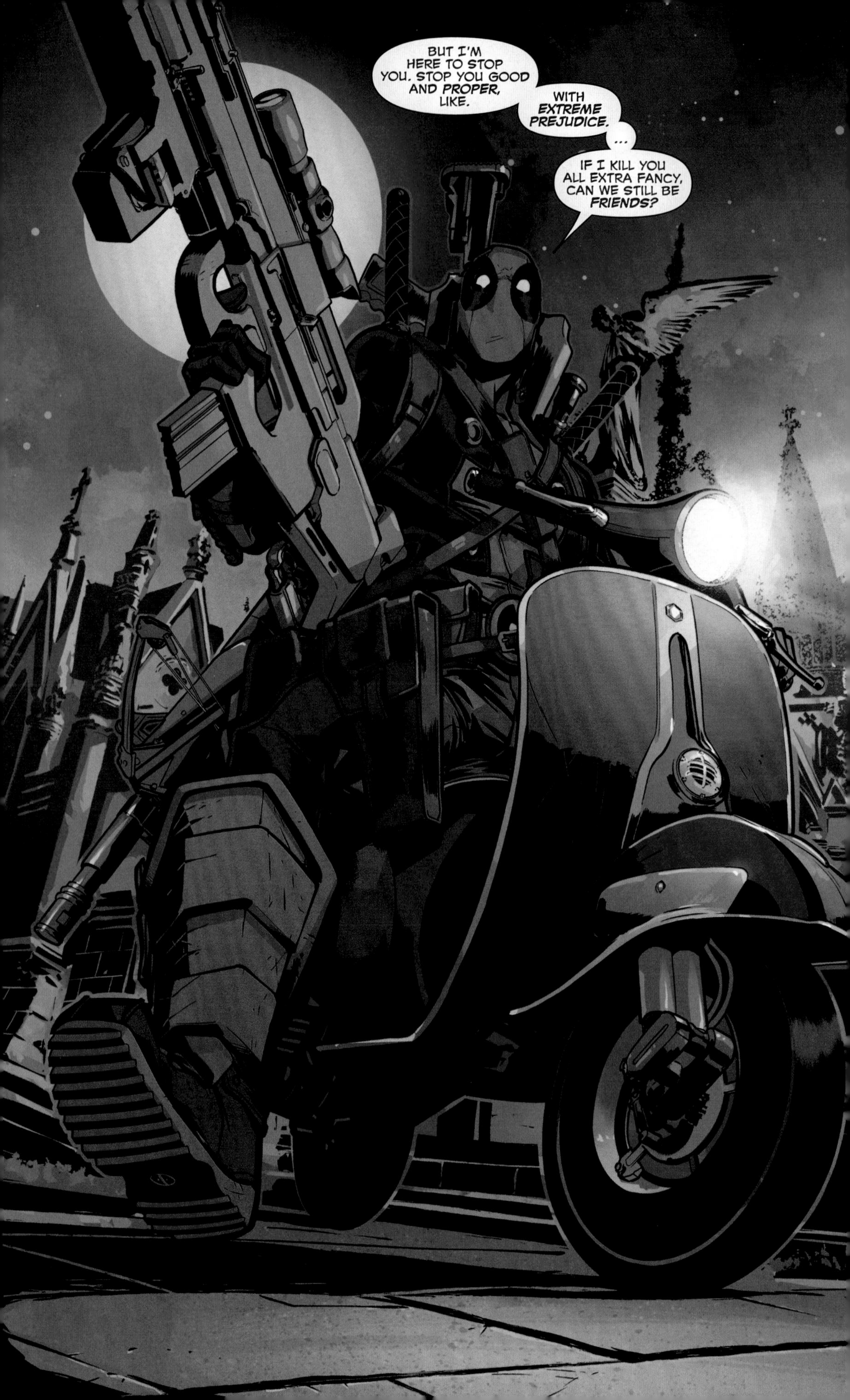
BUT I'M HERE TO STOP YOU. STOP YOU GOOD AND PROPER, LIKE.
WITH EXTREME PREJUDICE.
...
IF I KILL YOU ALL EXTRA FANCY, CAN WE STILL BE FRIENDS?

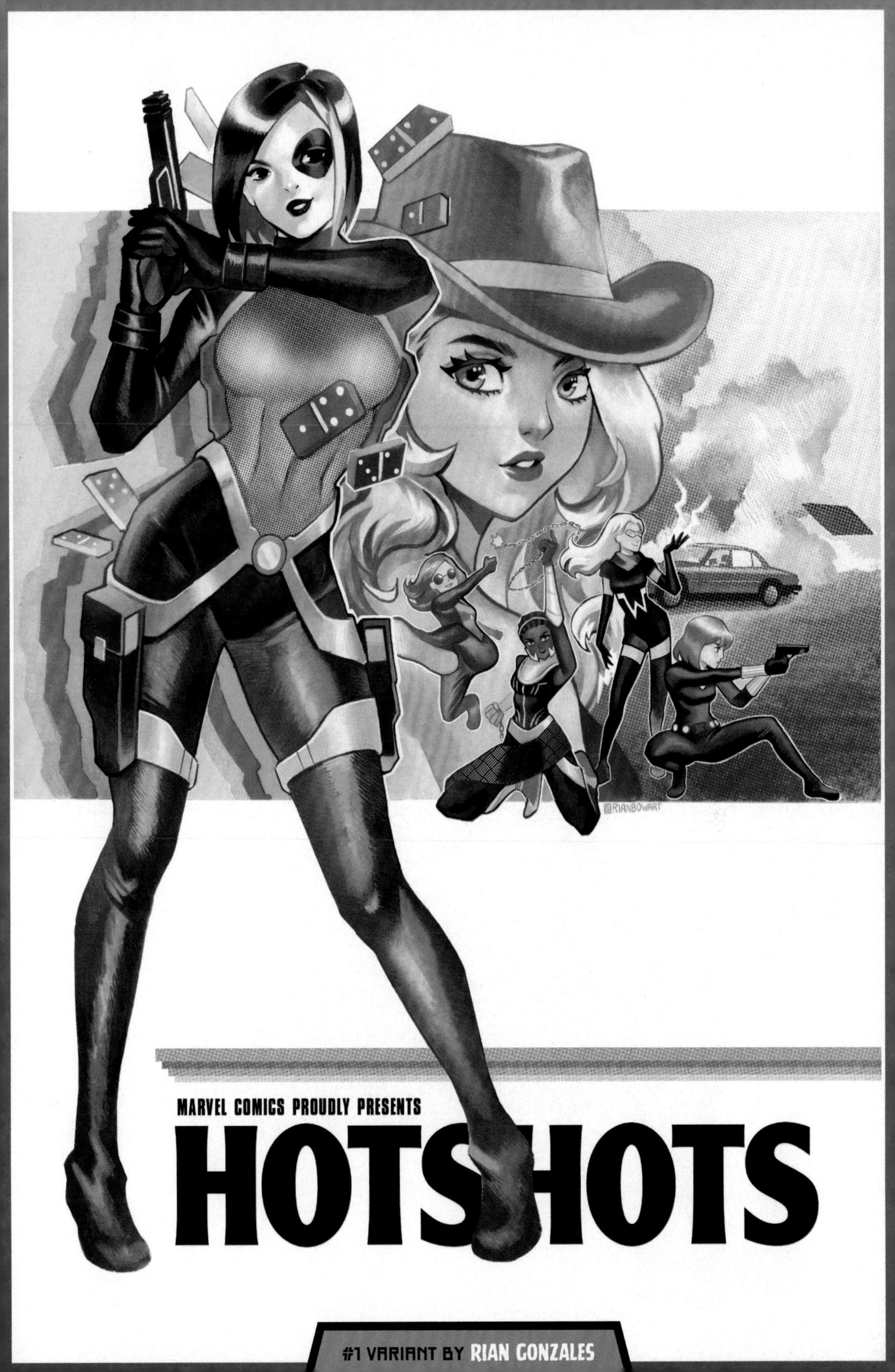
@RIANBOWART
MARVEL COMICS PROUDLY PRESENTS
HOTSHOTS
#1 VARIANT BY RIAN GONZALES

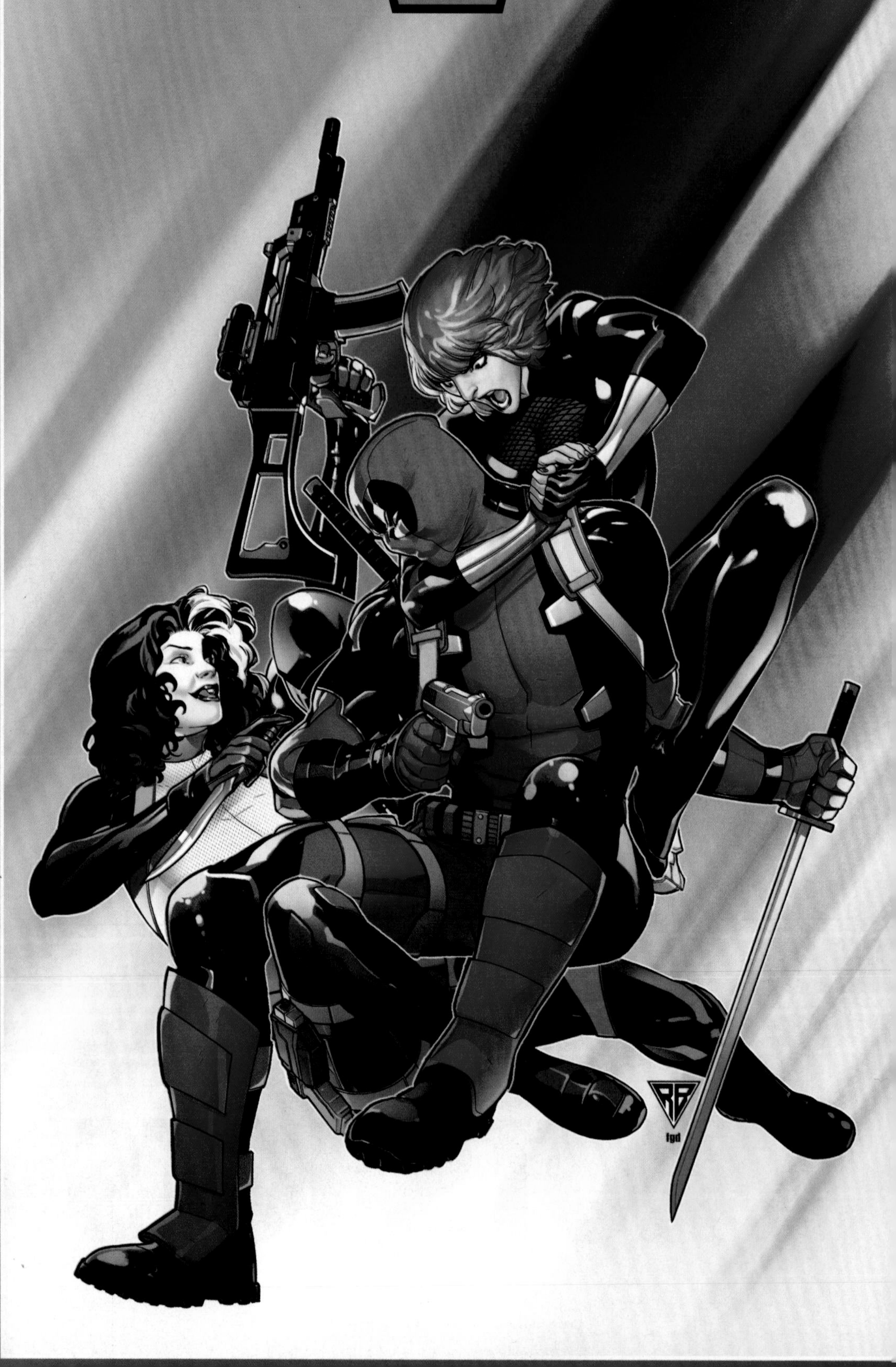

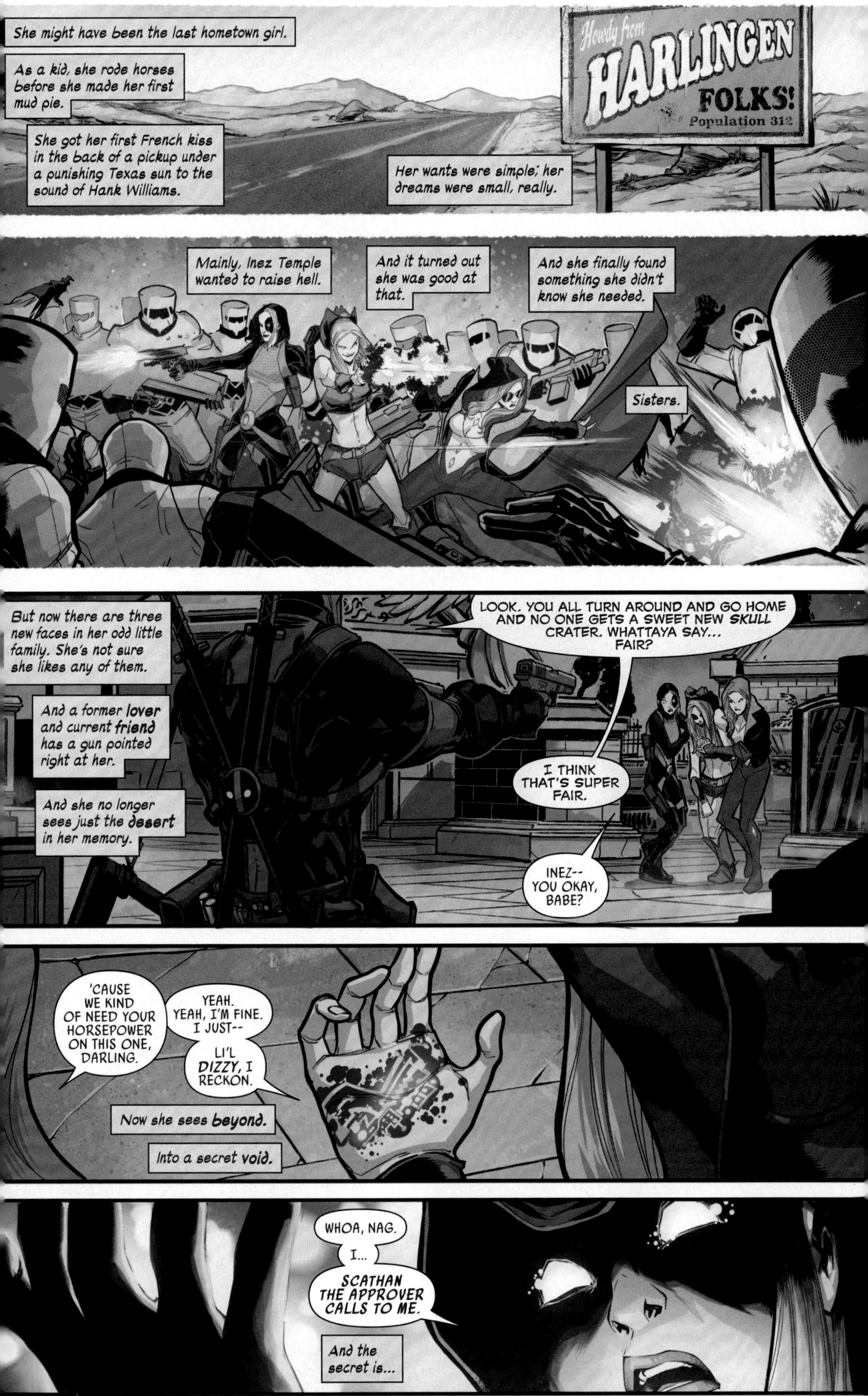

2

She might have been the last hometown girl.
As a kid, she rode horses before she made her first mud pie.
She got her first French kiss in the back of a pickup under a punishing Texas sun to the sound of Hank Williams.
Howdy from HARLINGEN FOLKS! Population 312
Her wants were simple; her dreams were small, really.
Mainly, Inez Temple wanted to raise hell.
And it turned out she was good at that.
And she finally found something she didn't know she needed.
Sisters.
But now there are three new faces in her odd little family. She's not sure she likes any of them.
And a former lover and current friend has a gun pointed right at her.
And she no longer sees just the desert in her memory.
LOOK. YOU ALL TURN AROUND AND GO HOME AND NO ONE GETS A SWEET NEW SKULL CRATER. WHATTAYA SAY... FAIR?
I THINK THAT'S SUPER FAIR.
INEZ-- YOU OKAY, BABE?
'CAUSE WE KIND OF NEED YOUR HORSEPOWER ON THIS ONE, DARLING.
YEAH. YEAH, I'M FINE. I JUST--
LI'L DIZZY, I RECKON.
Now she sees beyond.
Into a secret void.
WHOA, NAG.
I...
SCATHAN THE APPROVER CALLS TO ME.
And the secret is...

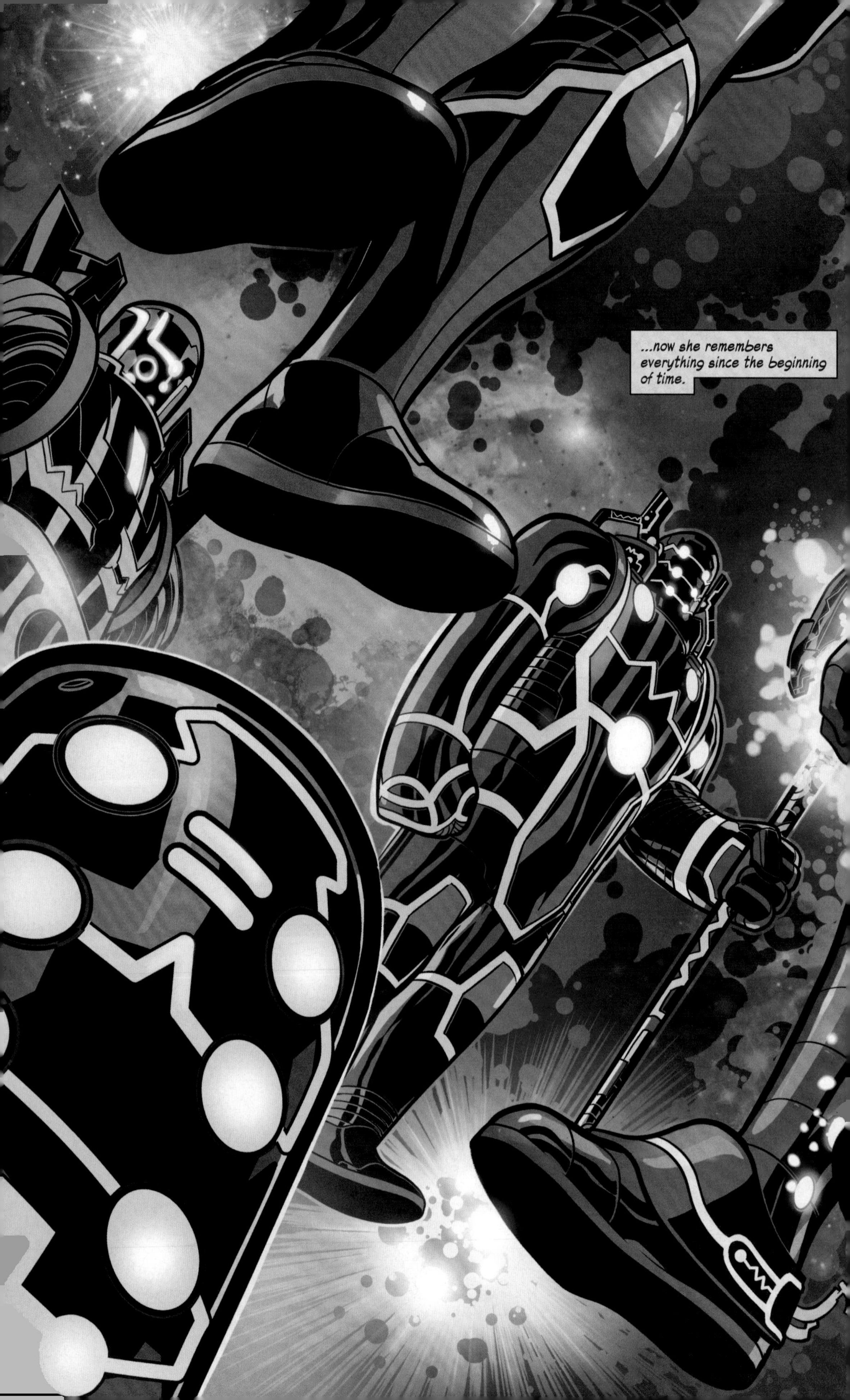
...now she remembers everything since the beginning of time.

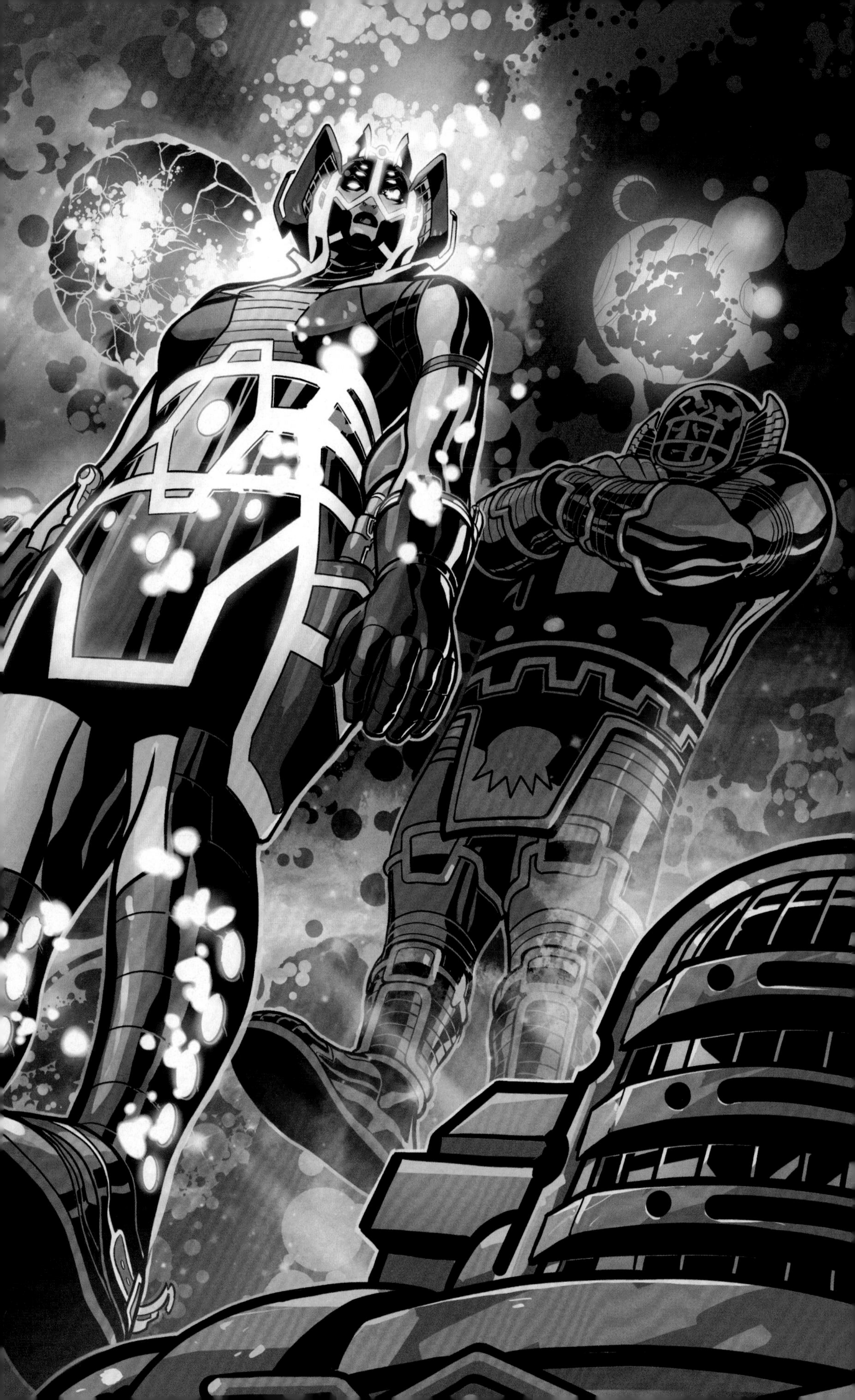

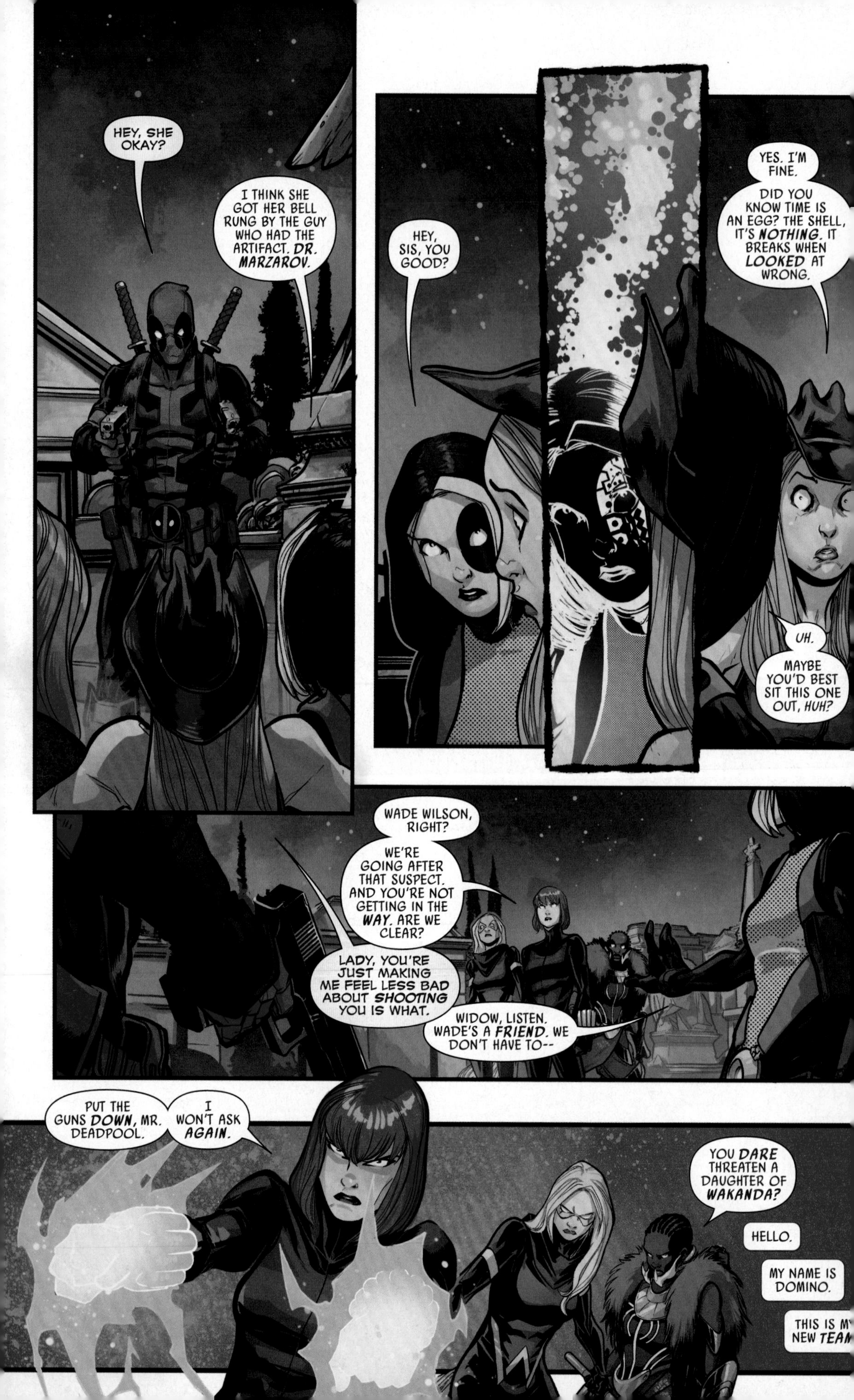

HEY, SHE OKAY?
I THINK SHE GOT HER BELL RUNG BY THE GUY WHO HAD THE ARTIFACT. DR. MARZAROV.
HEY, SIS, YOU GOOD?
YES. I'M FINE.
DID YOU KNOW TIME IS AN EGG? THE SHELL, IT'S NOTHING. IT BREAKS WHEN LOOKED AT WRONG.
UH.
MAYBE YOU'D BEST SIT THIS ONE OUT, HUH?
WADE WILSON, RIGHT?
WE'RE GOING AFTER THAT SUSPECT. AND YOU'RE NOT GETTING IN THE WAY. ARE WE CLEAR?
LADY, YOU'RE JUST MAKING ME FEEL LESS BAD ABOUT SHOOTING YOU IS WHAT.
WIDOW, LISTEN. WADE'S A FRIEND. WE DON'T HAVE TO--
PUT THE GUNS DOWN, MR. DEADPOOL.
I WON'T ASK AGAIN.
YOU DARE THREATEN A DAUGHTER OF WAKANDA?
HELLO.
MY NAME IS DOMINO.

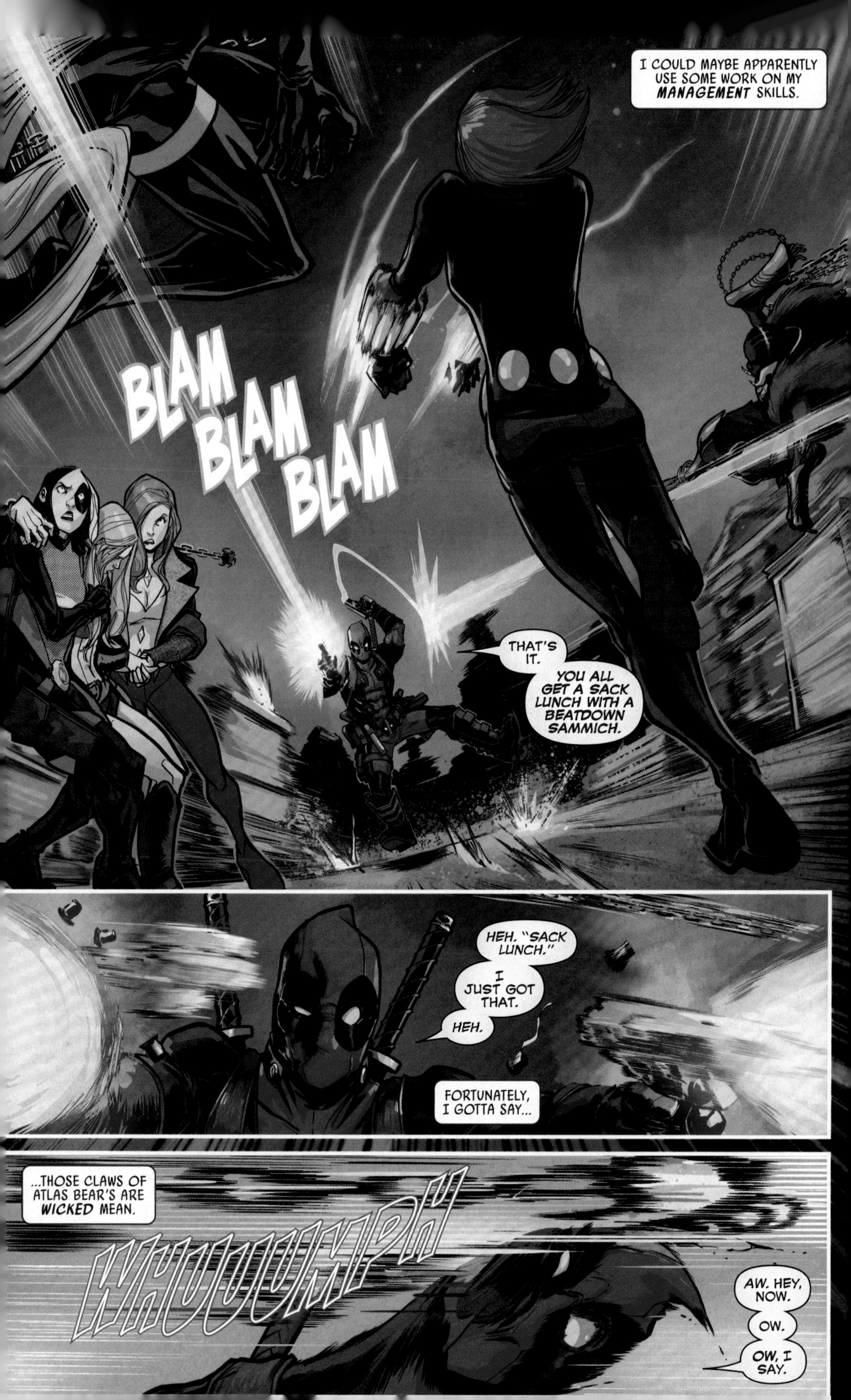

I COULD MAYBE APPARENTLY USE SOME WORK ON MY MANAGEMENT SKILLS.
BLAM BLAM BLAM
THAT'S IT.
YOU ALL GET A SACK LUNCH WITH A BEATDOWN SAMMICH.
HEH. "SACK LUNCH."
I JUST GOT THAT.
HEH.
FORTUNATELY, I GOTTA SAY...
...THOSE CLAWS OF ATLAS BEAR'S ARE WICKED MEAN.
WHUUUMPH
AW. HEY, NOW.
OW.
OW, I SAY.

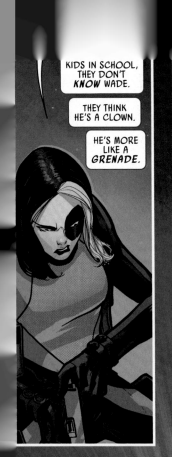

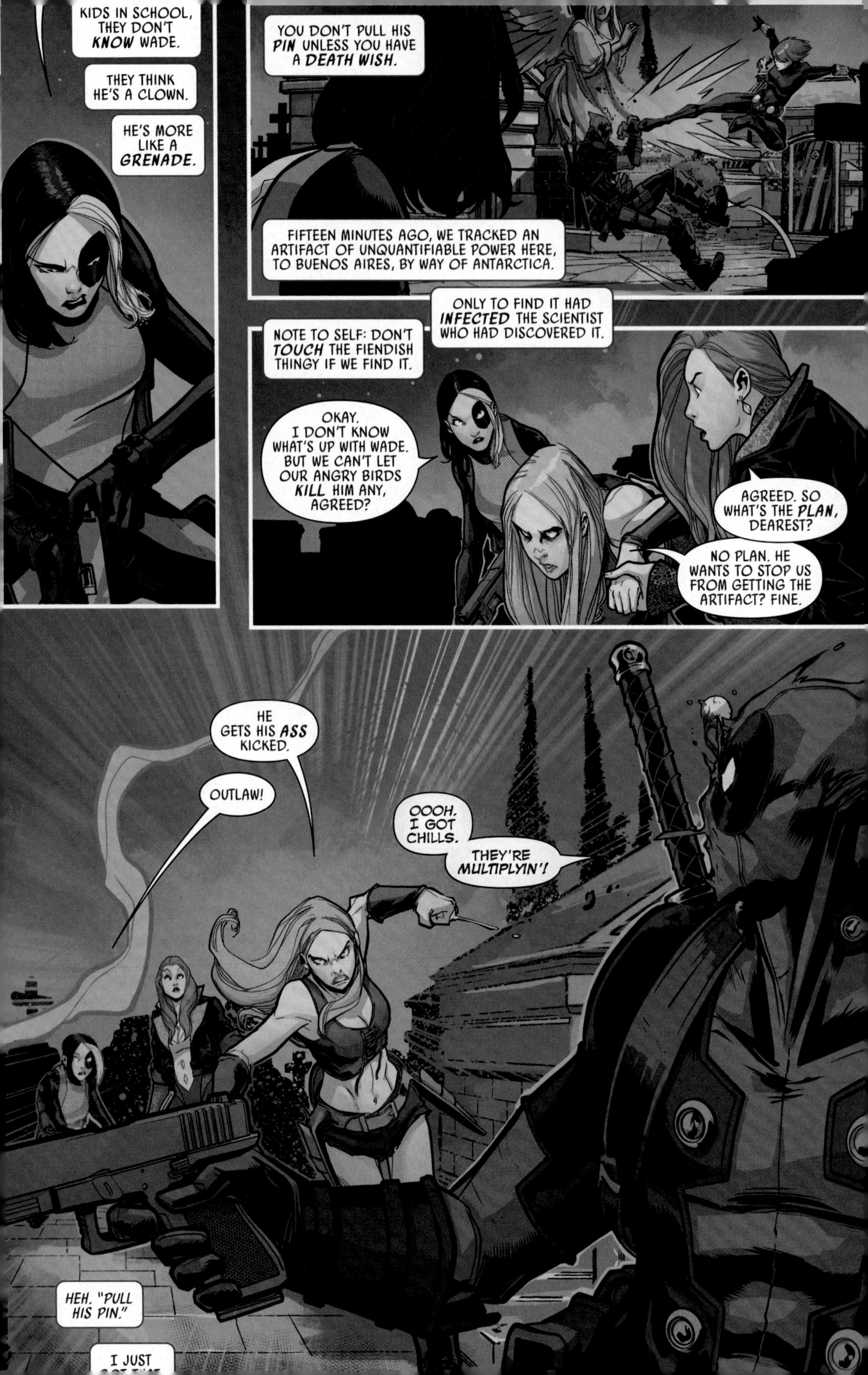
KIDS IN SCHOOL, THEY DON'T KNOW WADE.
THEY THINK HE'S A CLOWN.
HE'S MORE LIKE A GRENADE.
YOU DON'T PULL HIS PIN UNLESS YOU HAVE A DEATH WISH.
FIFTEEN MINUTES AGO, WE TRACKED AN ARTIFACT OF UNQUANTIFIABLE POWER HERE, TO BUENOS AIRES, BY WAY OF ANTARCTICA.
ONLY TO FIND IT HAD INFECTED THE SCIENTIST WHO HAD DISCOVERED IT.
NOTE TO SELF: DON'T TOUCH THE FIENDISH THINGY IF WE FIND IT.
OKAY. I DON'T KNOW WHAT'S UP WITH WADE. BUT WE CAN'T LET OUR ANGRY BIRDS KILL HIM ANY, AGREED?
AGREED. SO WHAT'S THE PLAN, DEAREST?
NO PLAN. HE WANTS TO STOP US FROM GETTING THE ARTIFACT? FINE.
HE GETS HIS ASS KICKED.
OUTLAW!
OOOH. I GOT CHILLS.
THEY'RE MULTIPLYIN'!
HEH. "PULL HIS PIN."
I JUST

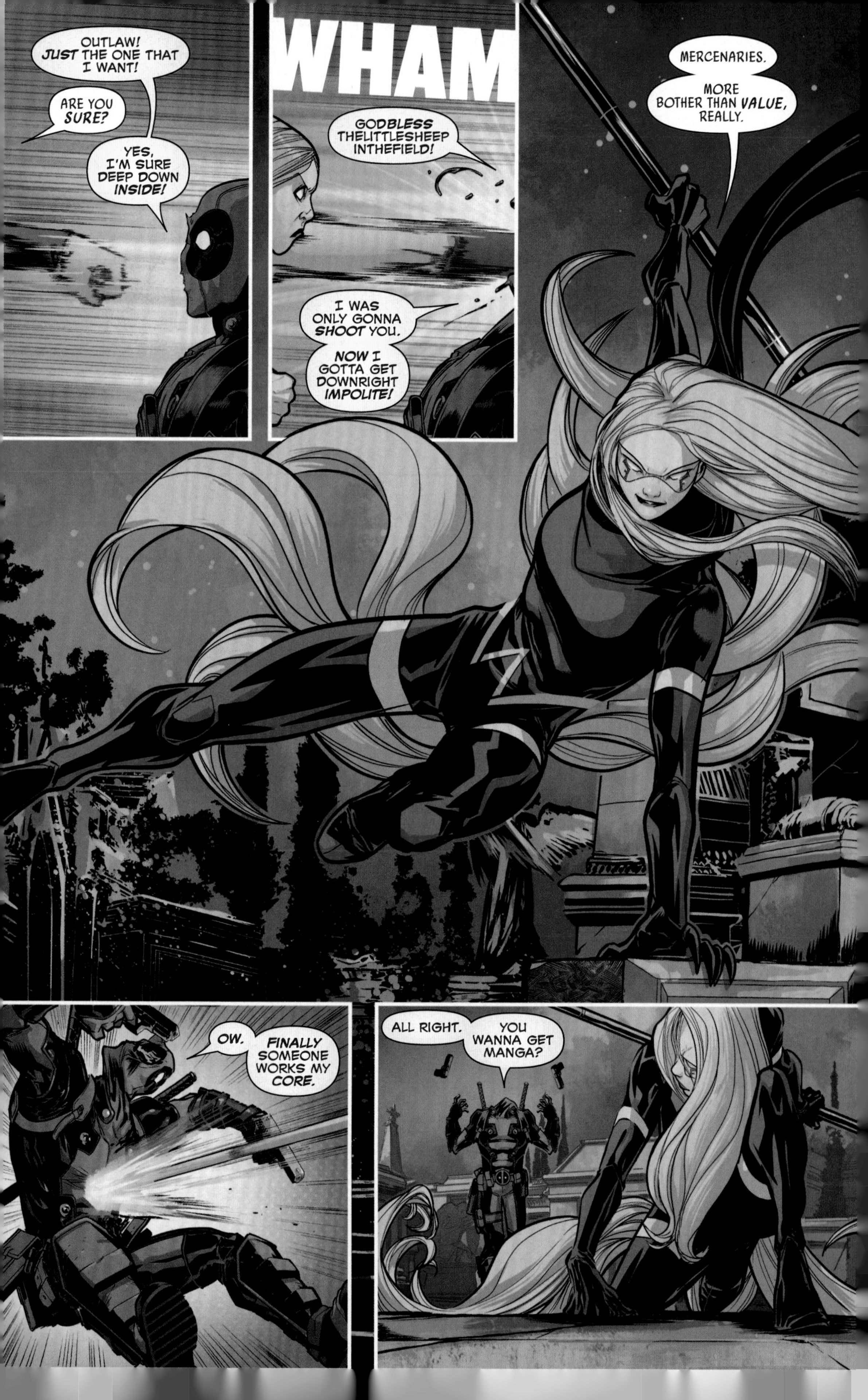
OUTLAW! JUST THE ONE THAT I WANT!
ARE YOU SURE?
YES, I'M SURE DEEP DOWN INSIDE!
WHAM
GODBLESS THELITTLESHEEP INTHEFIELD!
I WAS ONLY GONNA SHOOT YOU.
NOW I GOTTA GET DOWNRIGHT IMPOLITE!
MERCENARIES.
MORE BOTHER THAN VALUE, REALLY.
OW.
FINALLY SOMEONE WORKS MY CORE.
ALL RIGHT.
YOU WANNA GET MANGA?

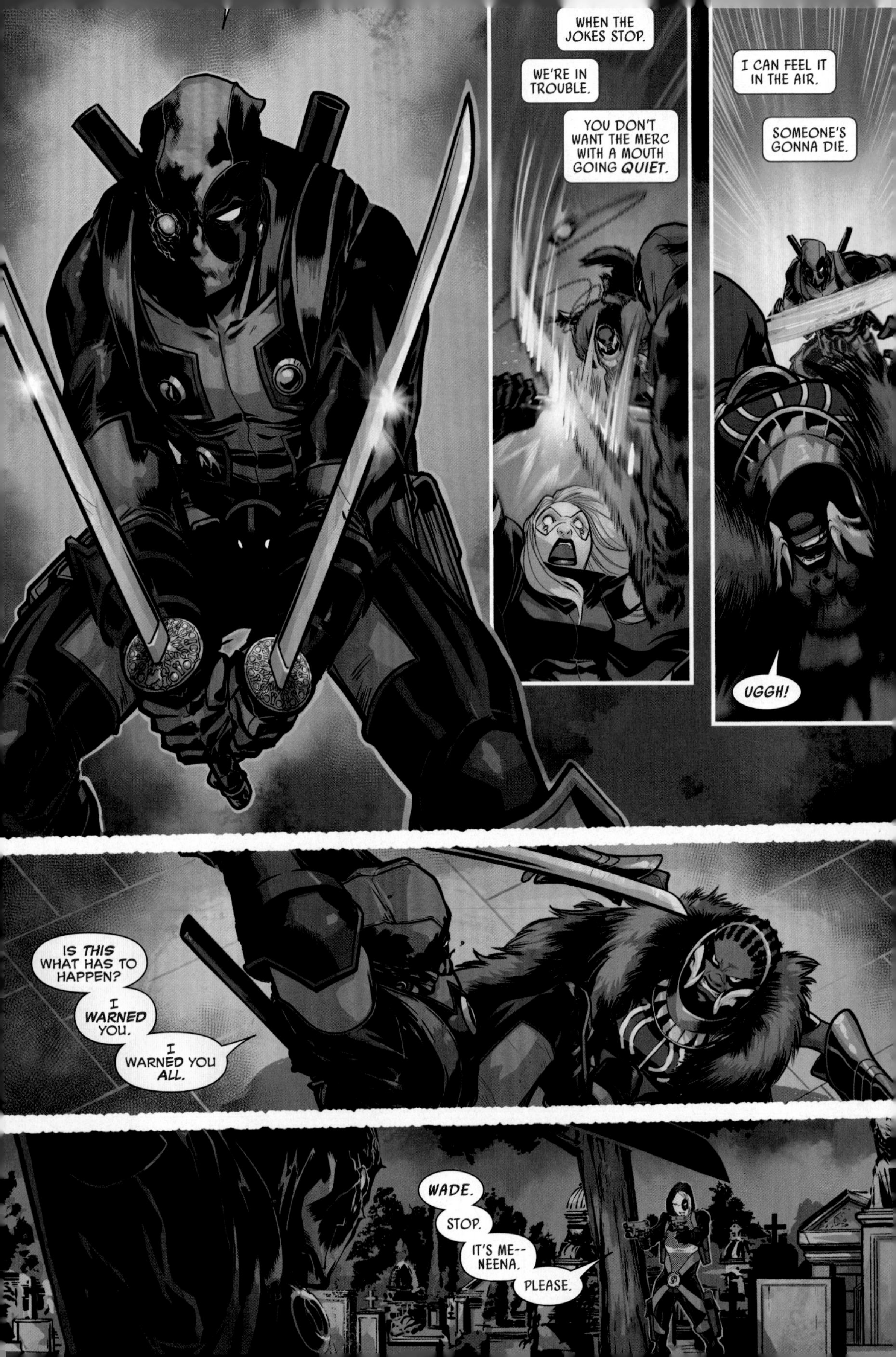
WHEN THE JOKES STOP.
WE'RE IN TROUBLE.
YOU DON'T WANT THE MERC WITH A MOUTH GOING QUIET.
I CAN FEEL IT IN THE AIR.
SOMEONE'S GONNA DIE.
UGGH!
IS THIS WHAT HAS TO HAPPEN?
I WARNED YOU.
I WARNED YOU ALL.
WADE.
STOP.
IT'S ME-- NEENA.
PLEASE.

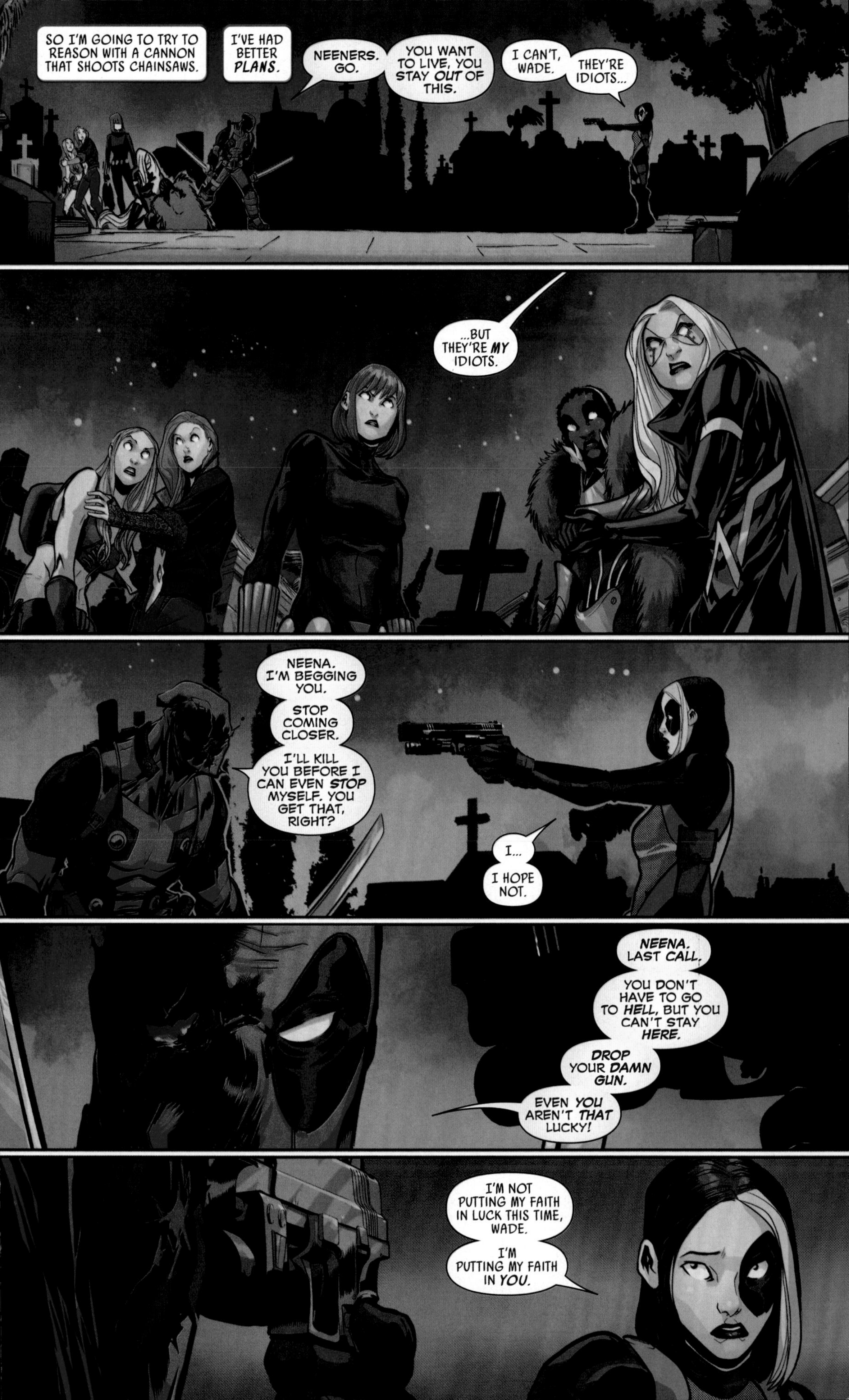
SO I'M GOING TO TRY TO REASON WITH A CANNON THAT SHOOTS CHAINSAWS.
I'VE HAD BETTER *PLANS.*
NEENERS. GO.
YOU WANT TO LIVE, YOU STAY *OUT* OF THIS.
I CAN'T, WADE.
THEY'RE IDIOTS...
...BUT THEY'RE *MY* IDIOTS.
NEENA. I'M BEGGING YOU.
STOP COMING CLOSER.
I'LL KILL YOU BEFORE I CAN EVEN *STOP* MYSELF. YOU GET THAT, RIGHT?
I...
I HOPE NOT.
NEENA. LAST *CALL.*
YOU *DON'T* HAVE TO GO TO *HELL,* BUT YOU CAN'T STAY *HERE.*
DROP YOUR *DAMN GUN.*
EVEN *YOU* AREN'T *THAT* LUCKY!
I'M NOT PUTTING MY FAITH IN LUCK THIS TIME, WADE.
I'M PUTTING MY FAITH IN *YOU.*

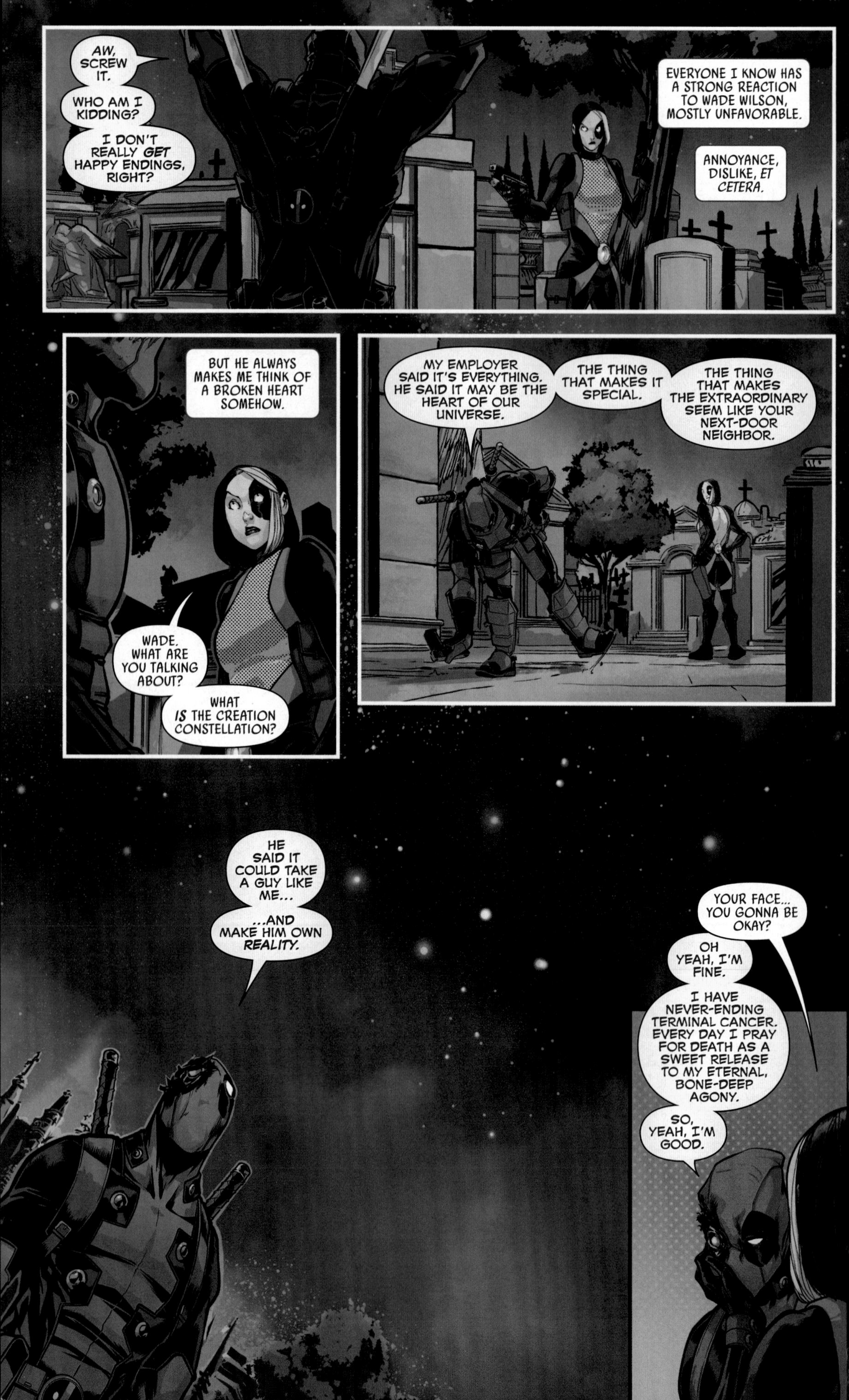
AW, SCREW IT.
WHO AM I KIDDING?
I DON'T REALLY GET HAPPY ENDINGS, RIGHT?
EVERYONE I KNOW HAS A STRONG REACTION TO WADE WILSON, MOSTLY UNFAVORABLE.
ANNOYANCE, DISLIKE, ET CETERA.
BUT HE ALWAYS MAKES ME THINK OF A BROKEN HEART SOMEHOW.
WADE. WHAT ARE YOU TALKING ABOUT?
WHAT IS THE CREATION CONSTELLATION?
MY EMPLOYER SAID IT'S EVERYTHING. HE SAID IT MAY BE THE HEART OF OUR UNIVERSE.
THE THING THAT MAKES IT SPECIAL.
THE THING THAT MAKES THE EXTRAORDINARY SEEM LIKE YOUR NEXT-DOOR NEIGHBOR.
HE SAID IT COULD TAKE A GUY LIKE ME...
...AND MAKE HIM OWN REALITY.
YOUR FACE... YOU GONNA BE OKAY?
OH YEAH, I'M FINE.
I HAVE NEVER-ENDING TERMINAL CANCER. EVERY DAY I PRAY FOR DEATH AS A SWEET RELEASE TO MY ETERNAL, BONE-DEEP AGONY.
SO, YEAH, I'M GOOD.

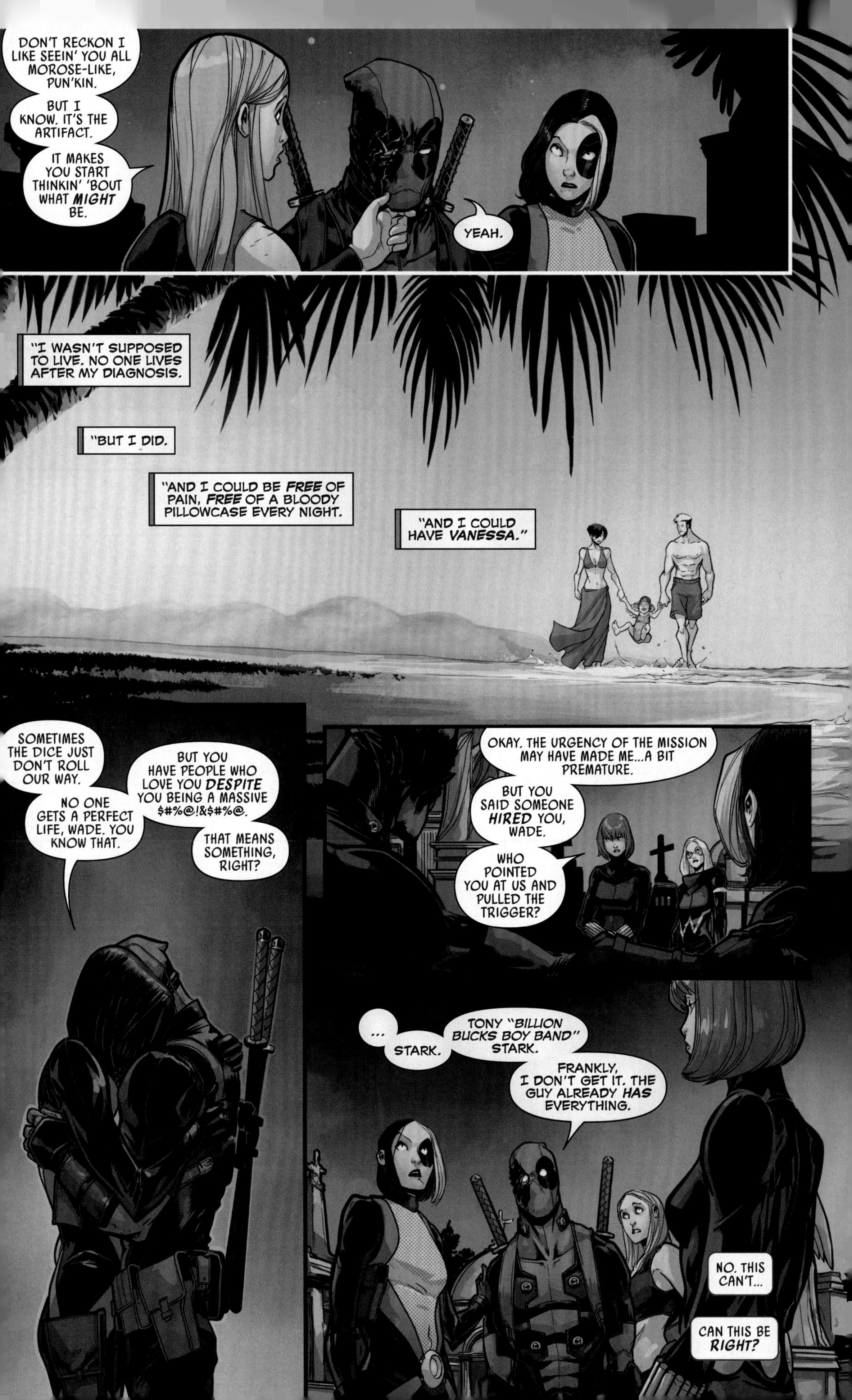

DON'T RECKON I LIKE SEEIN' YOU ALL MOROSE-LIKE, PUN'KIN.
BUT I KNOW. IT'S THE ARTIFACT.
IT MAKES YOU START THINKIN' 'BOUT WHAT MIGHT BE.
YEAH.
"I WASN'T SUPPOSED TO LIVE. NO ONE LIVES AFTER MY DIAGNOSIS.
"BUT I DID.
"AND I COULD BE FREE OF PAIN, FREE OF A BLOODY PILLOWCASE EVERY NIGHT.
"AND I COULD HAVE VANESSA."
SOMETIMES THE DICE JUST DON'T ROLL OUR WAY.
NO ONE GETS A PERFECT LIFE, WADE. YOU KNOW THAT.
BUT YOU HAVE PEOPLE WHO LOVE YOU DESPITE YOU BEING A MASSIVE $#%@!&$#%@.
THAT MEANS SOMETHING, RIGHT?
OKAY. THE URGENCY OF THE MISSION MAY HAVE MADE ME...A BIT PREMATURE.
BUT YOU SAID SOMEONE HIRED YOU, WADE.
WHO POINTED YOU AT US AND PULLED THE TRIGGER?
...
STARK.
TONY "BILLION BUCKS BOY BAND" STARK.
FRANKLY, I DON'T GET IT. THE GUY ALREADY HAS EVERYTHING.
NO. THIS CAN'T...
CAN THIS BE RIGHT?

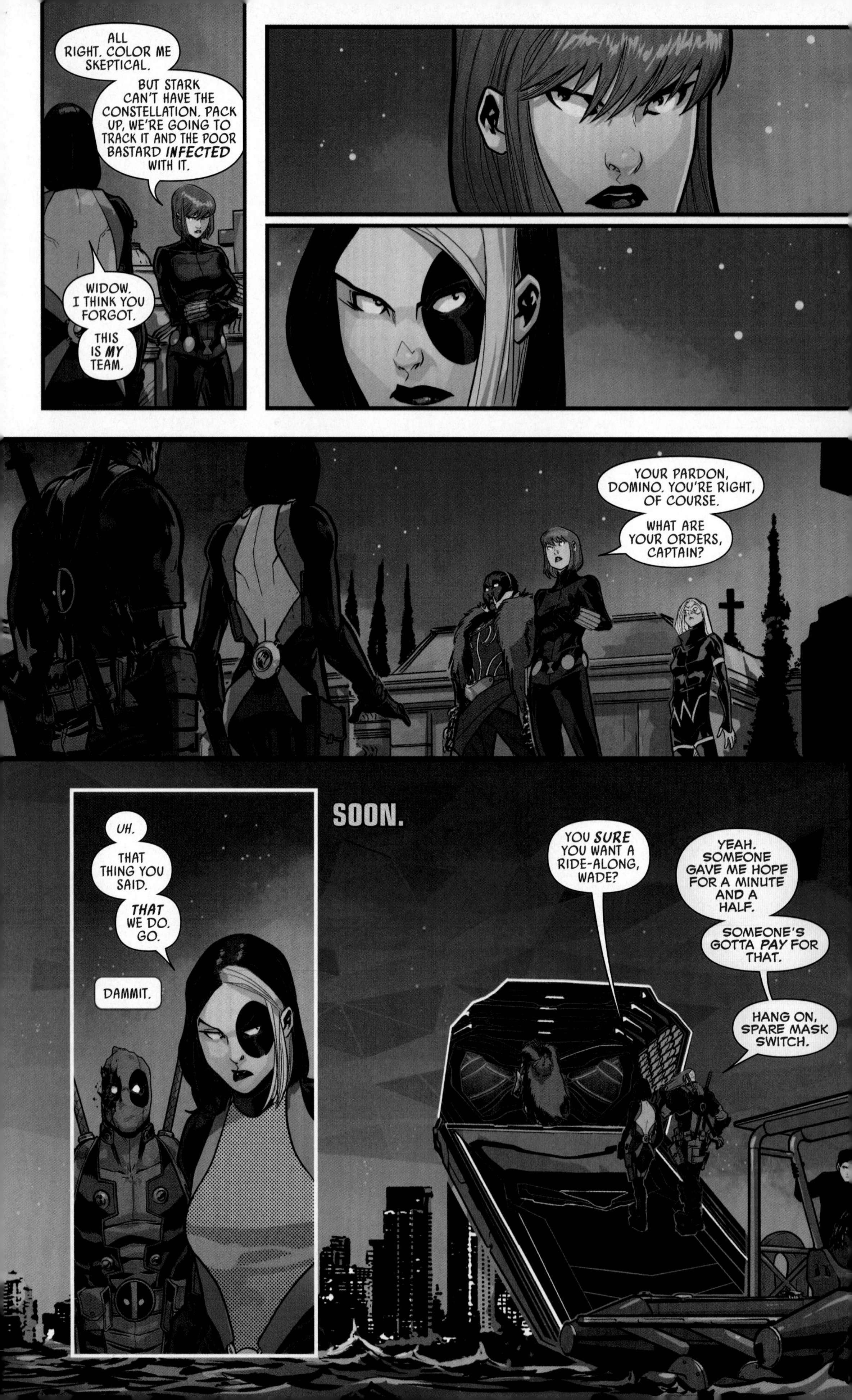
ALL RIGHT. COLOR ME SKEPTICAL.
BUT STARK CAN'T HAVE THE CONSTELLATION. PACK UP, WE'RE GOING TO TRACK IT AND THE POOR BASTARD INFECTED WITH IT.
WIDOW. I THINK YOU FORGOT.
THIS IS MY TEAM.
YOUR PARDON, DOMINO. YOU'RE RIGHT, OF COURSE.
WHAT ARE YOUR ORDERS, CAPTAIN?
SOON.
UH.
THAT THING YOU SAID.
THAT WE DO. GO.
DAMMIT.
YOU SURE YOU WANT A RIDE-ALONG, WADE?
YEAH. SOMEONE GAVE ME HOPE FOR A MINUTE AND A HALF.
SOMEONE'S GOTTA PAY FOR THAT.
HANG ON, SPARE MASK SWITCH.

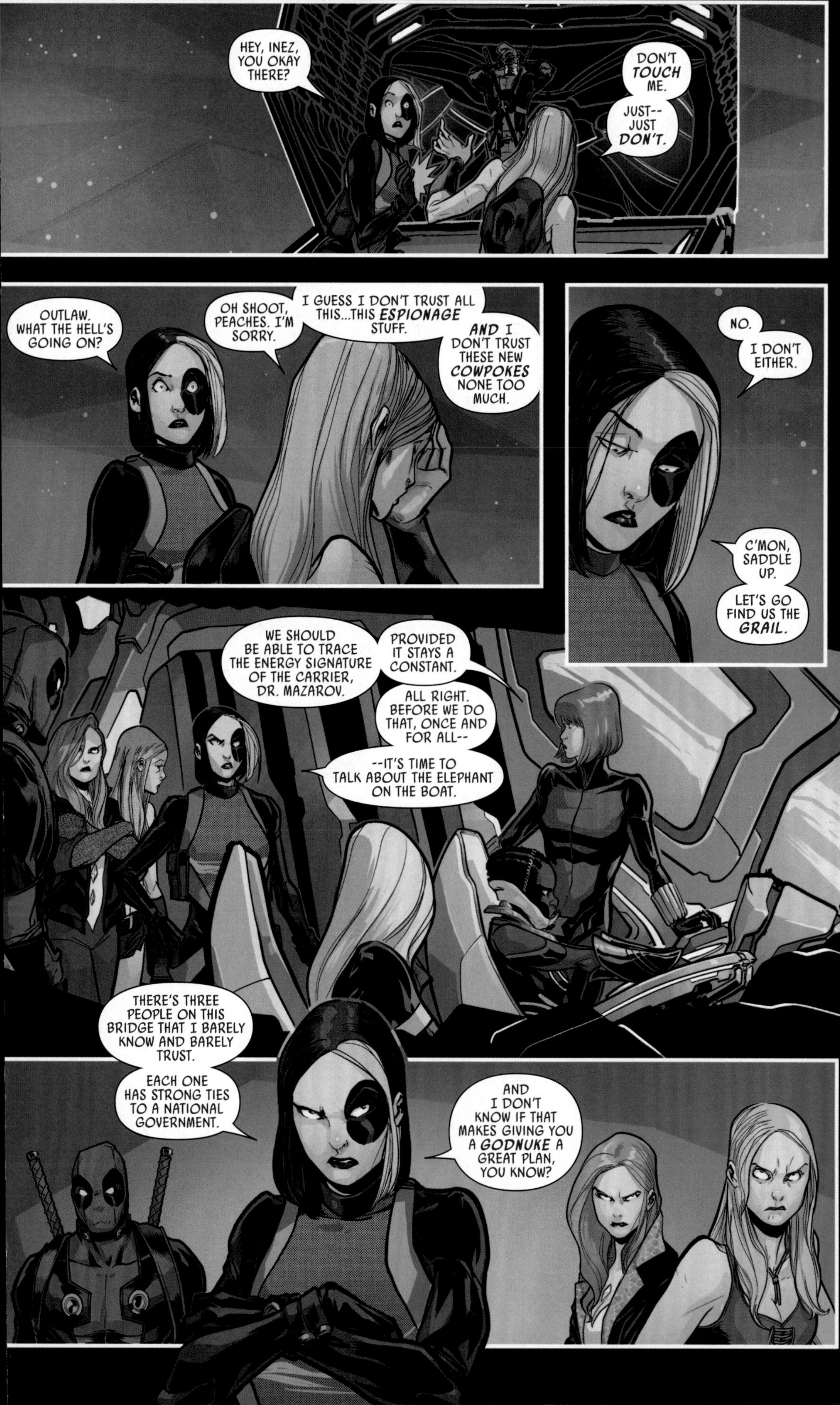
HEY, INEZ, YOU OKAY THERE?
DON'T TOUCH ME.
JUST-- JUST DON'T.
OUTLAW. WHAT THE HELL'S GOING ON?
OH SHOOT, PEACHES. I'M SORRY.
I GUESS I DON'T TRUST ALL THIS...THIS ESPIONAGE STUFF.
AND I DON'T TRUST THESE NEW COWPOKES NONE TOO MUCH.
NO.
I DON'T EITHER.
C'MON, SADDLE UP.
LET'S GO FIND US THE GRAIL.
WE SHOULD BE ABLE TO TRACE THE ENERGY SIGNATURE OF THE CARRIER, DR. MAZAROV.
PROVIDED IT STAYS A CONSTANT.
ALL RIGHT. BEFORE WE DO THAT, ONCE AND FOR ALL--
--IT'S TIME TO TALK ABOUT THE ELEPHANT ON THE BOAT.
THERE'S THREE PEOPLE ON THIS BRIDGE THAT I BARELY KNOW AND BARELY TRUST.
EACH ONE HAS STRONG TIES TO A NATIONAL GOVERNMENT.
AND I DON'T KNOW IF THAT MAKES GIVING YOU A GODNUKE A GREAT PLAN, YOU KNOW?

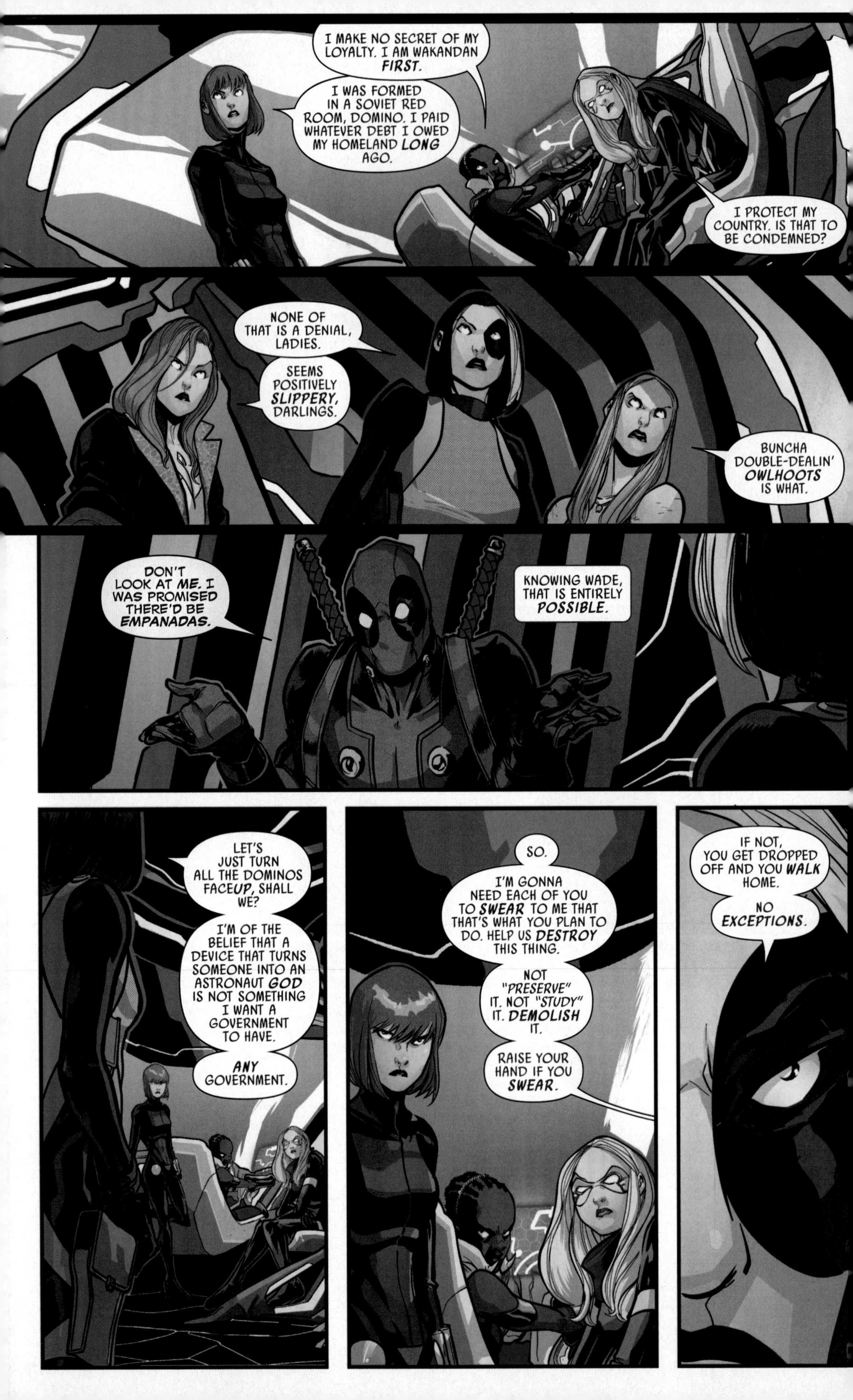
I MAKE NO SECRET OF MY LOYALTY. I AM WAKANDAN FIRST.
I WAS FORMED IN A SOVIET RED ROOM, DOMINO. I PAID WHATEVER DEBT I OWED MY HOMELAND LONG AGO.
I PROTECT MY COUNTRY. IS THAT TO BE CONDEMNED?
NONE OF THAT IS A DENIAL, LADIES.
SEEMS POSITIVELY SLIPPERY, DARLINGS.
BUNCHA DOUBLE-DEALIN' OWLHOOTS IS WHAT.
DON'T LOOK AT ME. I WAS PROMISED THERE'D BE EMPANADAS.
KNOWING WADE, THAT IS ENTIRELY POSSIBLE.
LET'S JUST TURN ALL THE DOMINOS FACEUP, SHALL WE?
I'M OF THE BELIEF THAT A DEVICE THAT TURNS SOMEONE INTO AN ASTRONAUT GOD IS NOT SOMETHING I WANT A GOVERNMENT TO HAVE.
ANY GOVERNMENT.
SO.
I'M GONNA NEED EACH OF YOU TO SWEAR TO ME THAT THAT'S WHAT YOU PLAN TO DO. HELP US DESTROY THIS THING.
NOT "PRESERVE" IT. NOT "STUDY" IT. DEMOLISH IT.
RAISE YOUR HAND IF YOU SWEAR.
IF NOT, YOU GET DROPPED OFF AND YOU WALK HOME.
NO EXCEPTIONS.

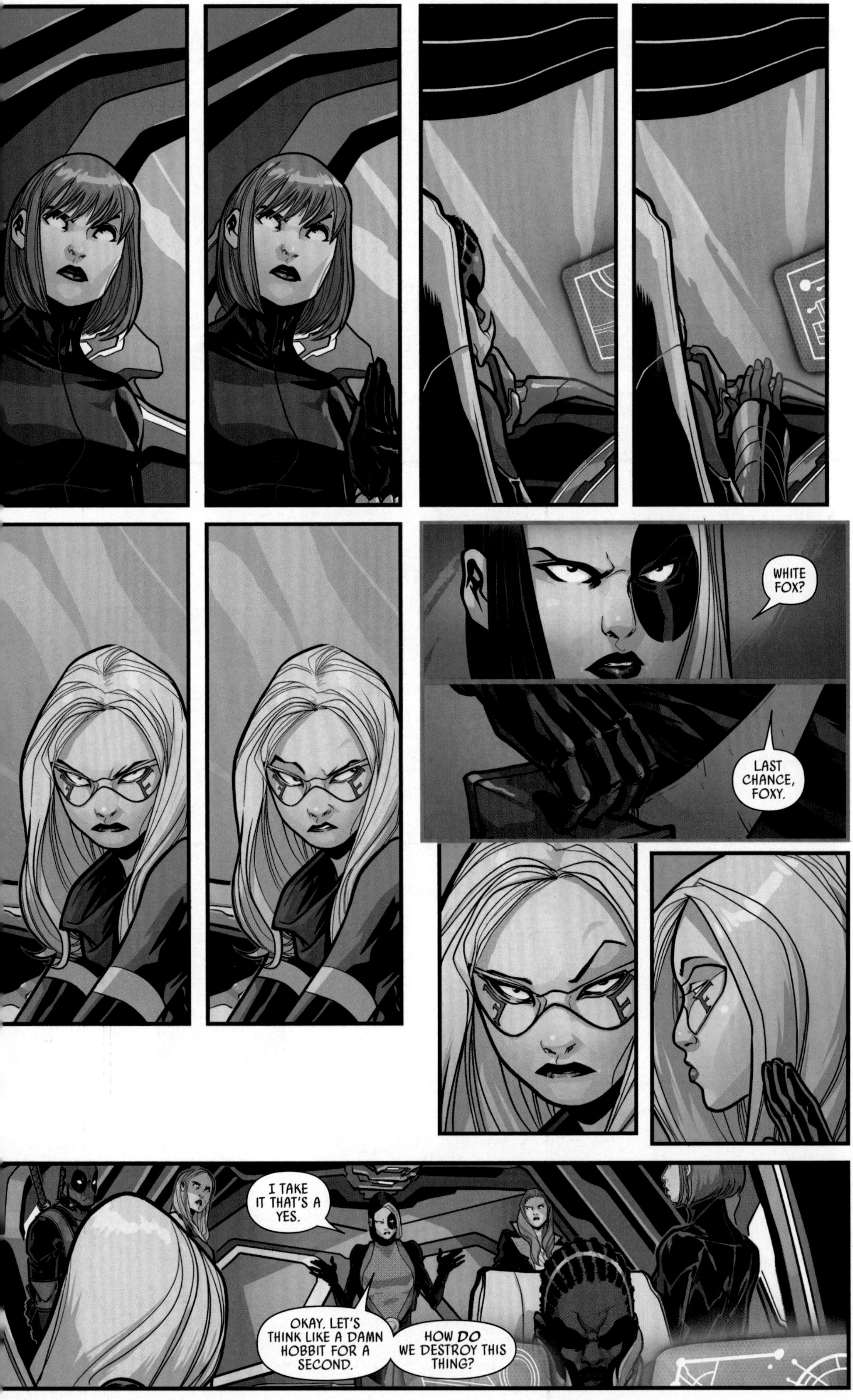
WHITE FOX?
LAST CHANCE, FOXY.
I TAKE IT THAT'S A YES.
OKAY. LET'S THINK LIKE A DAMN HOBBIT FOR A SECOND.
HOW DO WE DESTROY THIS THING?

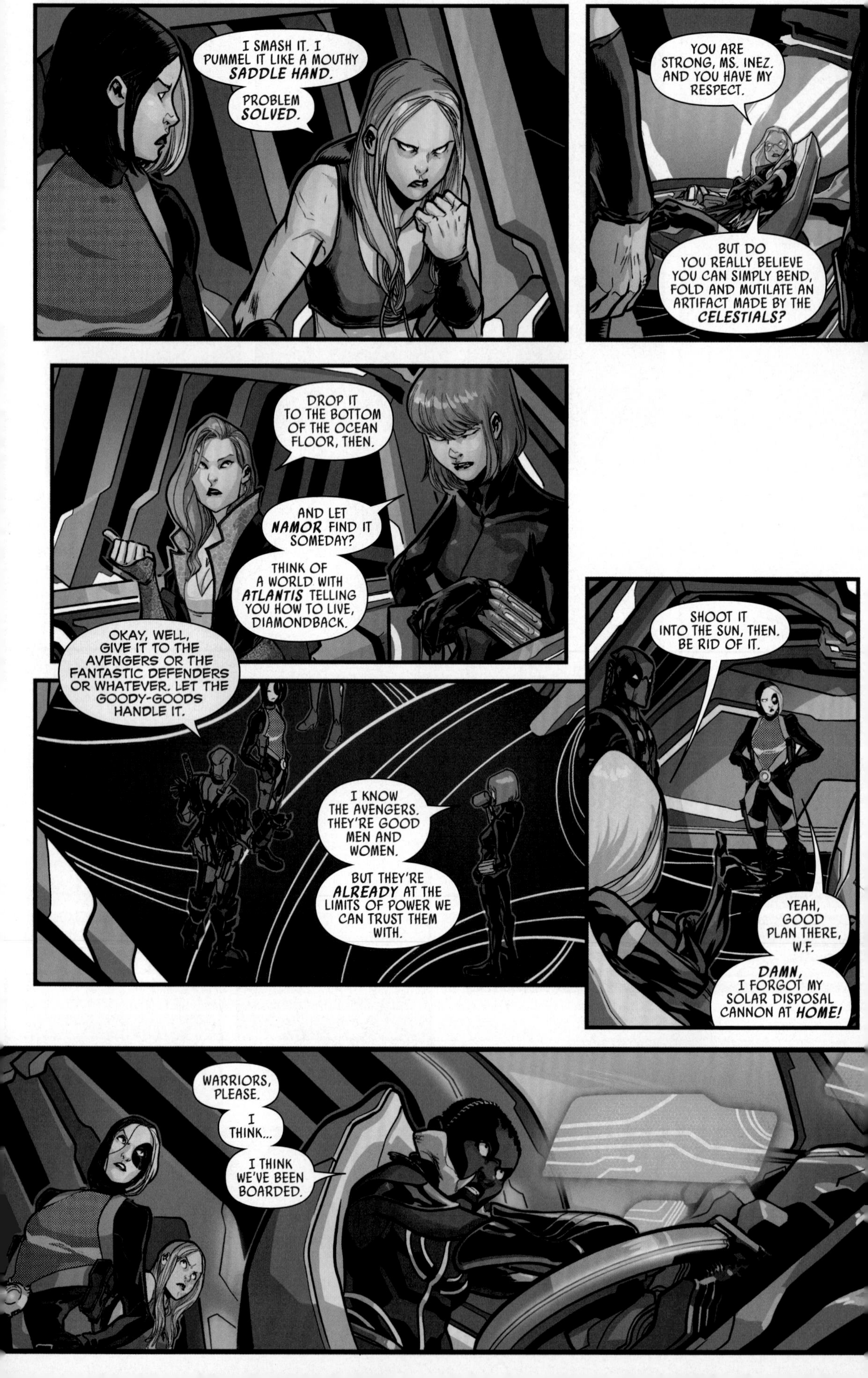
I SMASH IT. I PUMMEL IT LIKE A MOUTHY SADDLE HAND.
PROBLEM SOLVED.
YOU ARE STRONG, MS. INEZ. AND YOU HAVE MY RESPECT.
BUT DO YOU REALLY BELIEVE YOU CAN SIMPLY BEND, FOLD AND MUTILATE AN ARTIFACT MADE BY THE CELESTIALS?
DROP IT TO THE BOTTOM OF THE OCEAN FLOOR, THEN.
AND LET NAMOR FIND IT SOMEDAY?
THINK OF A WORLD WITH ATLANTIS TELLING YOU HOW TO LIVE, DIAMONDBACK.
OKAY, WELL, GIVE IT TO THE AVENGERS OR THE FANTASTIC DEFENDERS OR WHATEVER. LET THE GOODY-GOODS HANDLE IT.
I KNOW THE AVENGERS. THEY'RE GOOD MEN AND WOMEN.
BUT THEY'RE ALREADY AT THE LIMITS OF POWER WE CAN TRUST THEM WITH.
SHOOT IT INTO THE SUN, THEN. BE RID OF IT.
YEAH, GOOD PLAN THERE, W.F.
DAMN, I FORGOT MY SOLAR DISPOSAL CANNON AT HOME!
WARRIORS, PLEASE.
I THINK...
I THINK WE'VE BEEN BOARDED.

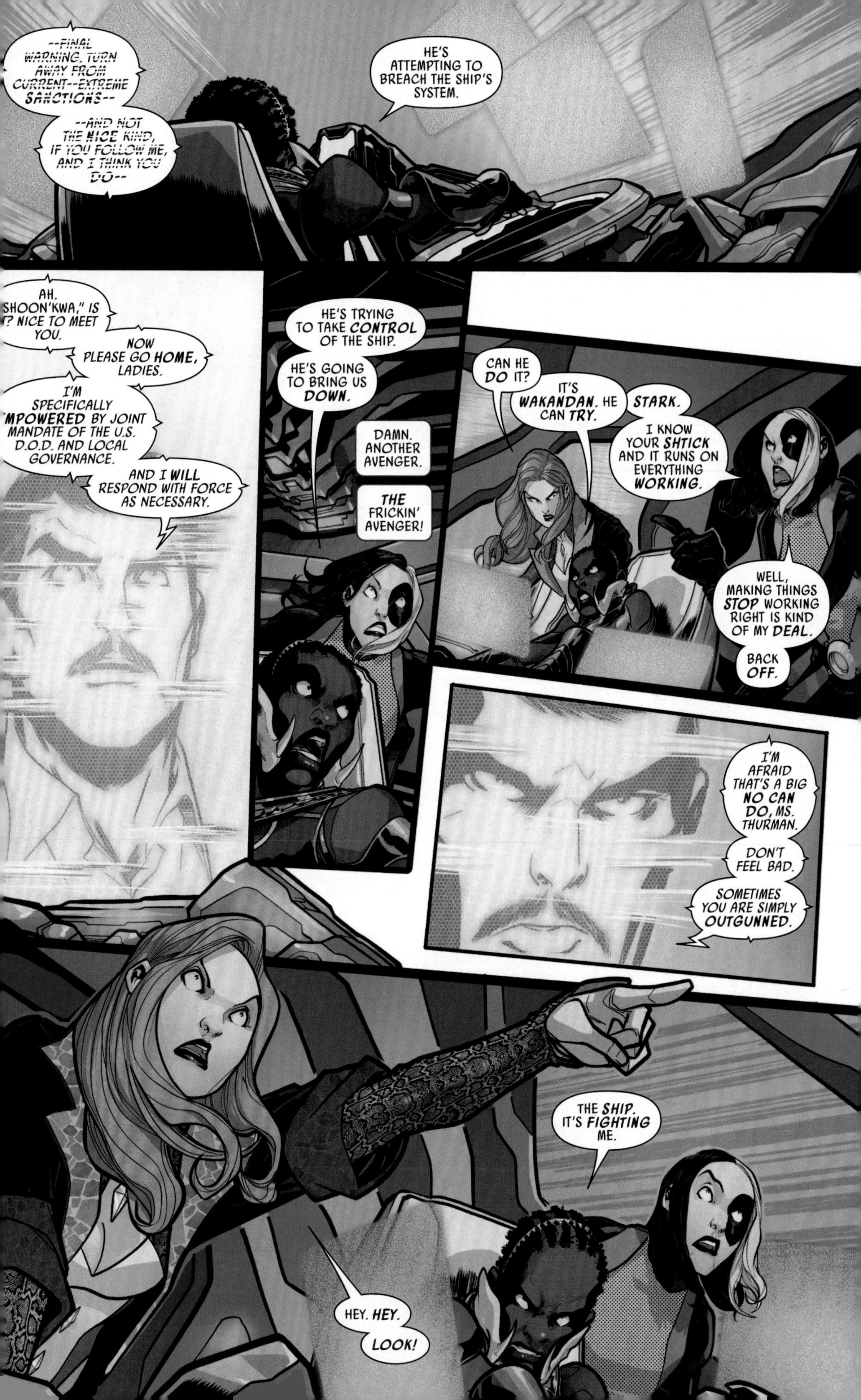
--FINAL WARNING. TURN AWAY FROM CURRENT--EXTREME SANCTIONS--
--AND NOT THE NICE KIND, IF YOU FOLLOW ME, AND I THINK YOU DO--
HE'S ATTEMPTING TO BREACH THE SHIP'S SYSTEM.
AH. "SHOON'KWA," IS IT? NICE TO MEET YOU.
NOW PLEASE GO HOME, LADIES.
I'M SPECIFICALLY EMPOWERED BY JOINT MANDATE OF THE U.S. D.O.D. AND LOCAL GOVERNANCE.
AND I WILL RESPOND WITH FORCE AS NECESSARY.
HE'S TRYING TO TAKE CONTROL OF THE SHIP.
HE'S GOING TO BRING US DOWN.
DAMN. ANOTHER AVENGER.
THE FRICKIN' AVENGER!
CAN HE DO IT?
IT'S WAKANDAN. HE CAN TRY.
STARK.
I KNOW YOUR SHTICK AND IT RUNS ON EVERYTHING WORKING.
WELL, MAKING THINGS STOP WORKING RIGHT IS KIND OF MY DEAL.
BACK OFF.
I'M AFRAID THAT'S A BIG NO CAN DO, MS. THURMAN.
DON'T FEEL BAD.
SOMETIMES YOU ARE SIMPLY OUTGUNNED.
THE SHIP. IT'S FIGHTING ME.
HEY. HEY.
LOOK!

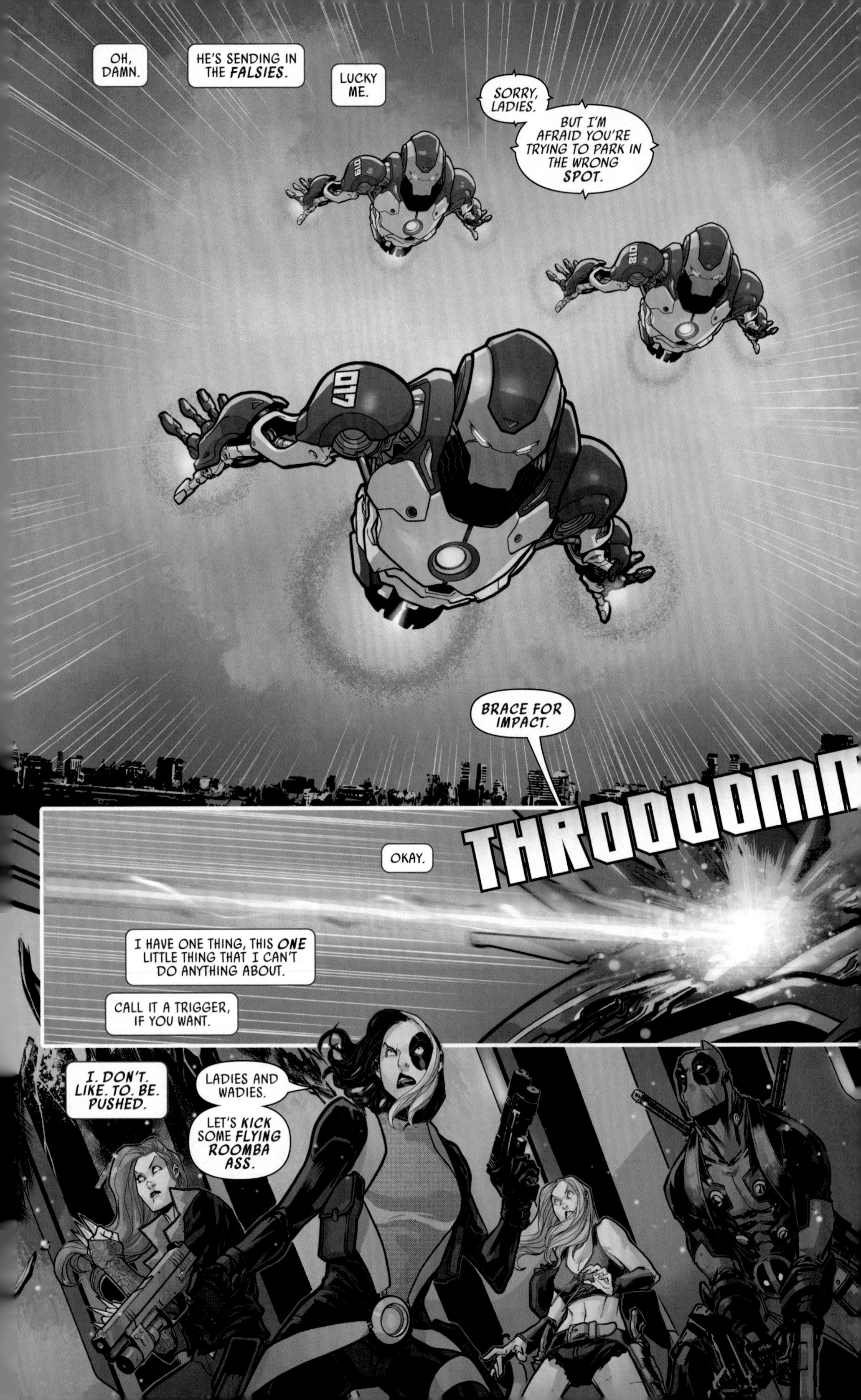
OH, DAMN.
HE'S SENDING IN THE FALSIES.
LUCKY ME.
SORRY, LADIES.
BUT I'M AFRAID YOU'RE TRYING TO PARK IN THE WRONG SPOT.
BRACE FOR IMPACT.
THROOOOMM
OKAY.
I HAVE ONE THING, THIS ONE LITTLE THING THAT I CAN'T DO ANYTHING ABOUT.
CALL IT A TRIGGER, IF YOU WANT.
I. DON'T. LIKE. TO. BE. PUSHED.
LADIES AND WADIES.
LET'S KICK SOME FLYING ROOMBA ASS.

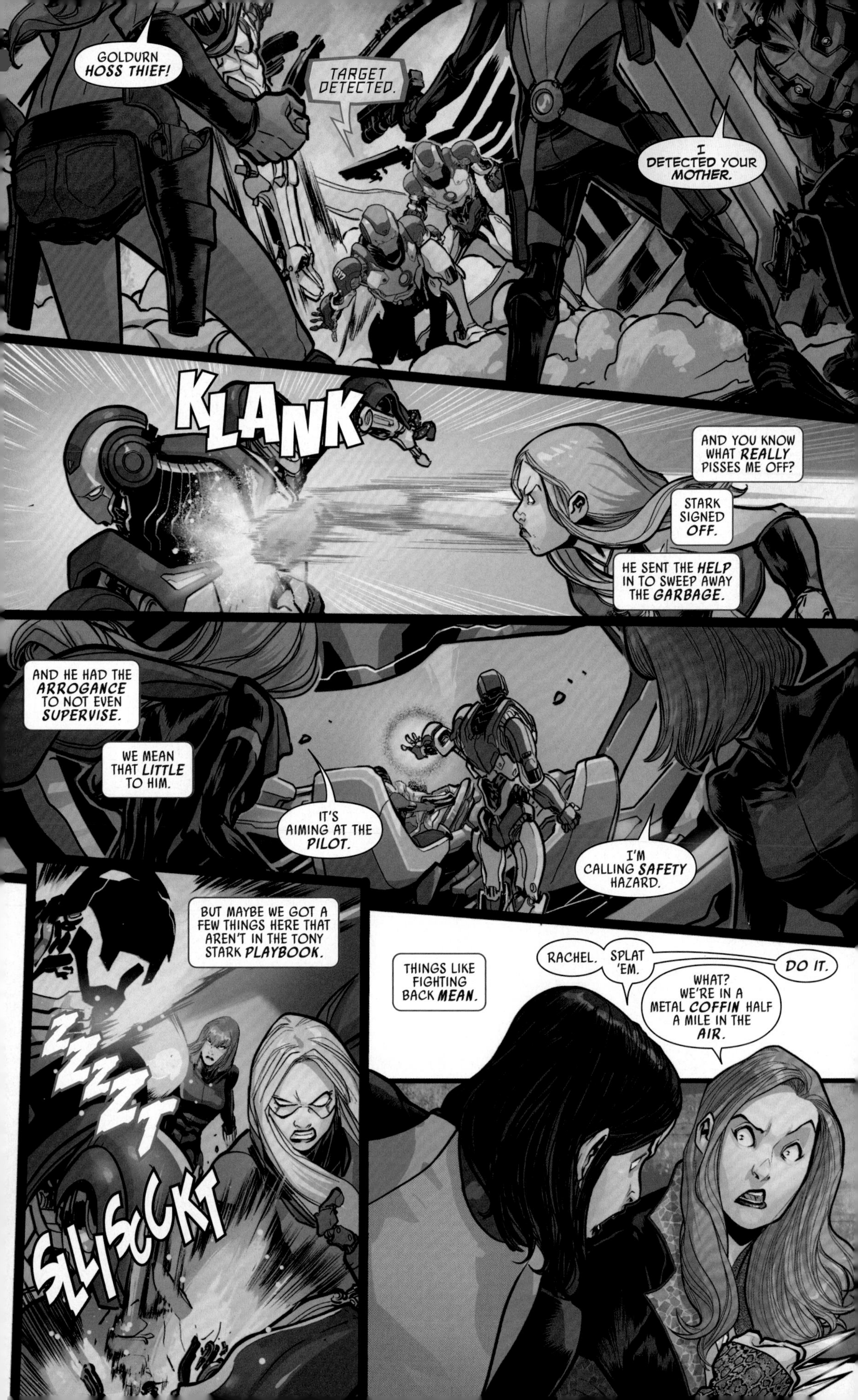

GOLDURN HOSS THIEF!
TARGET DETECTED.
I DETECTED YOUR MOTHER.
KLANK
AND YOU KNOW WHAT REALLY PISSES ME OFF?
STARK SIGNED OFF.
HE SENT THE HELP IN TO SWEEP AWAY THE GARBAGE.
AND HE HAD THE ARROGANCE TO NOT EVEN SUPERVISE.
WE MEAN THAT LITTLE TO HIM.
IT'S AIMING AT THE PILOT.
I'M CALLING SAFETY HAZARD.
BUT MAYBE WE GOT A FEW THINGS HERE THAT AREN'T IN THE TONY STARK PLAYBOOK.
ZZZZZT
SLLISCCKT
THINGS LIKE FIGHTING BACK MEAN.
RACHEL.
SPLAT 'EM.
DO IT.
WHAT? WE'RE IN A METAL COFFIN HALF A MILE IN THE AIR.

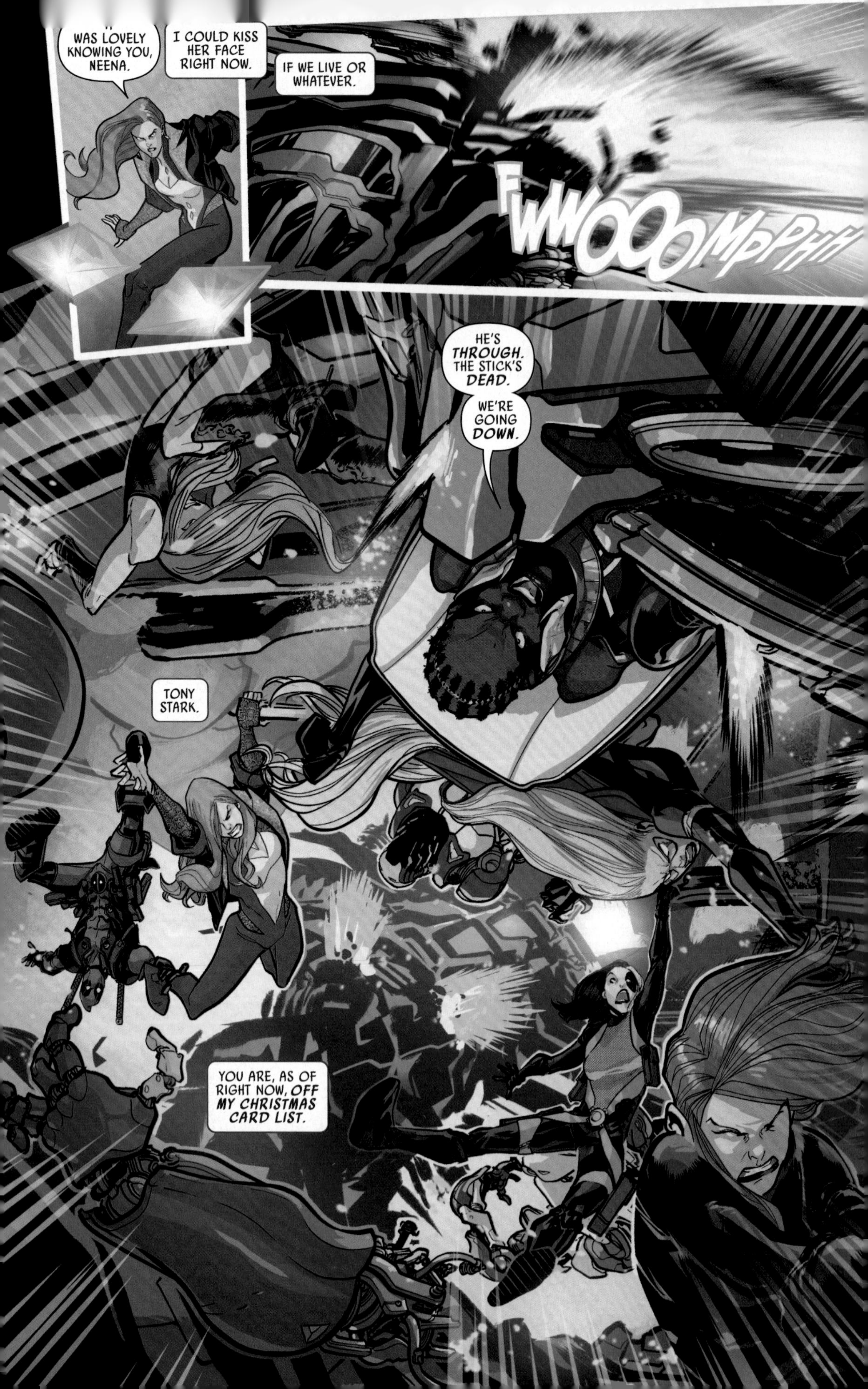

WAS LOVELY KNOWING YOU, NEENA.
I COULD KISS HER FACE RIGHT NOW.
IF WE LIVE OR WHATEVER.
FWWOOOMPPHH
HE'S THROUGH. THE STICK'S DEAD.
WE'RE GOING DOWN.
TONY STARK.
YOU ARE, AS OF RIGHT NOW, OFF MY CHRISTMAS CARD LIST.

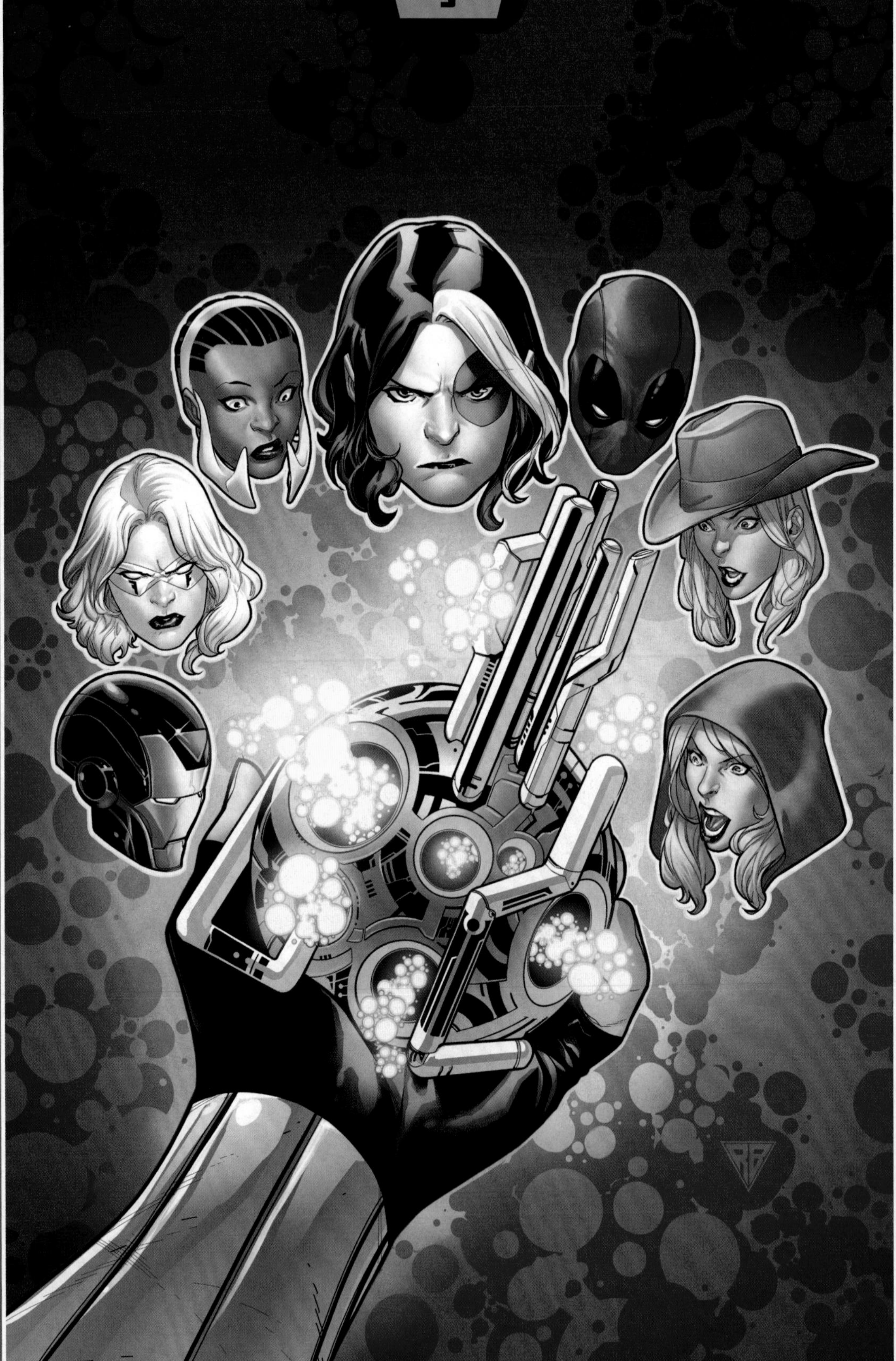

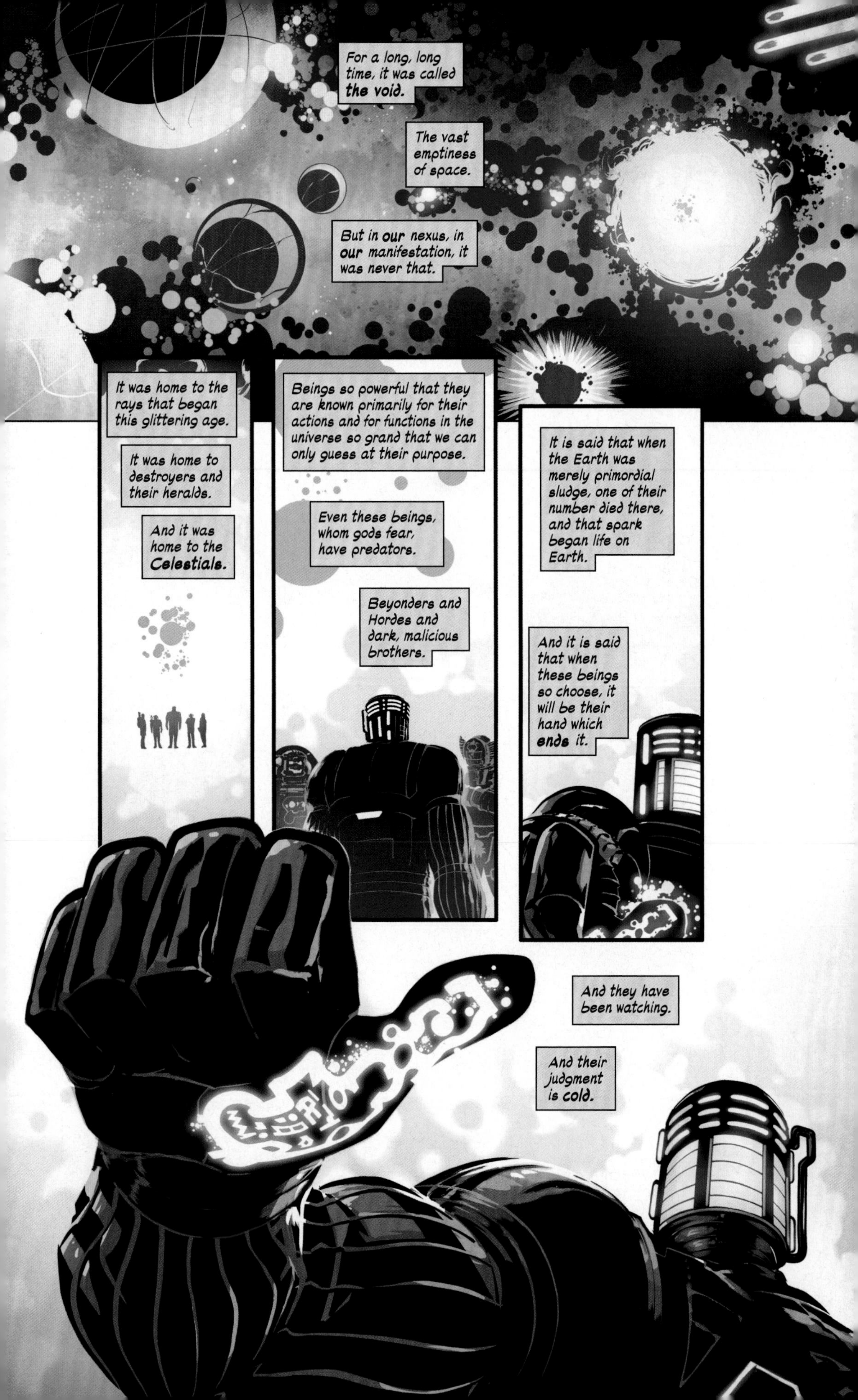
For a long, long time, it was called the void.
The vast emptiness of space.
But in our nexus, in our manifestation, it was never that.
It was home to the rays that began this glittering age.
It was home to destroyers and their heralds.
And it was home to the Celestials.
Beings so powerful that they are known primarily for their actions and for functions in the universe so grand that we can only guess at their purpose.
Even these beings, whom gods fear, have predators.
Beyonders and Hordes and dark, malicious brothers.
It is said that when the Earth was merely primordial sludge, one of their number died there, and that spark began life on Earth.
And it is said that when these beings so choose, it will be their hand which ends it.
And they have been watching.
And their judgment is cold.

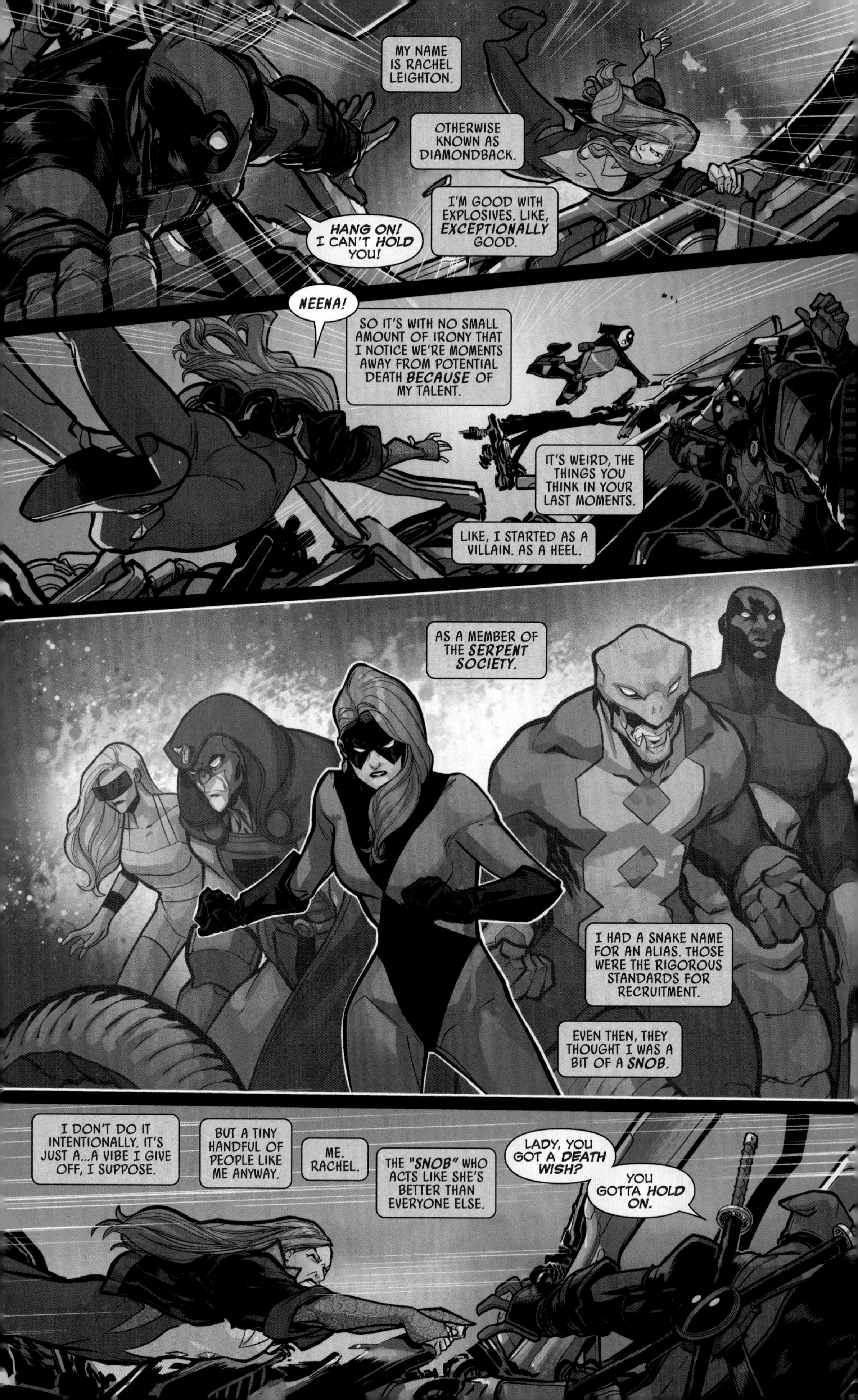
MY NAME IS RACHEL LEIGHTON.
OTHERWISE KNOWN AS DIAMONDBACK.
I'M GOOD WITH EXPLOSIVES. LIKE, EXCEPTIONALLY GOOD.
HANG ON! I CAN'T HOLD YOU!
NEENA!
SO IT'S WITH NO SMALL AMOUNT OF IRONY THAT I NOTICE WE'RE MOMENTS AWAY FROM POTENTIAL DEATH BECAUSE OF MY TALENT.
IT'S WEIRD, THE THINGS YOU THINK IN YOUR LAST MOMENTS.
LIKE, I STARTED AS A VILLAIN. AS A HEEL.
AS A MEMBER OF THE SERPENT SOCIETY.
I HAD A SNAKE NAME FOR AN ALIAS. THOSE WERE THE RIGOROUS STANDARDS FOR RECRUITMENT.
EVEN THEN, THEY THOUGHT I WAS A BIT OF A SNOB.
I DON'T DO IT INTENTIONALLY. IT'S JUST A...A VIBE I GIVE OFF, I SUPPOSE.
BUT A TINY HANDFUL OF PEOPLE LIKE ME ANYWAY.
ME. RACHEL.
THE "SNOB" WHO ACTS LIKE SHE'S BETTER THAN EVERYONE ELSE.
LADY, YOU GOT A DEATH WISH?
YOU GOTTA HOLD ON.

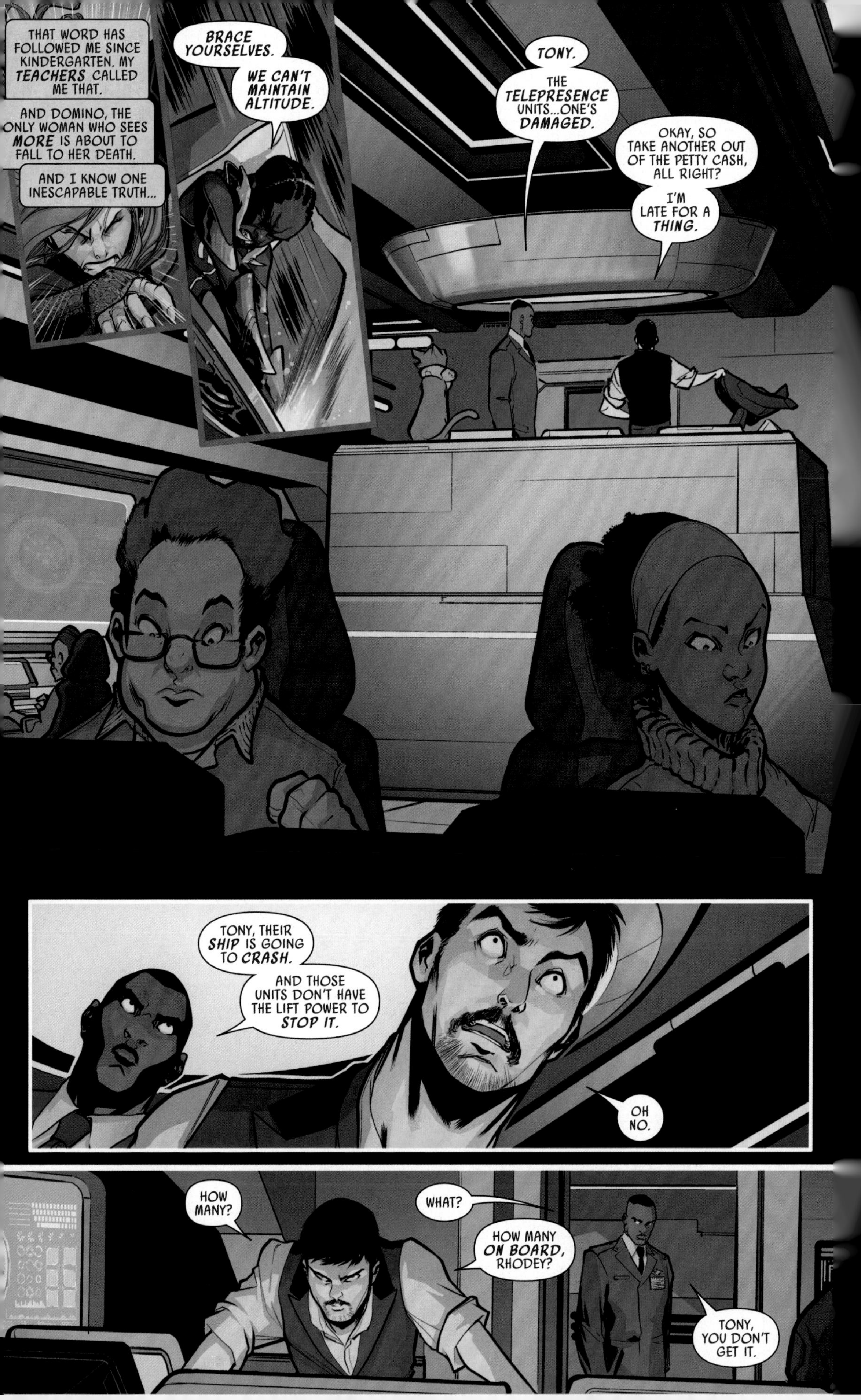
THAT WORD HAS FOLLOWED ME SINCE KINDERGARTEN. MY TEACHERS CALLED ME THAT.
AND DOMINO, THE ONLY WOMAN WHO SEES MORE IS ABOUT TO FALL TO HER DEATH.
AND I KNOW ONE INESCAPABLE TRUTH...
BRACE YOURSELVES.
WE CAN'T MAINTAIN ALTITUDE.
TONY.
THE TELEPRESENCE UNITS...ONE'S DAMAGED.
OKAY, SO TAKE ANOTHER OUT OF THE PETTY CASH, ALL RIGHT?
I'M LATE FOR A THING.
TONY, THEIR SHIP IS GOING TO CRASH.
AND THOSE UNITS DON'T HAVE THE LIFT POWER TO STOP IT.
OH NO.
HOW MANY?
WHAT?
HOW MANY ON BOARD, RHODEY?
TONY, YOU DON'T GET IT.

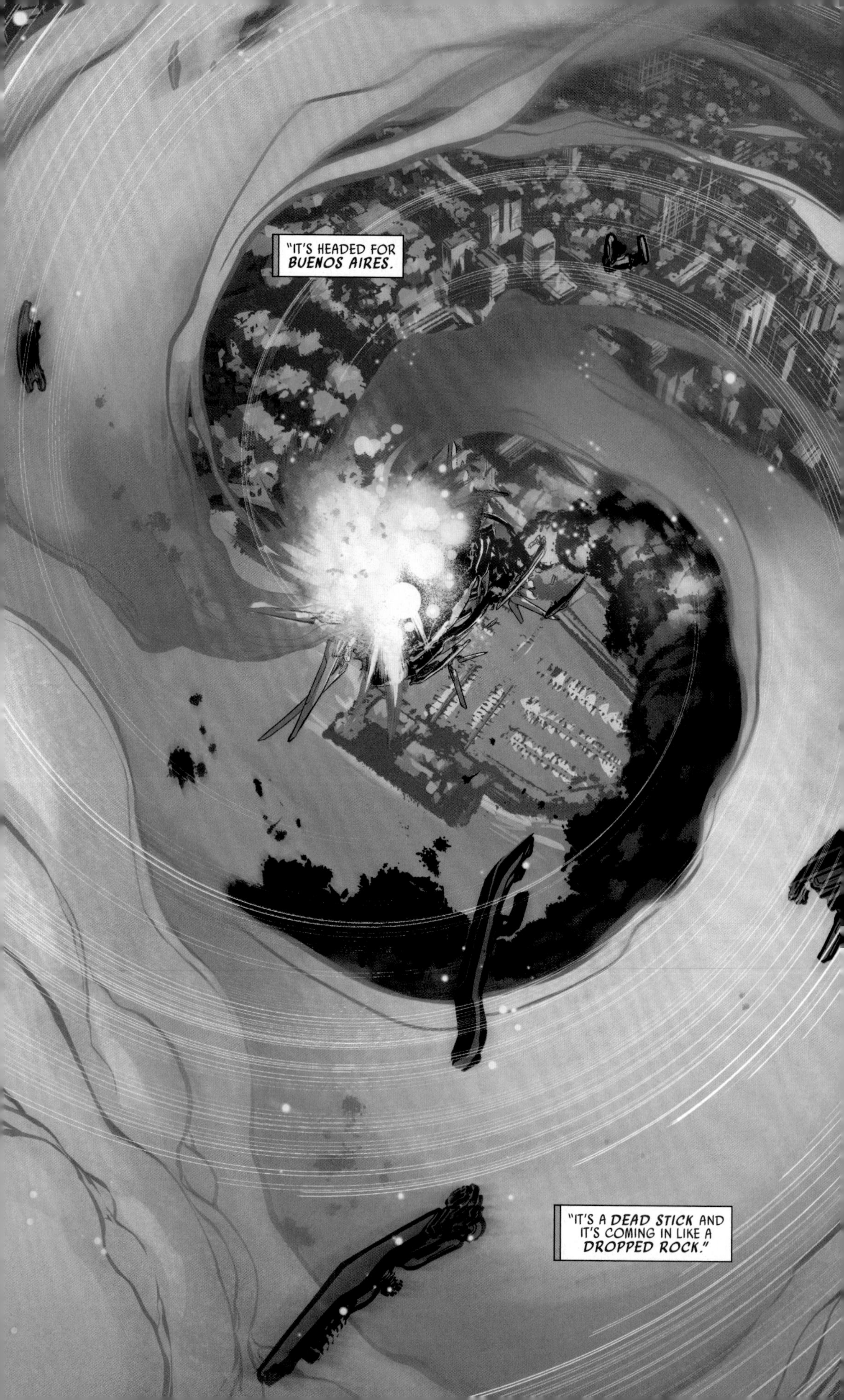
"IT'S HEADED FOR BUENOS AIRES.
"IT'S A DEAD STICK AND IT'S COMING IN LIKE A DROPPED ROCK."

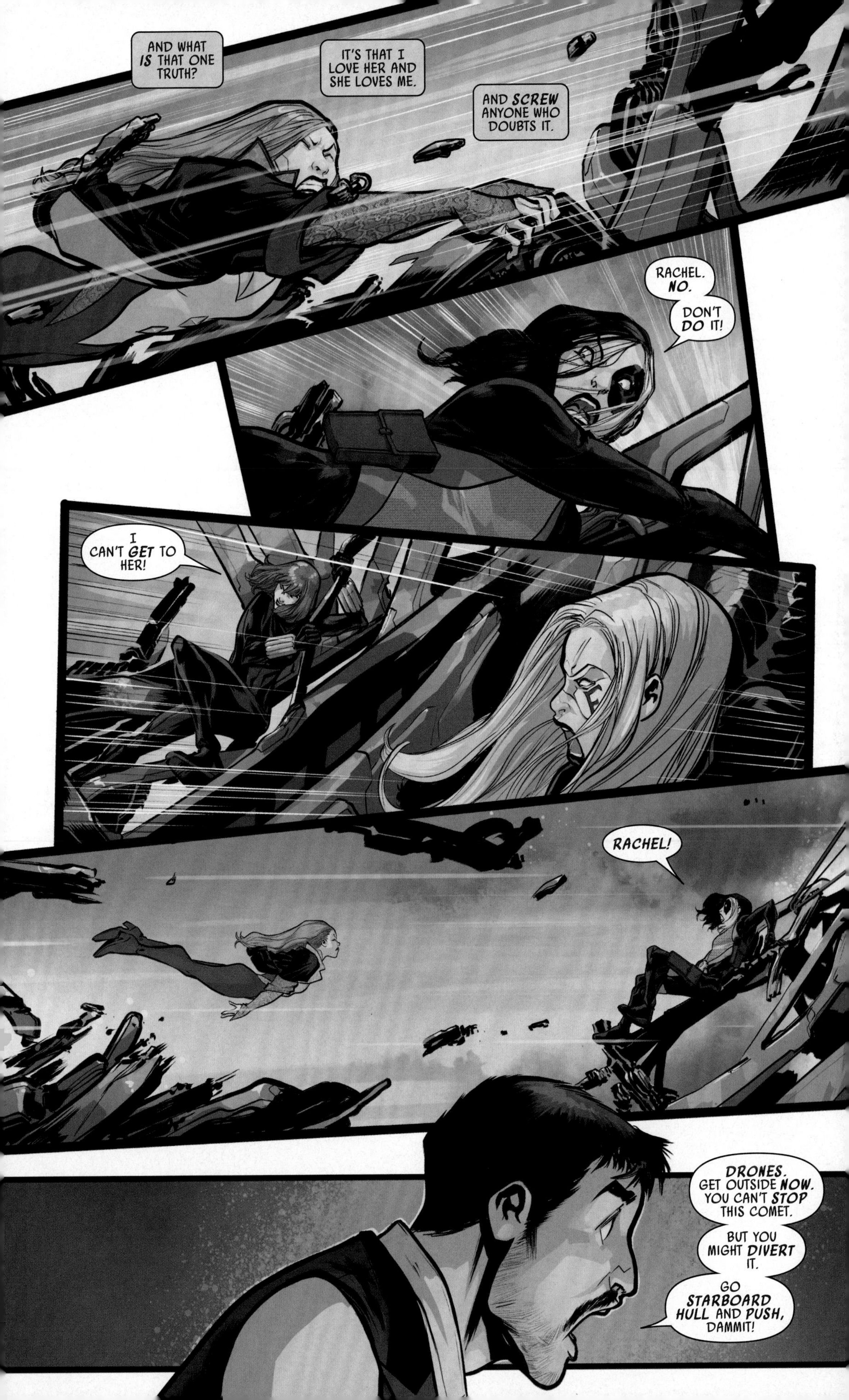
AND WHAT IS THAT ONE TRUTH?
IT'S THAT I LOVE HER AND SHE LOVES ME.
AND SCREW ANYONE WHO DOUBTS IT.
RACHEL. NO.
DON'T DO IT!
I CAN'T GET TO HER!
RACHEL!
DRONES. GET OUTSIDE NOW. YOU CAN'T STOP THIS COMET.
BUT YOU MIGHT DIVERT IT.
GO STARBOARD HULL AND PUSH, DAMMIT!

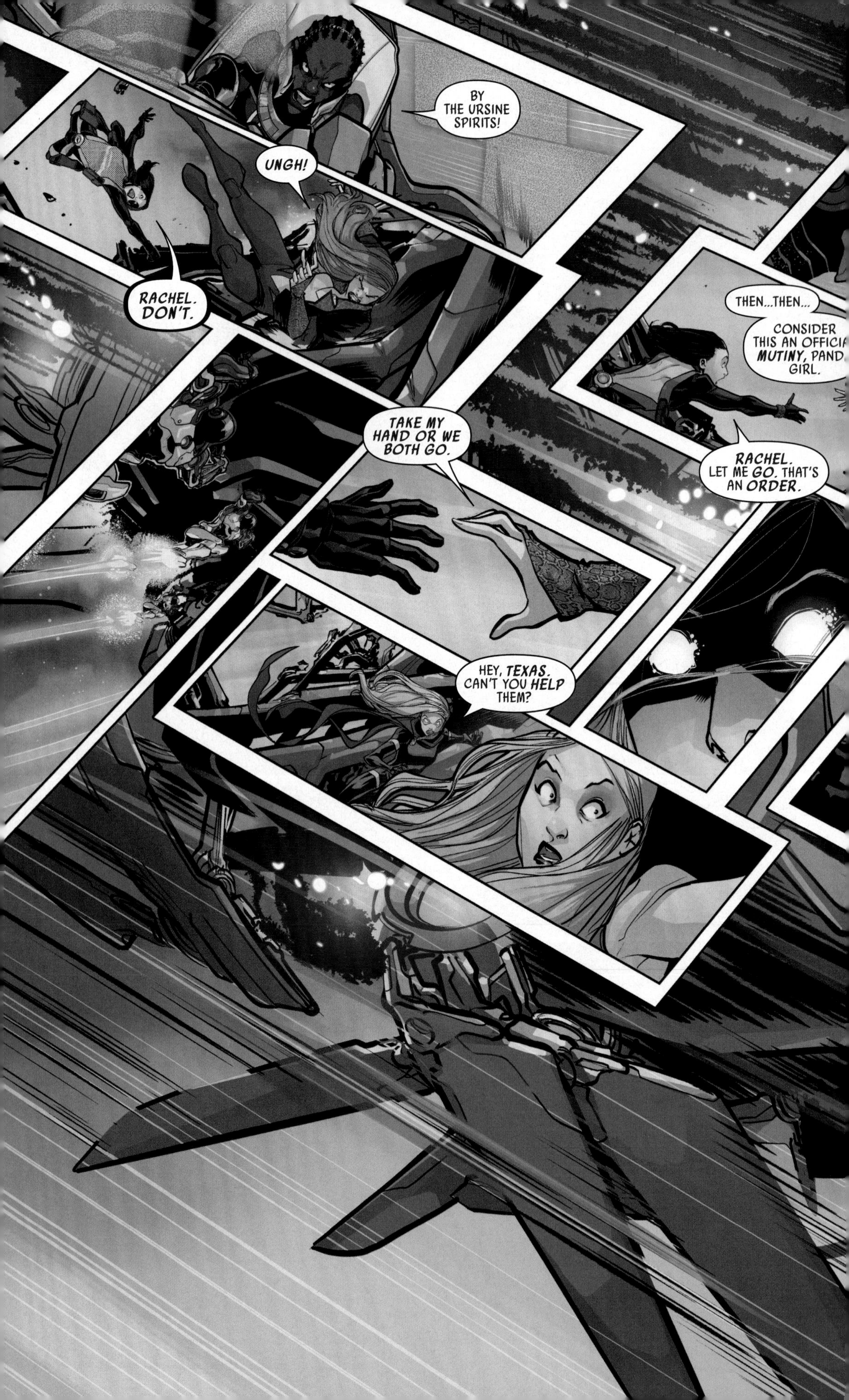
BY THE URSINE SPIRITS!
UNGH!
RACHEL. DON'T.
THEN...THEN...
CONSIDER THIS AN OFFICIA MUTINY, PAND GIRL.
TAKE MY HAND OR WE BOTH GO.
RACHEL. LET ME GO. THAT'S AN ORDER.
HEY, TEXAS. CAN'T YOU HELP THEM?

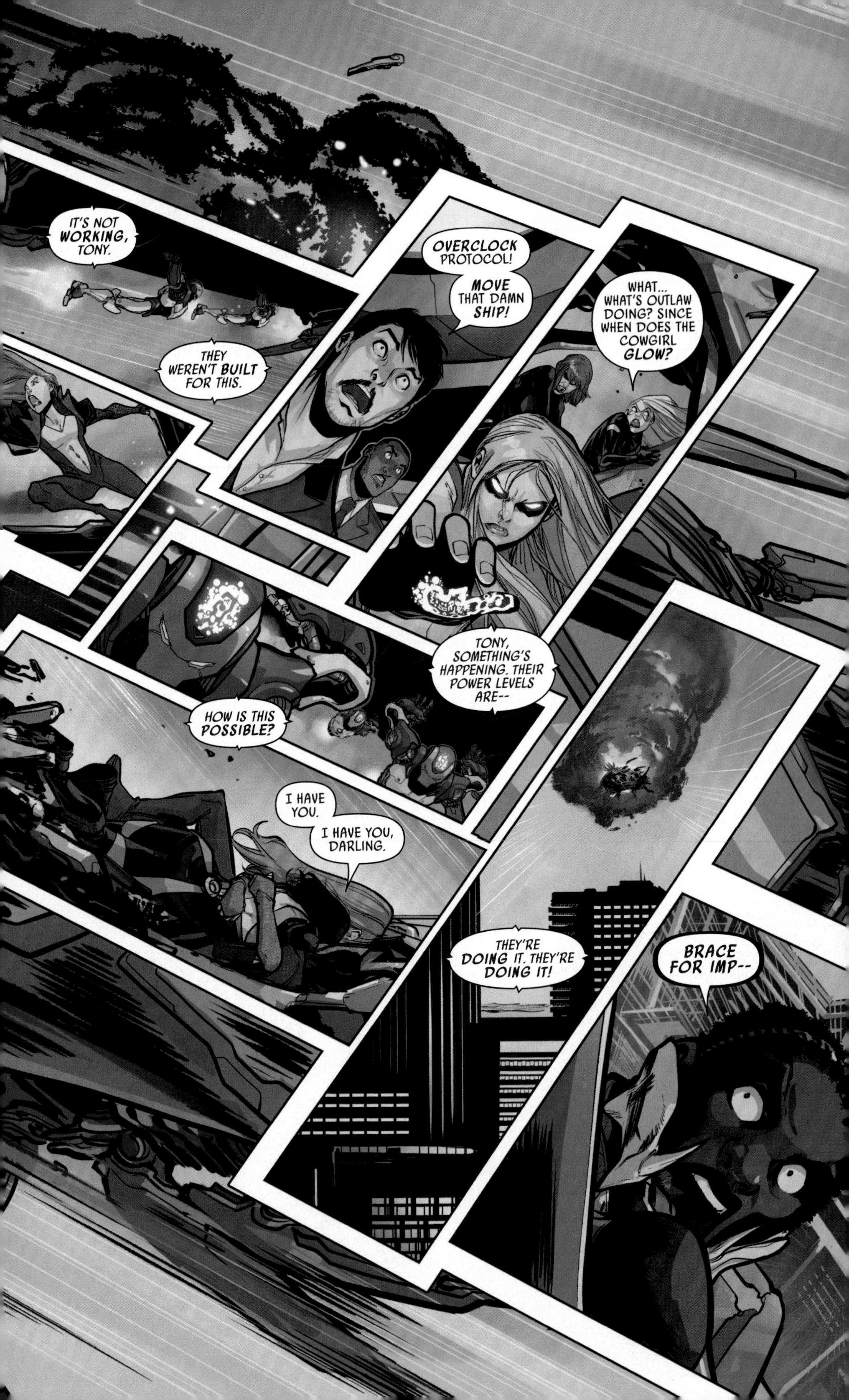

IT'S NOT WORKING, TONY.
THEY WEREN'T BUILT FOR THIS.
OVERCLOCK PROTOCOL!
MOVE THAT DAMN SHIP!
WHAT... WHAT'S OUTLAW DOING? SINCE WHEN DOES THE COWGIRL GLOW?
TONY, SOMETHING'S HAPPENING. THEIR POWER LEVELS ARE--
HOW IS THIS POSSIBLE?
I HAVE YOU.
I HAVE YOU, DARLING.
THEY'RE DOING IT. THEY'RE DOING IT!
BRACE FOR IMP--

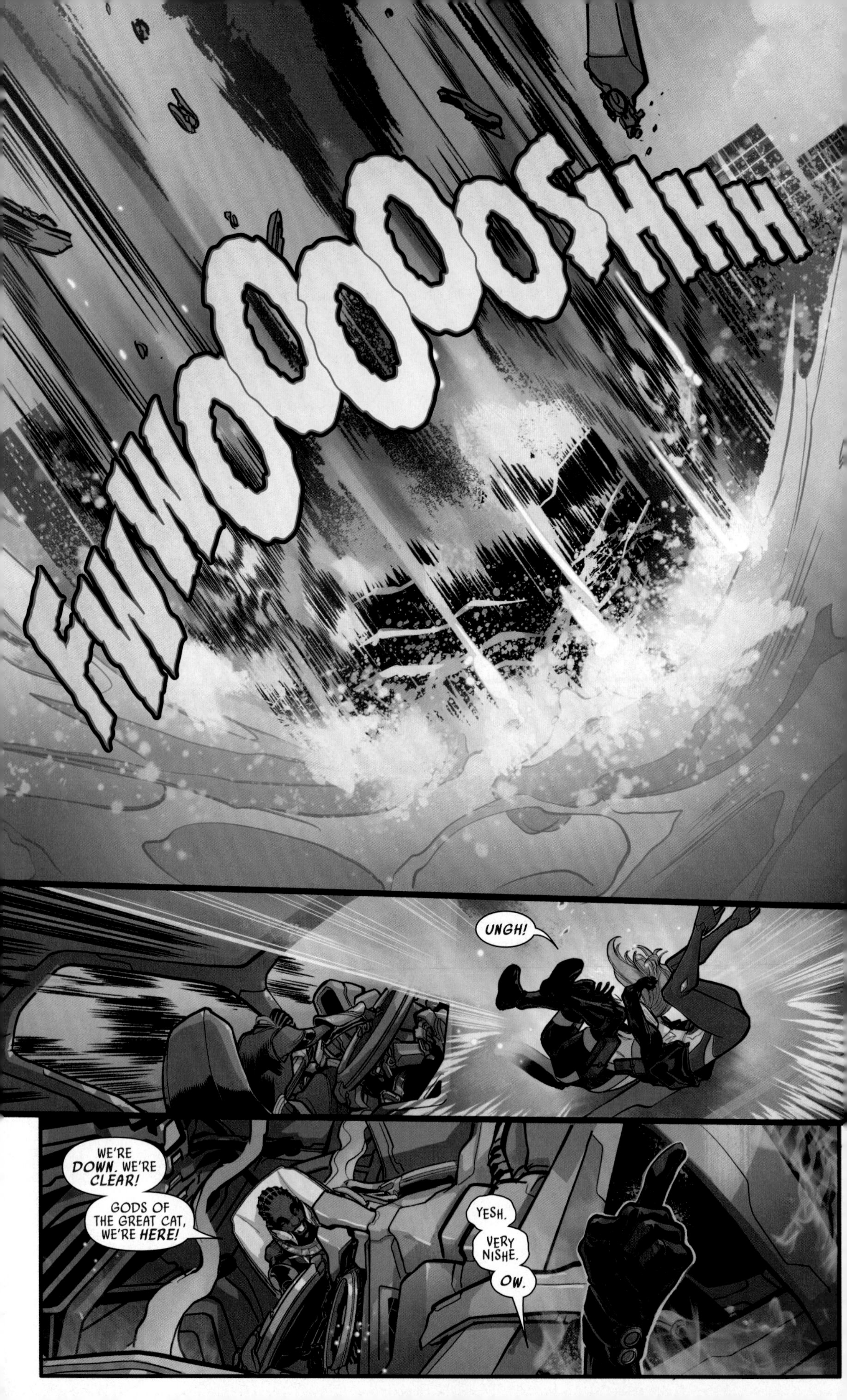
FWWOOOOOSHHH
UNGH!
WE'RE DOWN. WE'RE CLEAR!
GODS OF THE GREAT CAT, WE'RE HERE!
YESH.
VERY NISHE.
OW.

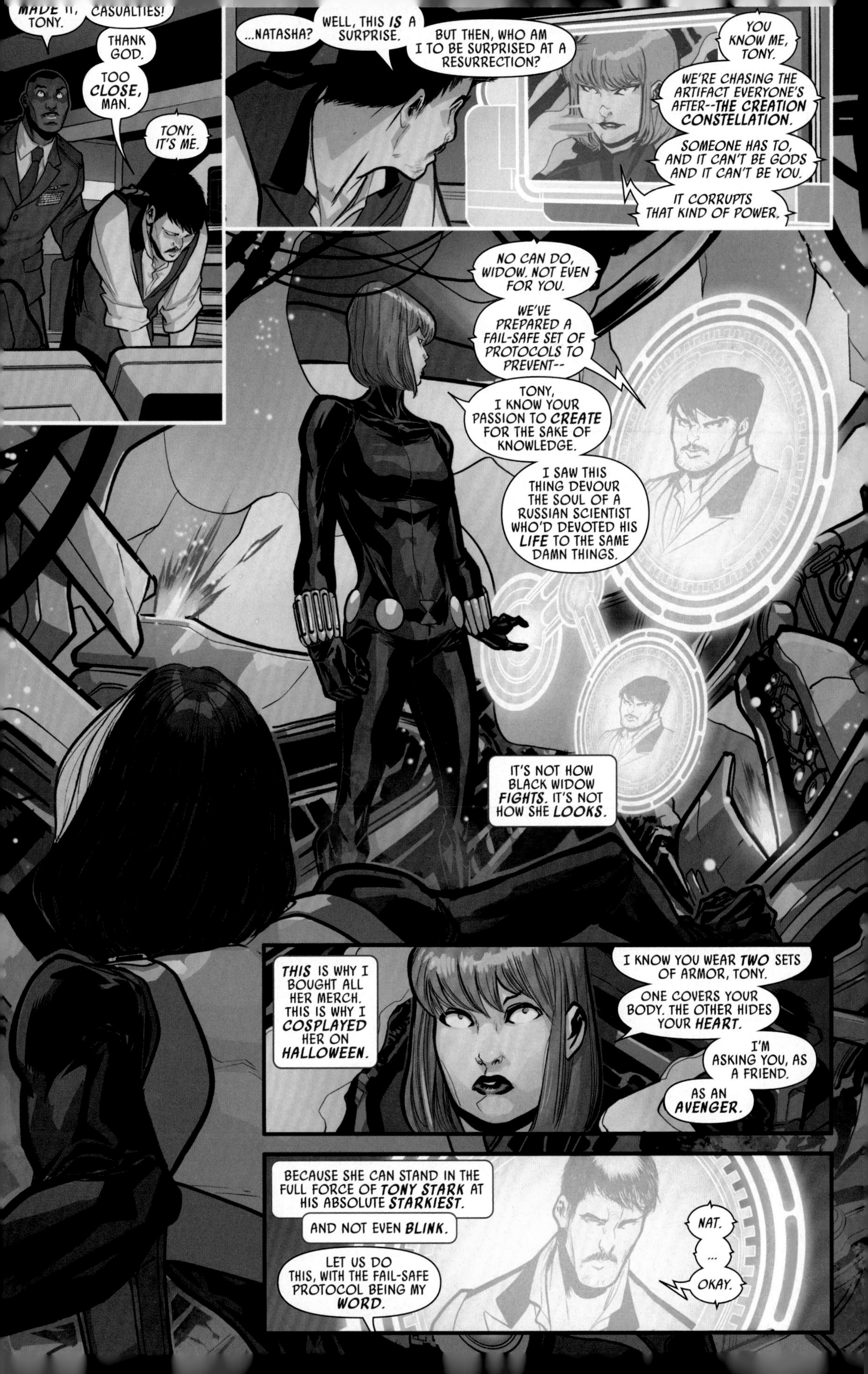
MADE IT, TONY.
CASUALTIES!
THANK GOD.
TOO CLOSE, MAN.
TONY. IT'S ME.
...NATASHA?
WELL, THIS IS A SURPRISE.
BUT THEN, WHO AM I TO BE SURPRISED AT A RESURRECTION?
YOU KNOW ME, TONY.
WE'RE CHASING THE ARTIFACT EVERYONE'S AFTER--THE CREATION CONSTELLATION.
SOMEONE HAS TO, AND IT CAN'T BE GODS AND IT CAN'T BE YOU.
IT CORRUPTS THAT KIND OF POWER.
NO CAN DO, WIDOW. NOT EVEN FOR YOU.
WE'VE PREPARED A FAIL-SAFE SET OF PROTOCOLS TO PREVENT--
TONY, I KNOW YOUR PASSION TO CREATE FOR THE SAKE OF KNOWLEDGE.
I SAW THIS THING DEVOUR THE SOUL OF A RUSSIAN SCIENTIST WHO'D DEVOTED HIS LIFE TO THE SAME DAMN THINGS.
IT'S NOT HOW BLACK WIDOW FIGHTS. IT'S NOT HOW SHE LOOKS.
THIS IS WHY I BOUGHT ALL HER MERCH. THIS IS WHY I COSPLAYED HER ON HALLOWEEN.
I KNOW YOU WEAR TWO SETS OF ARMOR, TONY.
ONE COVERS YOUR BODY. THE OTHER HIDES YOUR HEART.
I'M ASKING YOU, AS A FRIEND.
AS AN AVENGER.
BECAUSE SHE CAN STAND IN THE FULL FORCE OF TONY STARK AT HIS ABSOLUTE STARKIEST.
AND NOT EVEN BLINK.
LET US DO THIS, WITH THE FAIL-SAFE PROTOCOL BEING MY WORD.
NAT.
...
OKAY.

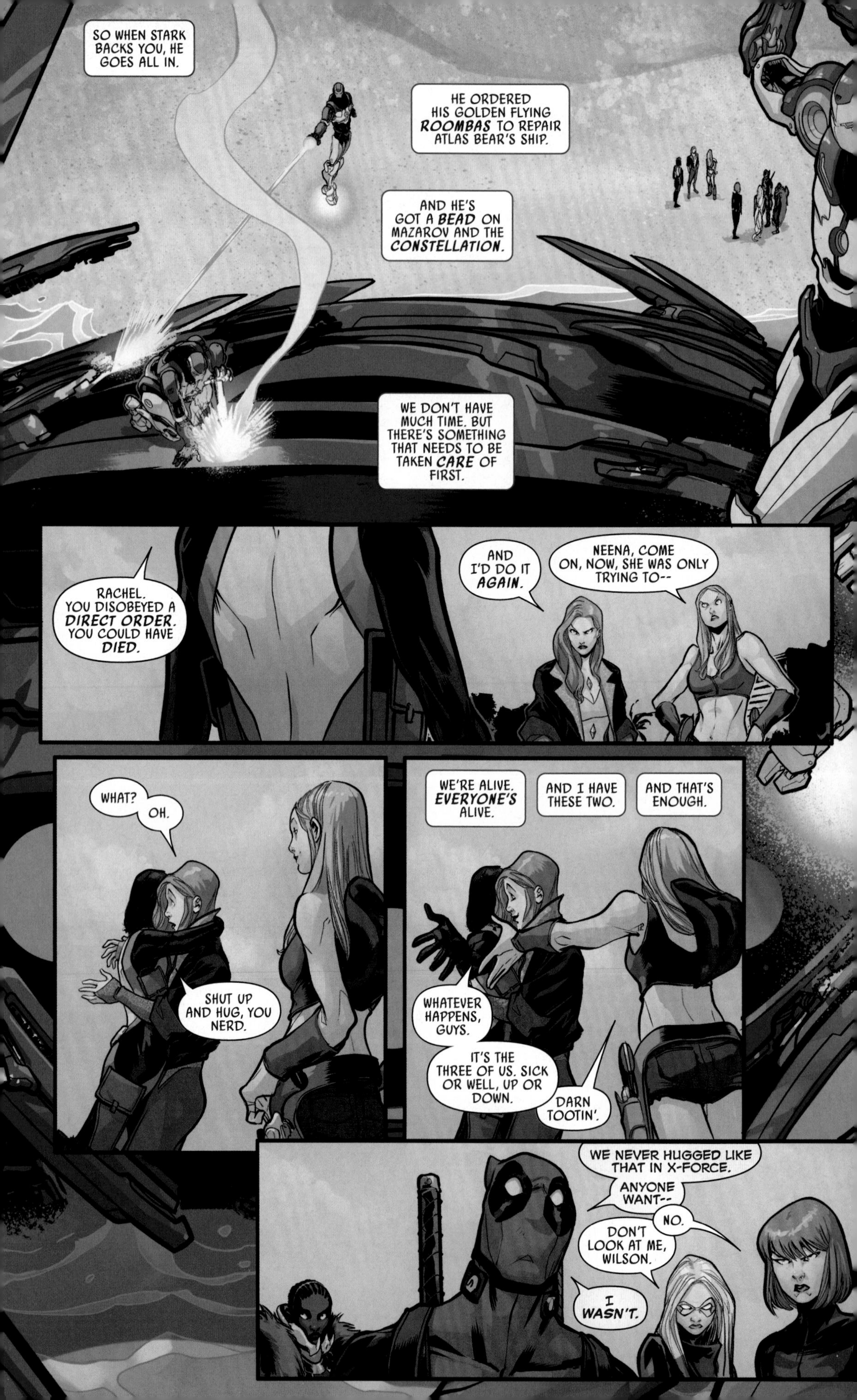
SO WHEN STARK BACKS YOU, HE GOES ALL IN.
HE ORDERED HIS GOLDEN FLYING ROOMBAS TO REPAIR ATLAS BEAR'S SHIP.
AND HE'S GOT A BEAD ON MAZAROV AND THE CONSTELLATION.
WE DON'T HAVE MUCH TIME. BUT THERE'S SOMETHING THAT NEEDS TO BE TAKEN CARE OF FIRST.
RACHEL. YOU DISOBEYED A DIRECT ORDER. YOU COULD HAVE DIED.
AND I'D DO IT AGAIN.
NEENA, COME ON, NOW, SHE WAS ONLY TRYING TO--
WHAT?
OH.
SHUT UP AND HUG, YOU NERD.
WE'RE ALIVE. EVERYONE'S ALIVE.
AND I HAVE THESE TWO.
AND THAT'S ENOUGH.
WHATEVER HAPPENS, GUYS.
IT'S THE THREE OF US. SICK OR WELL, UP OR DOWN.
DARN TOOTIN'.
WE NEVER HUGGED LIKE THAT IN X-FORCE.
ANYONE WANT--
NO.
DON'T LOOK AT ME, WILSON.
I WASN'T.

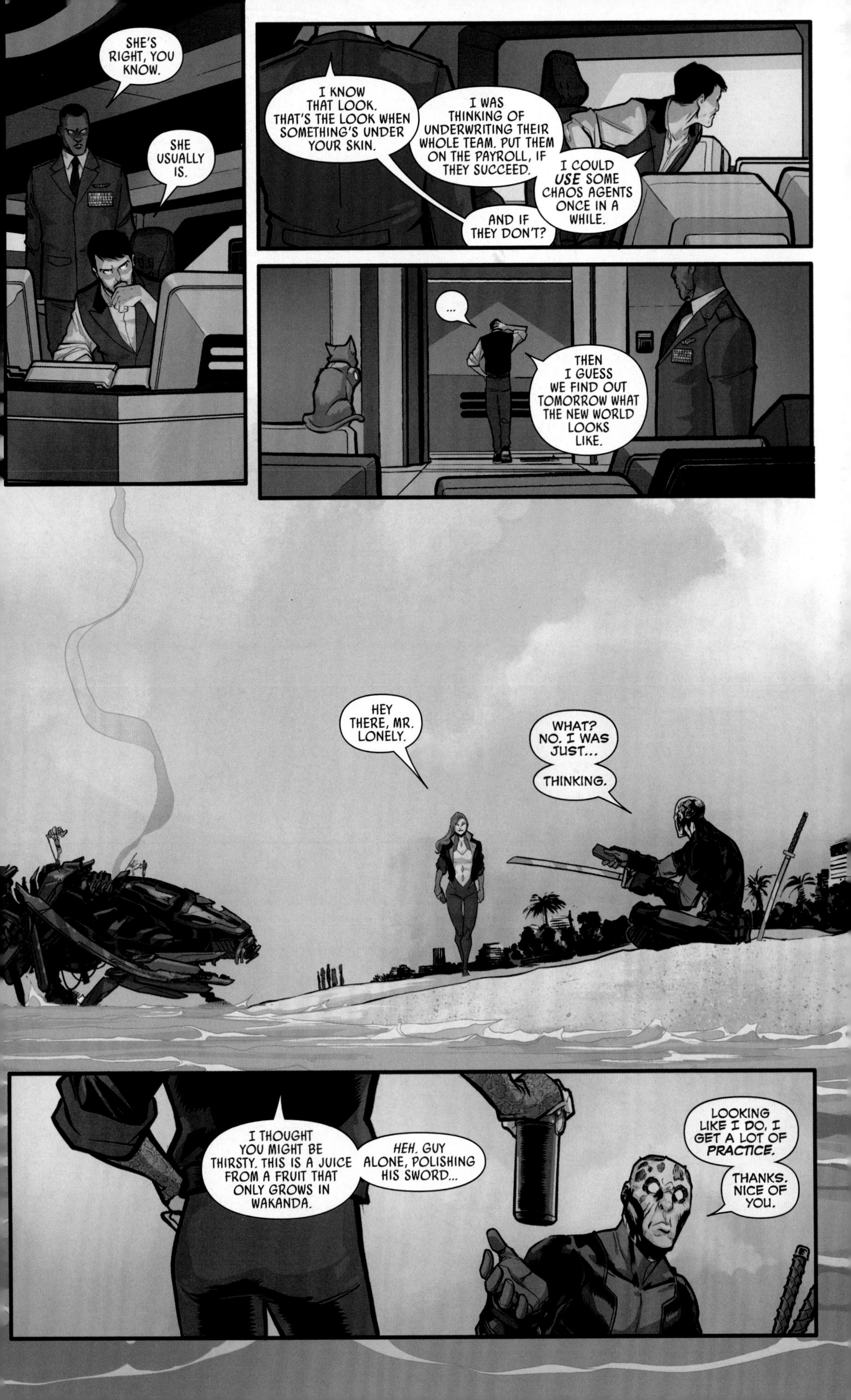
SHE'S RIGHT, YOU KNOW.
SHE USUALLY IS.
I KNOW THAT LOOK. THAT'S THE LOOK WHEN SOMETHING'S UNDER YOUR SKIN.
I WAS THINKING OF UNDERWRITING THEIR WHOLE TEAM. PUT THEM ON THE PAYROLL, IF THEY SUCCEED.
I COULD USE SOME CHAOS AGENTS ONCE IN A WHILE.
AND IF THEY DON'T?
...
THEN I GUESS WE FIND OUT TOMORROW WHAT THE NEW WORLD LOOKS LIKE.
HEY THERE, MR. LONELY.
WHAT? NO. I WAS JUST...
THINKING.
I THOUGHT YOU MIGHT BE THIRSTY. THIS IS A JUICE FROM A FRUIT THAT ONLY GROWS IN WAKANDA.
HEH. GUY ALONE, POLISHING HIS SWORD...
LOOKING LIKE I DO, I GET A LOT OF PRACTICE.
THANKS. NICE OF YOU.

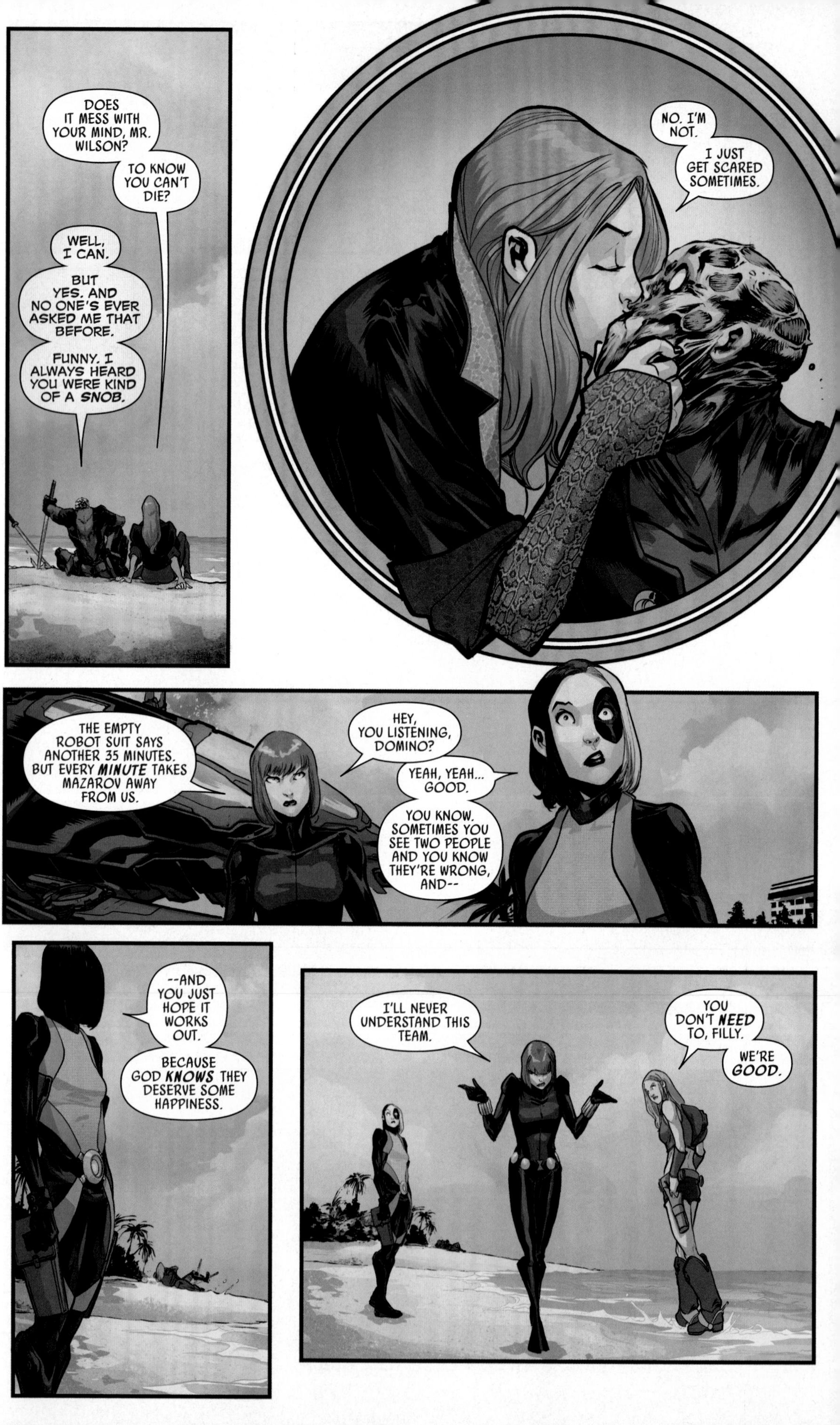
DOES IT MESS WITH YOUR MIND, MR. WILSON?
TO KNOW YOU CAN'T DIE?
WELL, I CAN.
BUT YES. AND NO ONE'S EVER ASKED ME THAT BEFORE.
FUNNY. I ALWAYS HEARD YOU WERE KIND OF A SNOB.
NO. I'M NOT.
I JUST GET SCARED SOMETIMES.
THE EMPTY ROBOT SUIT SAYS ANOTHER 35 MINUTES. BUT EVERY MINUTE TAKES MAZAROV AWAY FROM US.
HEY, YOU LISTENING, DOMINO?
YEAH, YEAH... GOOD.
YOU KNOW. SOMETIMES YOU SEE TWO PEOPLE AND YOU KNOW THEY'RE WRONG, AND--
--AND YOU JUST HOPE IT WORKS OUT.
BECAUSE GOD KNOWS THEY DESERVE SOME HAPPINESS.
I'LL NEVER UNDERSTAND THIS TEAM.
YOU DON'T NEED TO, FILLY.
WE'RE GOOD.

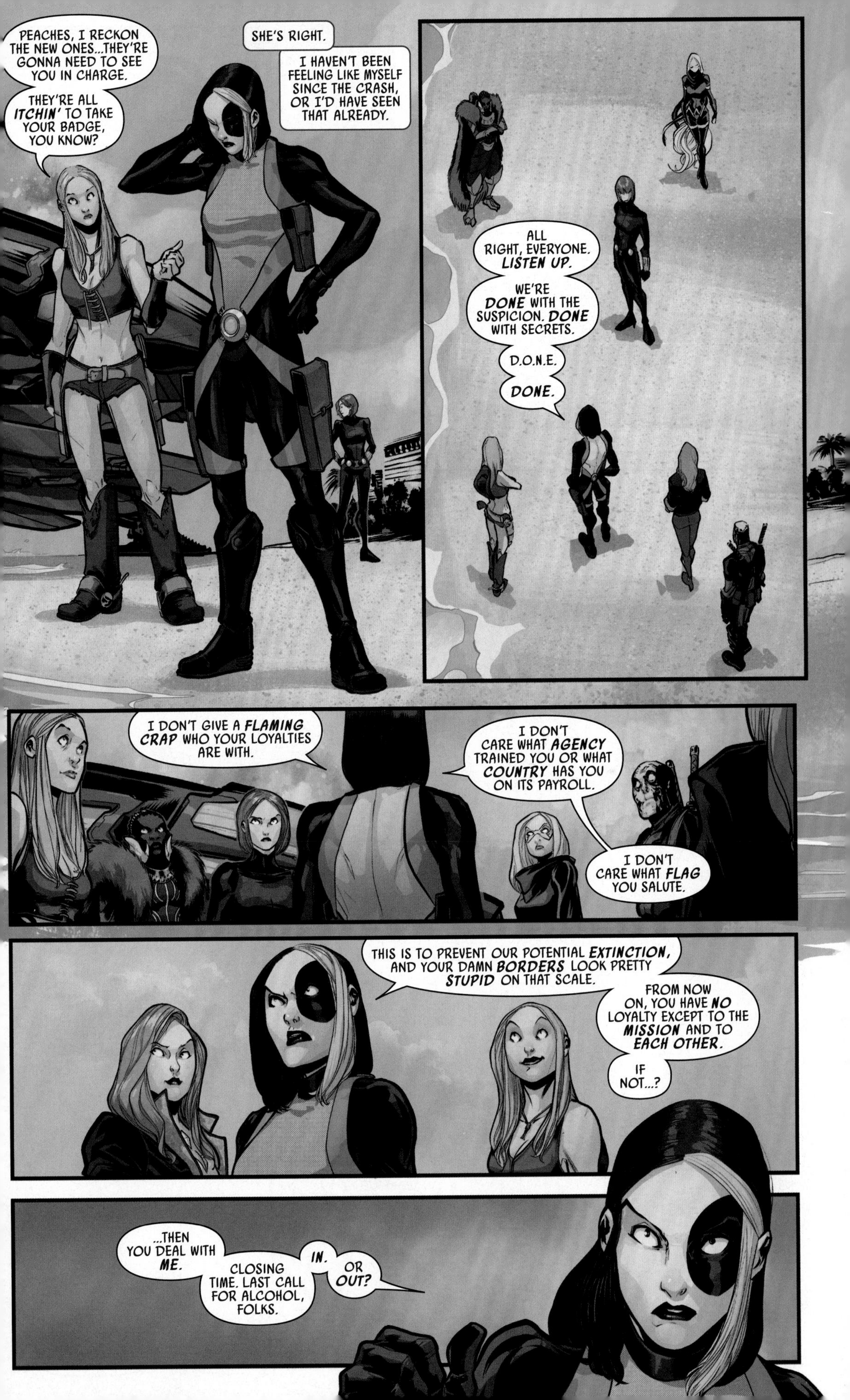
PEACHES, I RECKON THE NEW ONES...THEY'RE GONNA NEED TO SEE YOU IN CHARGE.
THEY'RE ALL ITCHIN' TO TAKE YOUR BADGE, YOU KNOW?
SHE'S RIGHT.
I HAVEN'T BEEN FEELING LIKE MYSELF SINCE THE CRASH, OR I'D HAVE SEEN THAT ALREADY.
ALL RIGHT, EVERYONE. LISTEN UP.
WE'RE DONE WITH THE SUSPICION. DONE WITH SECRETS.
D.O.N.E.
DONE.
I DON'T GIVE A FLAMING CRAP WHO YOUR LOYALTIES ARE WITH.
I DON'T CARE WHAT AGENCY TRAINED YOU OR WHAT COUNTRY HAS YOU ON ITS PAYROLL.
I DON'T CARE WHAT FLAG YOU SALUTE.
THIS IS TO PREVENT OUR POTENTIAL EXTINCTION, AND YOUR DAMN BORDERS LOOK PRETTY STUPID ON THAT SCALE.
FROM NOW ON, YOU HAVE NO LOYALTY EXCEPT TO THE MISSION AND TO EACH OTHER.
IF NOT...?
...THEN YOU DEAL WITH ME.
CLOSING TIME. LAST CALL FOR ALCOHOL, FOLKS.
IN.
OR OUT?

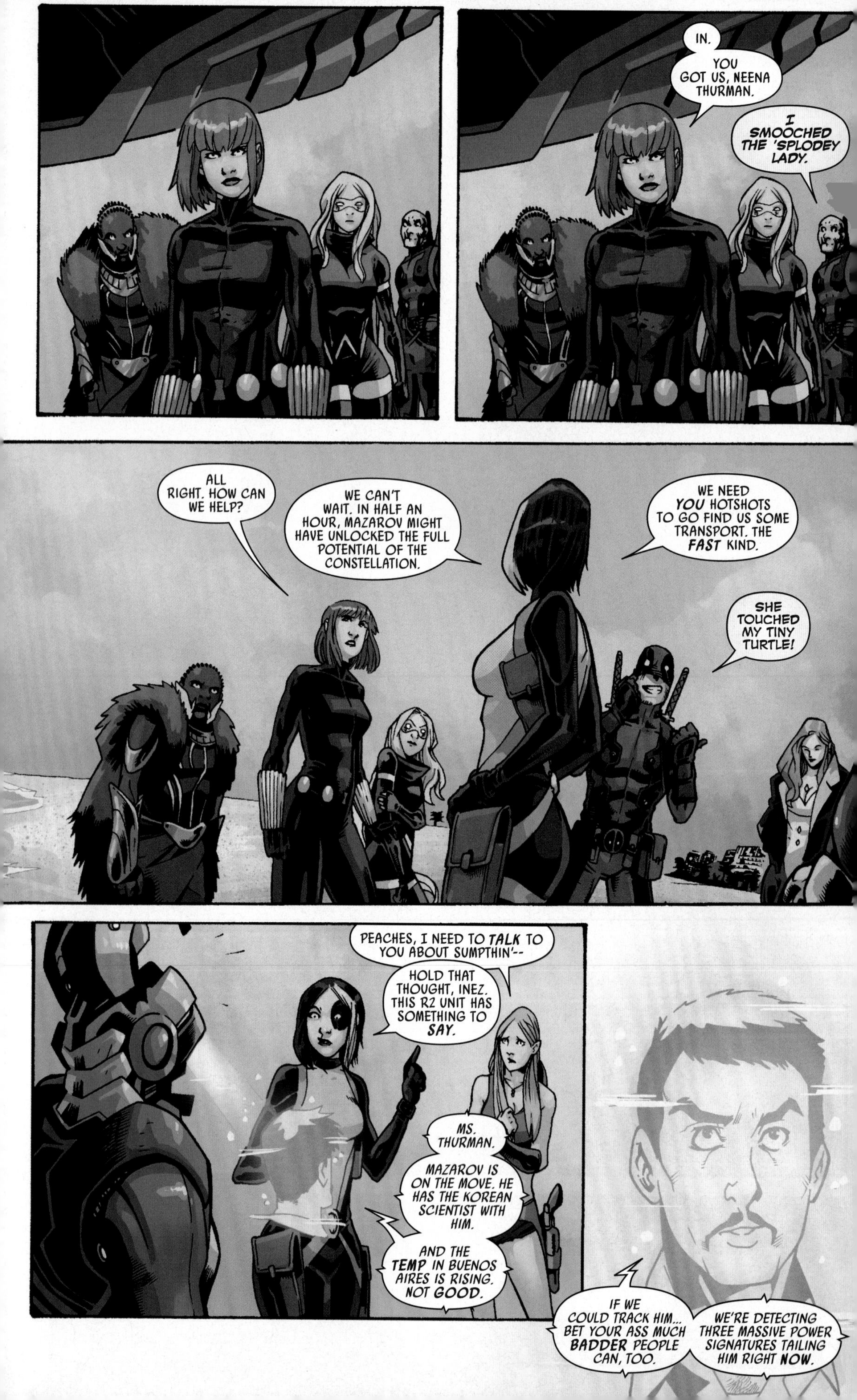
IN.
YOU GOT US, NEENA THURMAN.
I SMOOCHED THE 'SPLODEY LADY.
ALL RIGHT. HOW CAN WE HELP?
WE CAN'T WAIT. IN HALF AN HOUR, MAZAROV MIGHT HAVE UNLOCKED THE FULL POTENTIAL OF THE CONSTELLATION.
WE NEED YOU HOTSHOTS TO GO FIND US SOME TRANSPORT. THE FAST KIND.
SHE TOUCHED MY TINY TURTLE!
PEACHES, I NEED TO TALK TO YOU ABOUT SUMPTHIN'--
HOLD THAT THOUGHT, INEZ. THIS R2 UNIT HAS SOMETHING TO SAY.
MS. THURMAN.
MAZAROV IS ON THE MOVE. HE HAS THE KOREAN SCIENTIST WITH HIM.
AND THE TEMP IN BUENOS AIRES IS RISING. NOT GOOD.
WE'RE DETECTING THREE MASSIVE POWER SIGNATURES TAILING HIM RIGHT NOW.
IF WE COULD TRACK HIM... BET YOUR ASS MUCH BADDER PEOPLE CAN, TOO.

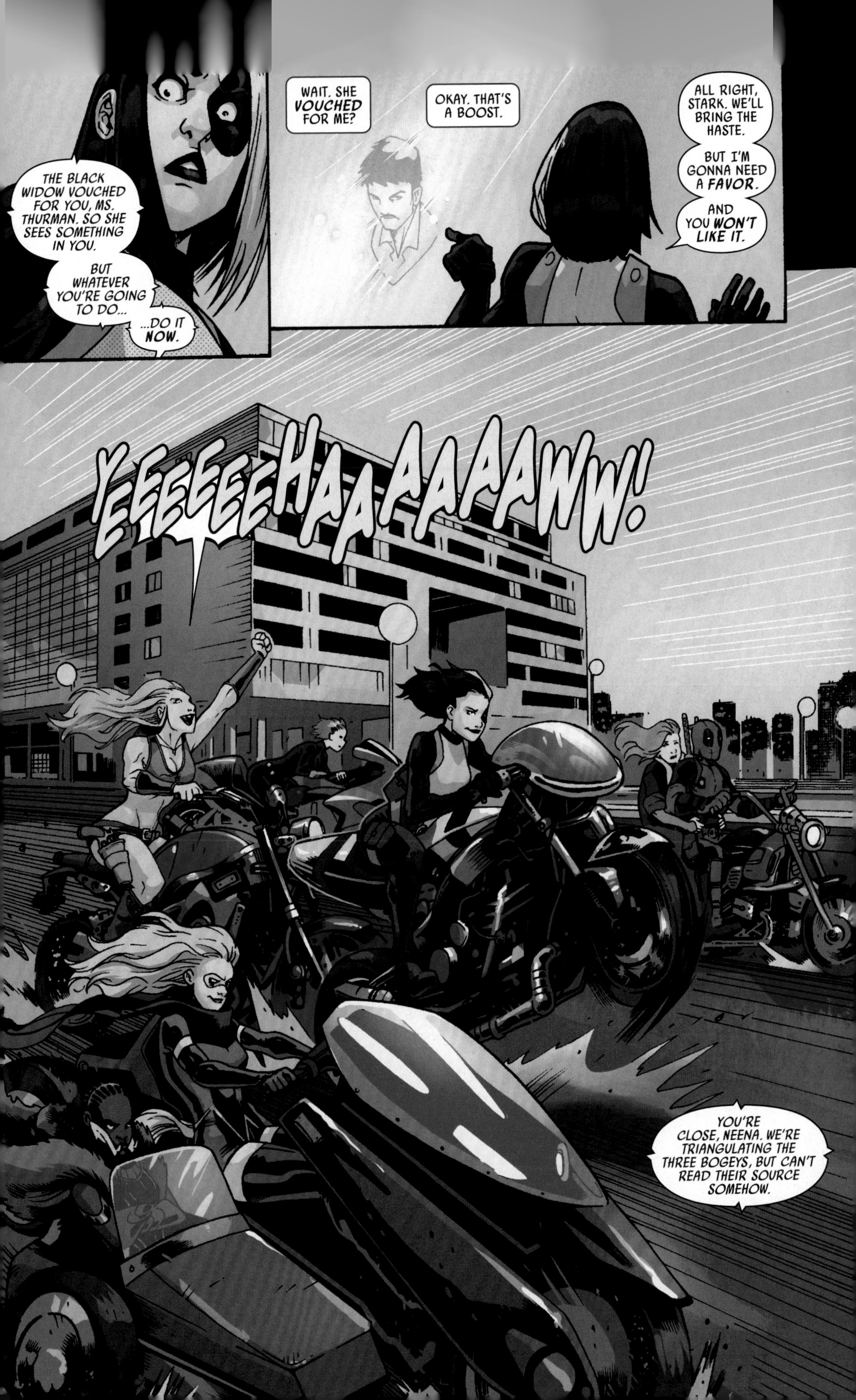

THE BLACK WIDOW VOUCHED FOR YOU, MS. THURMAN. SO SHE SEES SOMETHING IN YOU.
BUT WHATEVER YOU'RE GOING TO DO...
...DO IT NOW.
WAIT. SHE VOUCHED FOR ME?
OKAY. THAT'S A BOOST.
ALL RIGHT, STARK. WE'LL BRING THE HASTE.
BUT I'M GONNA NEED A FAVOR.
AND YOU WON'T LIKE IT.
YEEEEEEHAAAAAAAWW!
YOU'RE CLOSE, NEENA. WE'RE TRIANGULATING THE THREE BOGEYS, BUT CAN'T READ THEIR SOURCE SOMEHOW.

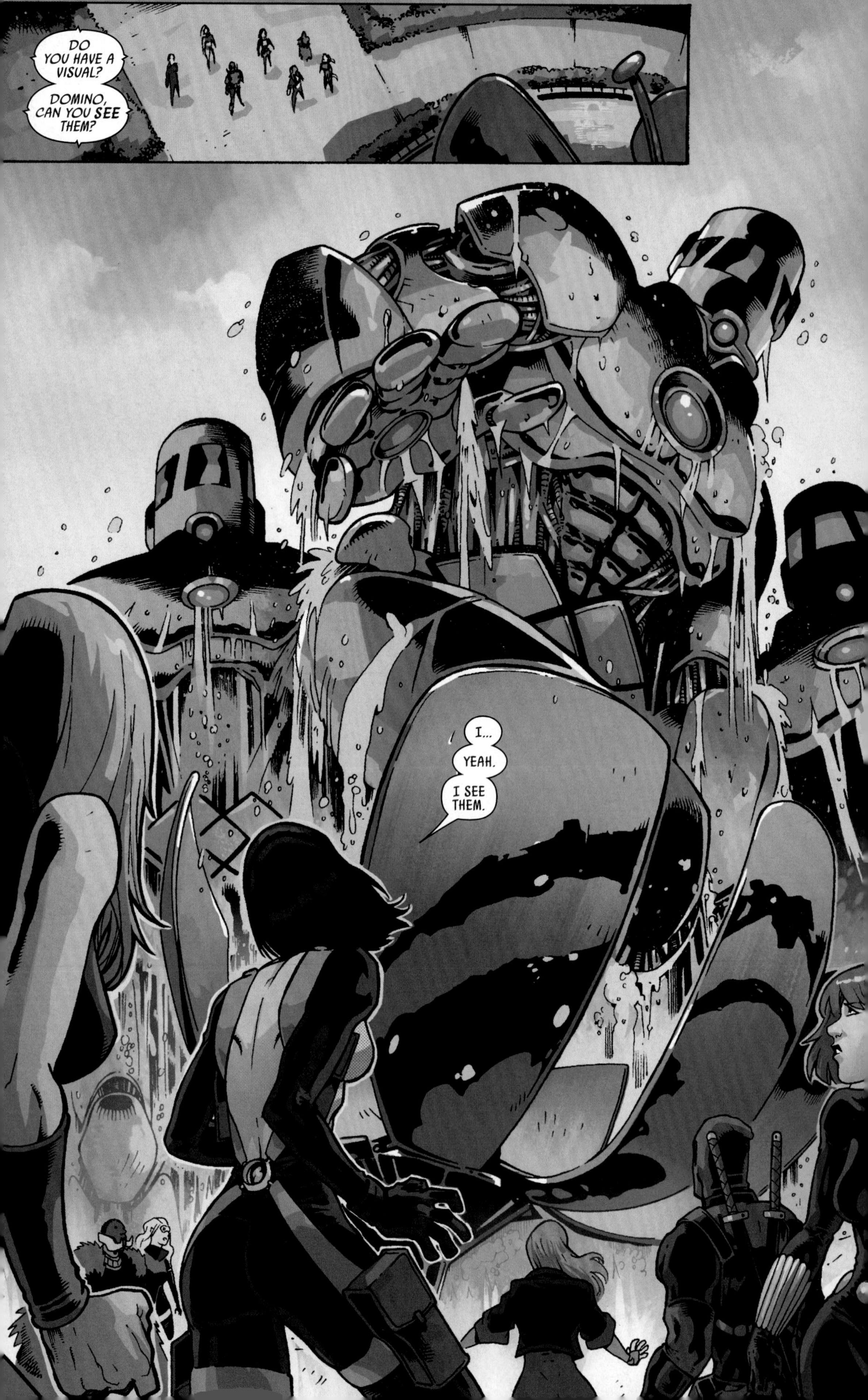
DO YOU HAVE A VISUAL?
DOMINO, CAN YOU SEE THEM?
I...
YEAH.
I SEE THEM.

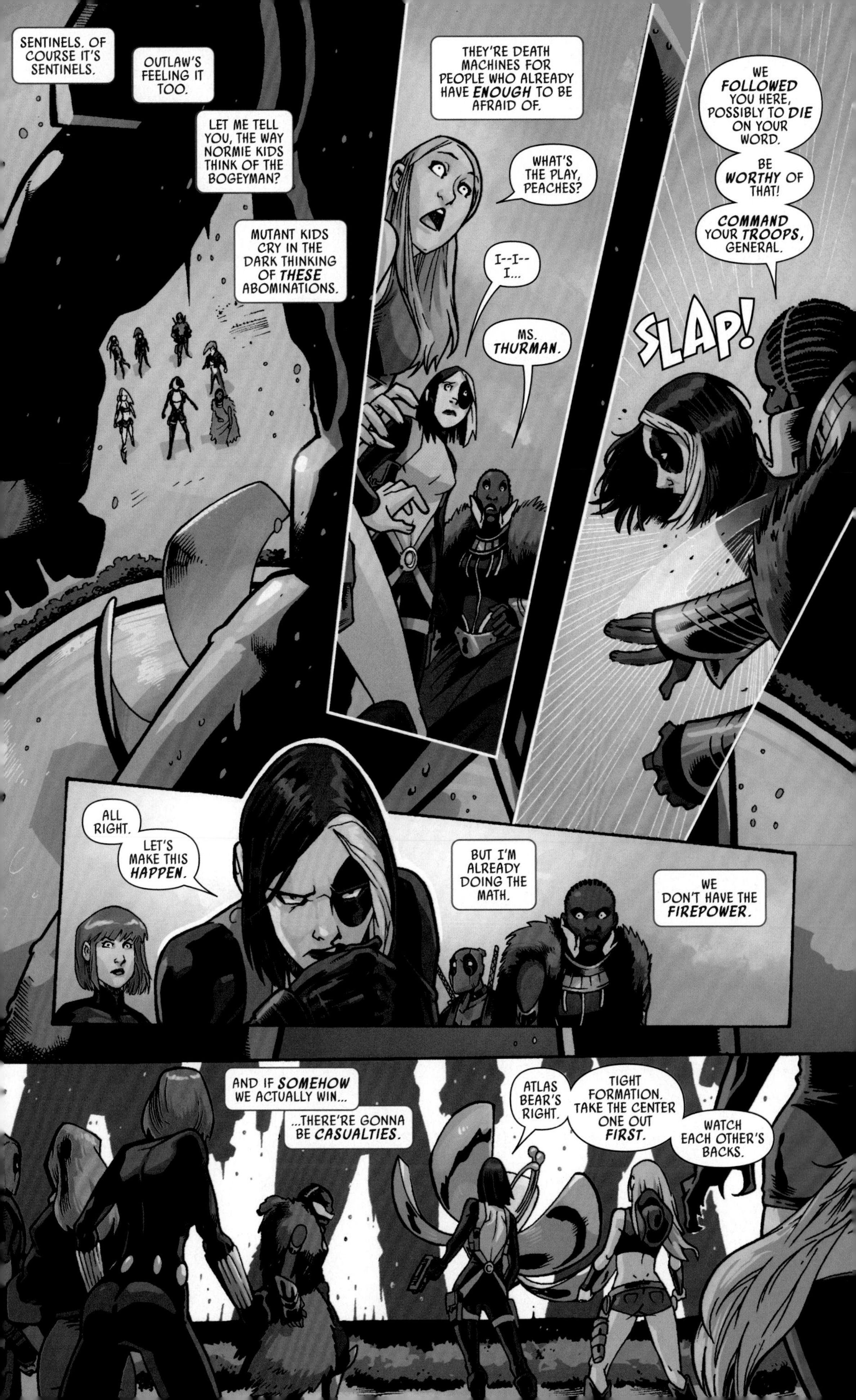
SENTINELS. OF COURSE IT'S SENTINELS.
OUTLAW'S FEELING IT TOO.
LET ME TELL YOU, THE WAY NORMIE KIDS THINK OF THE BOGEYMAN?
MUTANT KIDS CRY IN THE DARK THINKING OF THESE ABOMINATIONS.
THEY'RE DEATH MACHINES FOR PEOPLE WHO ALREADY HAVE ENOUGH TO BE AFRAID OF.
WHAT'S THE PLAY, PEACHES?
I--I-- I...
MS. THURMAN.
WE FOLLOWED YOU HERE, POSSIBLY TO DIE ON YOUR WORD.
BE WORTHY OF THAT!
COMMAND YOUR TROOPS, GENERAL.
SLAP!
ALL RIGHT.
LET'S MAKE THIS HAPPEN.
BUT I'M ALREADY DOING THE MATH.
WE DON'T HAVE THE FIREPOWER.
AND IF SOMEHOW WE ACTUALLY WIN...
...THERE'RE GONNA BE CASUALTIES.
ATLAS BEAR'S RIGHT.
TIGHT FORMATION. TAKE THE CENTER ONE OUT FIRST.
WATCH EACH OTHER'S BACKS.

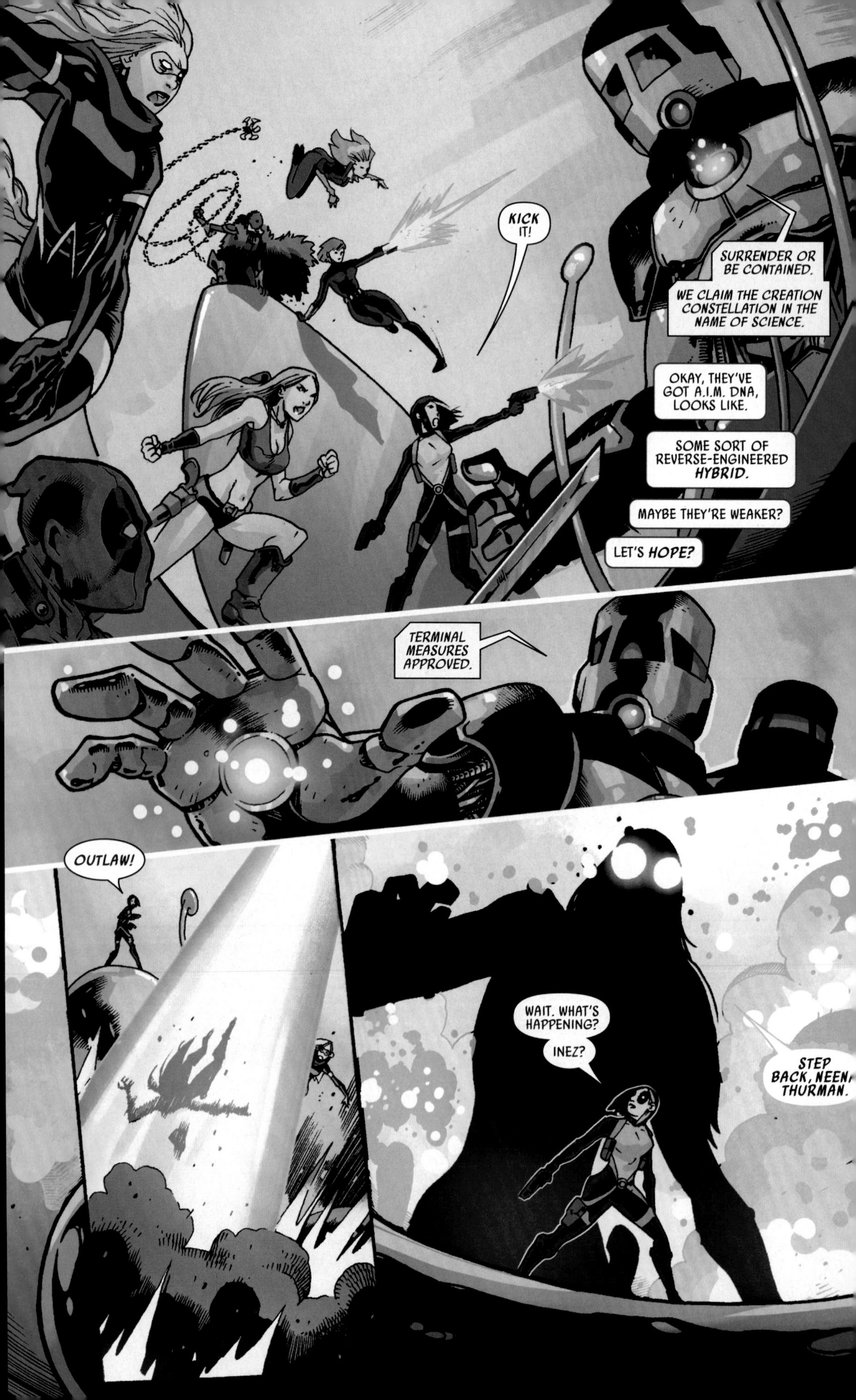
KICK IT!
SURRENDER OR BE CONTAINED.
WE CLAIM THE CREATION CONSTELLATION IN THE NAME OF SCIENCE.
OKAY, THEY'VE GOT A.I.M. DNA, LOOKS LIKE.
SOME SORT OF REVERSE-ENGINEERED HYBRID.
MAYBE THEY'RE WEAKER?
LET'S HOPE?
TERMINAL MEASURES APPROVED.
OUTLAW!
WAIT. WHAT'S HAPPENING?
INEZ?
STEP BACK, NEEN, THURMAN.

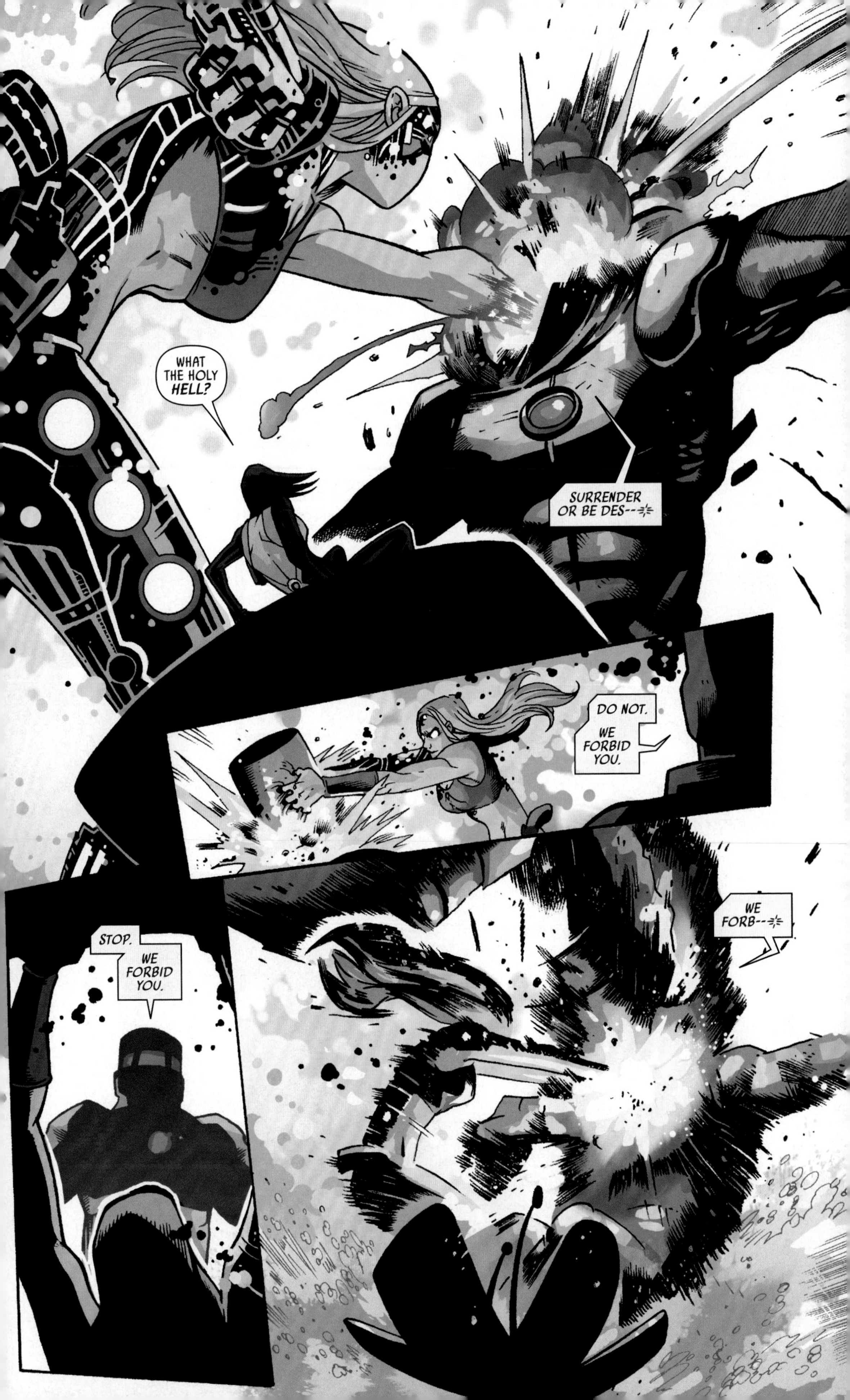
WHAT THE HOLY HELL?
SURRENDER OR BE DES--
DO NOT. WE FORBID YOU.
STOP. WE FORBID YOU.
WE FORB--

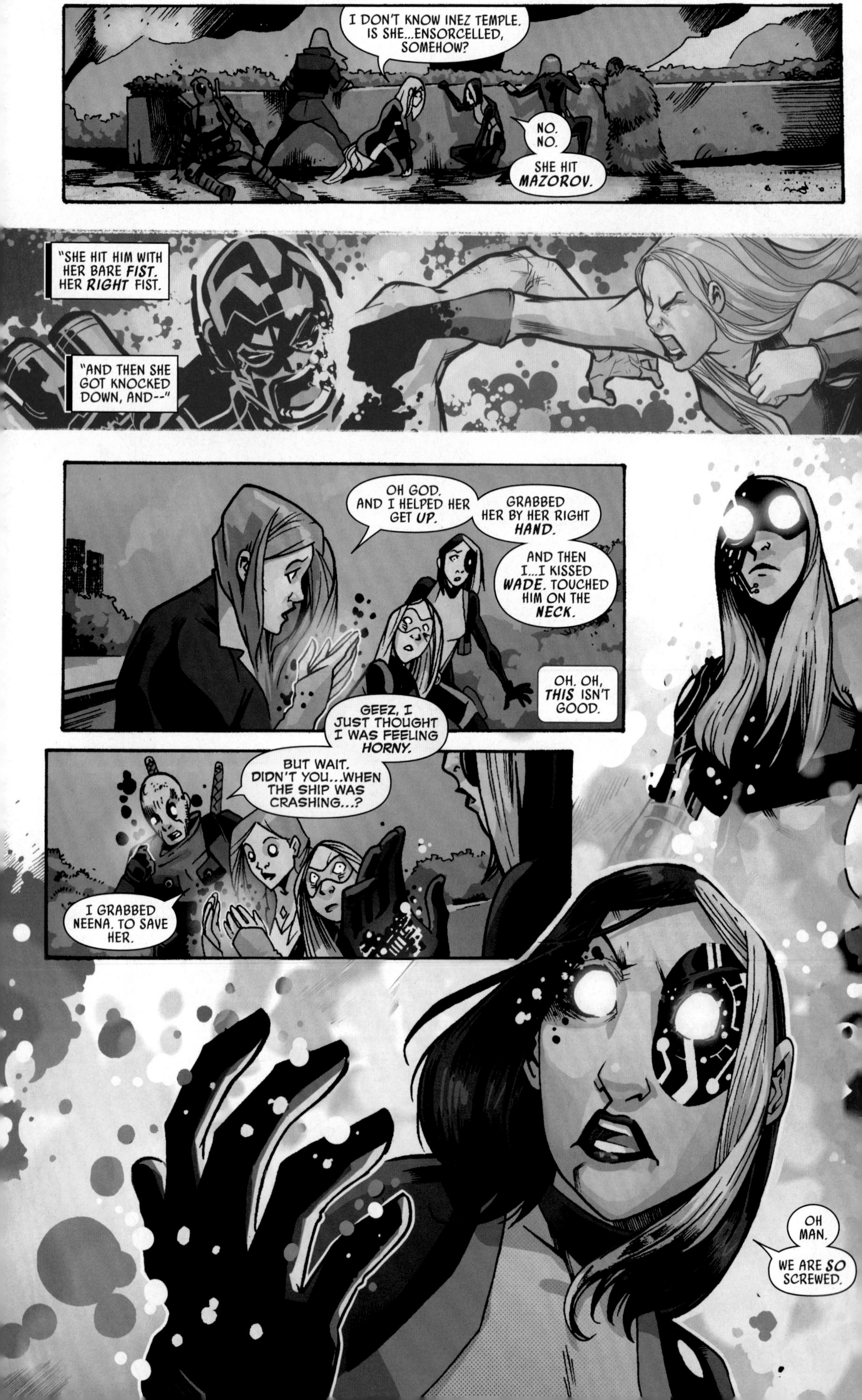
I DON'T KNOW INEZ TEMPLE. IS SHE...ENSORCELLED, SOMEHOW?
NO. NO.
SHE HIT MAZOROV.
"SHE HIT HIM WITH HER BARE FIST. HER RIGHT FIST.
"AND THEN SHE GOT KNOCKED DOWN, AND--"
OH GOD. AND I HELPED HER GET UP.
GRABBED HER BY HER RIGHT HAND.
AND THEN I...I KISSED WADE. TOUCHED HIM ON THE NECK.
OH. OH, THIS ISN'T GOOD.
GEEZ, I JUST THOUGHT I WAS FEELING HORNY.
BUT WAIT. DIDN'T YOU...WHEN THE SHIP WAS CRASHING...?
I GRABBED NEENA. TO SAVE HER.
OH MAN.
WE ARE SO SCREWED.

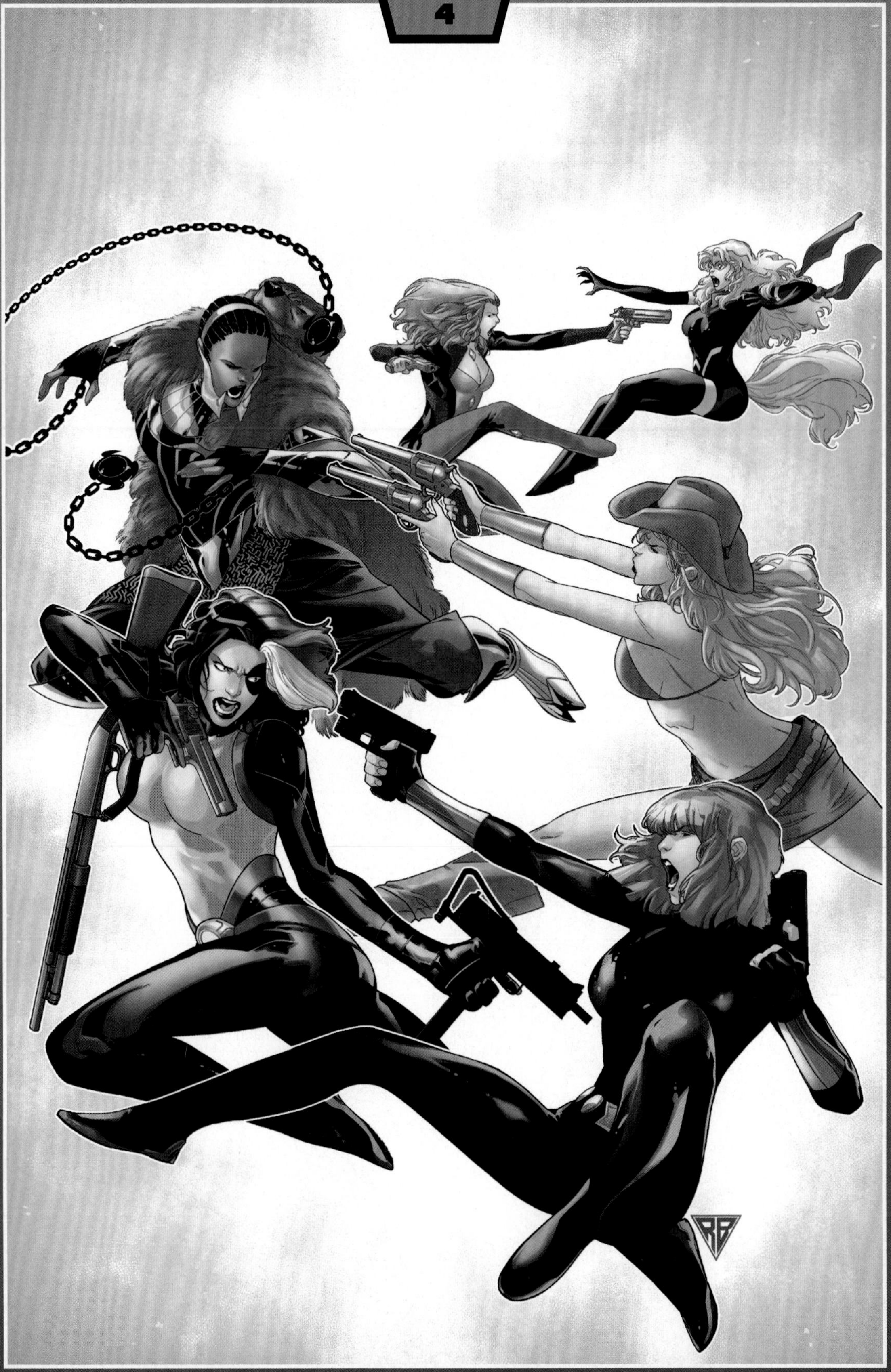

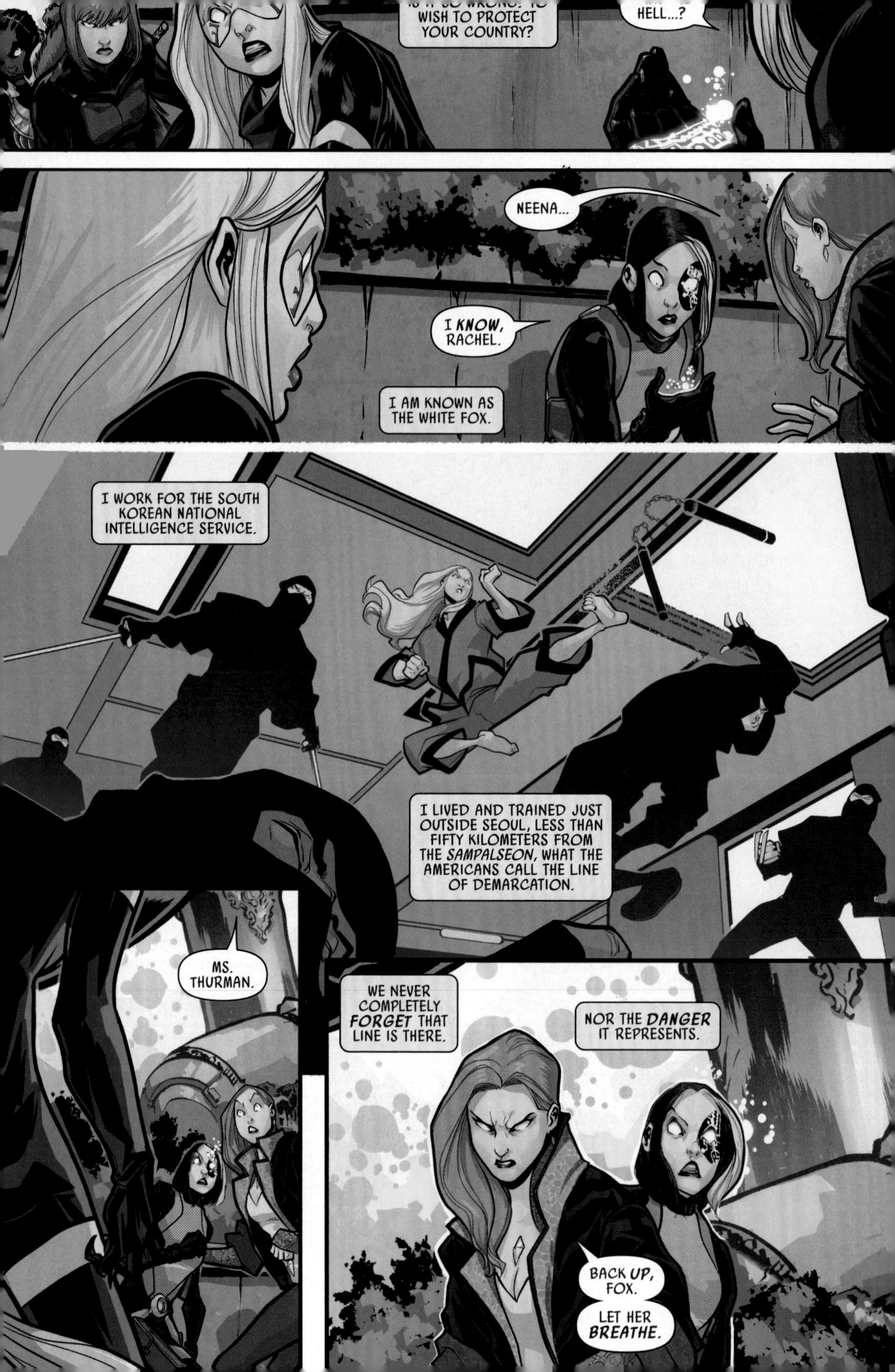

WISH TO PROTECT YOUR COUNTRY?
HELL...?
NEENA...
I KNOW, RACHEL.
I AM KNOWN AS THE WHITE FOX.
I WORK FOR THE SOUTH KOREAN NATIONAL INTELLIGENCE SERVICE.
I LIVED AND TRAINED JUST OUTSIDE SEOUL, LESS THAN FIFTY KILOMETERS FROM THE SAMPALSEON, WHAT THE AMERICANS CALL THE LINE OF DEMARCATION.
MS. THURMAN.
WE NEVER COMPLETELY FORGET THAT LINE IS THERE.
NOR THE DANGER IT REPRESENTS.
BACK UP, FOX.
LET HER BREATHE.

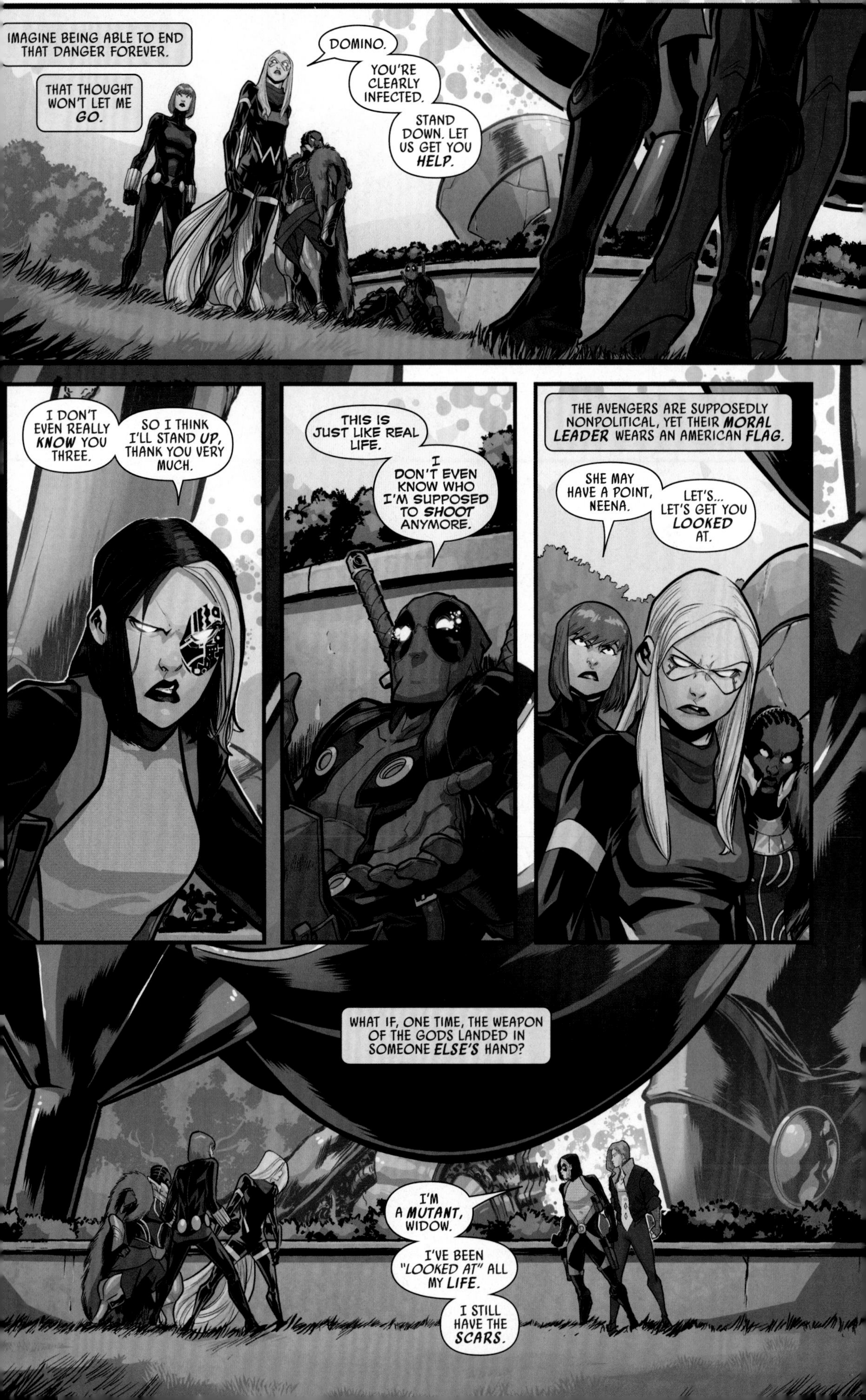

IMAGINE BEING ABLE TO END THAT DANGER FOREVER.
THAT THOUGHT WON'T LET ME GO.
DOMINO.
YOU'RE CLEARLY INFECTED.
STAND DOWN. LET US GET YOU HELP.
I DON'T EVEN REALLY KNOW YOU THREE.
SO I THINK I'LL STAND UP, THANK YOU VERY MUCH.
THIS IS JUST LIKE REAL LIFE.
I DON'T EVEN KNOW WHO I'M SUPPOSED TO SHOOT ANYMORE.
THE AVENGERS ARE SUPPOSEDLY NONPOLITICAL, YET THEIR MORAL LEADER WEARS AN AMERICAN FLAG.
SHE MAY HAVE A POINT, NEENA.
LET'S... LET'S GET YOU LOOKED AT.
WHAT IF, ONE TIME, THE WEAPON OF THE GODS LANDED IN SOMEONE ELSE'S HAND?
I'M A MUTANT, WIDOW.
I'VE BEEN "LOOKED AT" ALL MY LIFE.
I STILL HAVE THE SCARS.

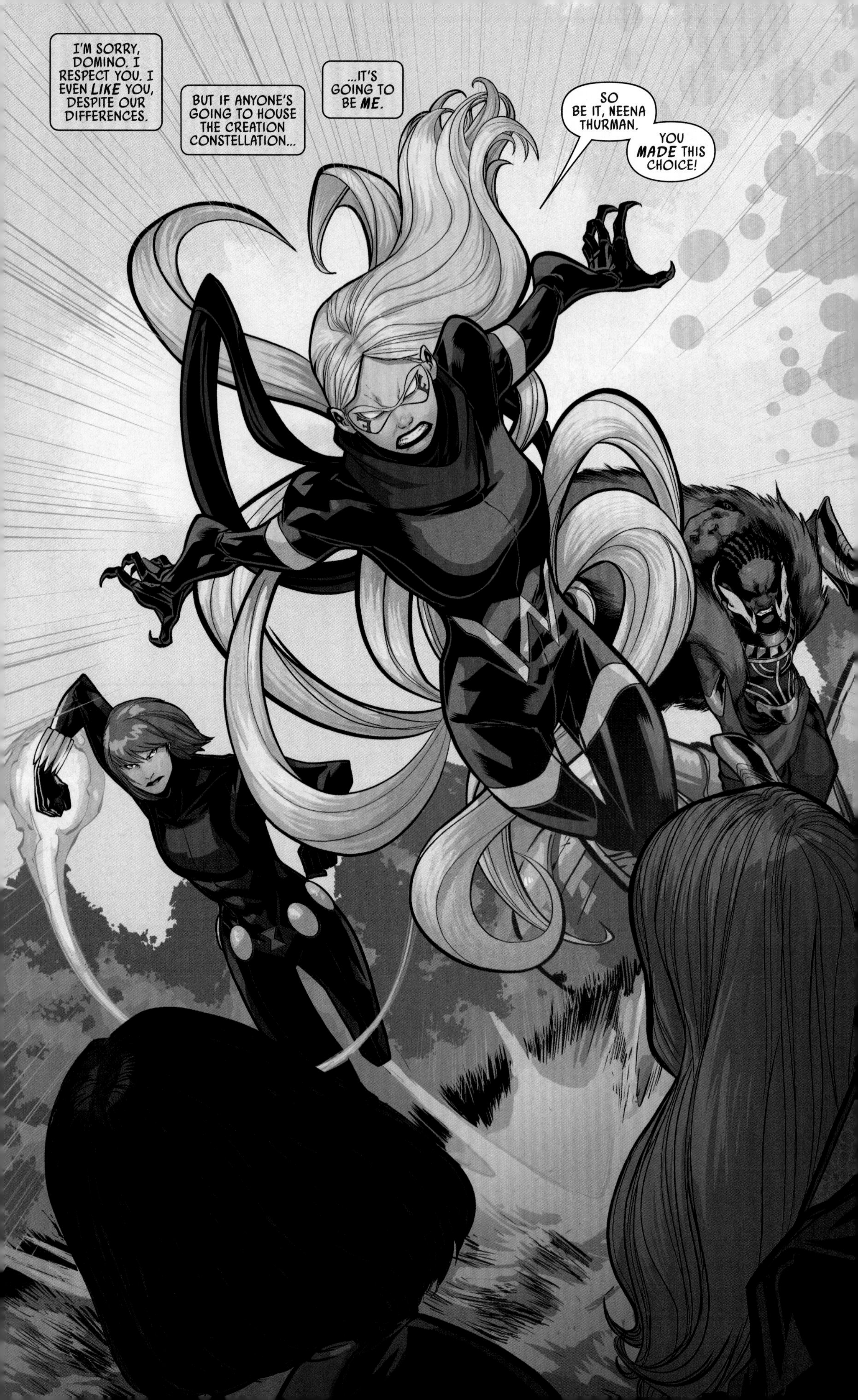
I'M SORRY, DOMINO. I RESPECT YOU. I EVEN LIKE YOU, DESPITE OUR DIFFERENCES.
BUT IF ANYONE'S GOING TO HOUSE THE CREATION CONSTELLATION...
...IT'S GOING TO BE ME.
SO BE IT, NEENA THURMAN.
YOU MADE THIS CHOICE!

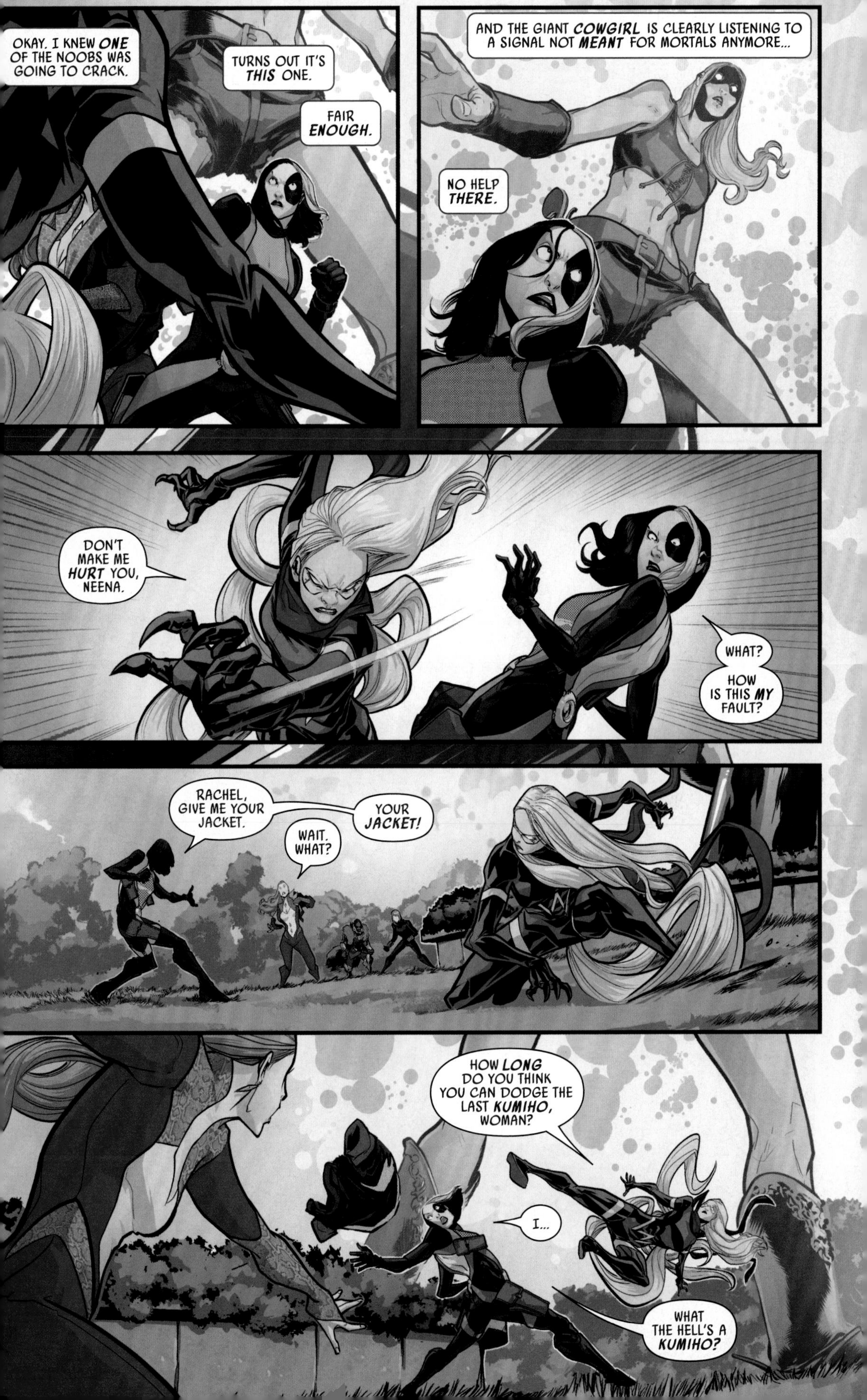
OKAY. I KNEW ONE OF THE NOOBS WAS GOING TO CRACK.
TURNS OUT IT'S THIS ONE.
FAIR ENOUGH.
AND THE GIANT COWGIRL IS CLEARLY LISTENING TO A SIGNAL NOT MEANT FOR MORTALS ANYMORE...
NO HELP THERE.
DON'T MAKE ME HURT YOU, NEENA.
WHAT?
HOW IS THIS MY FAULT?
RACHEL, GIVE ME YOUR JACKET.
YOUR JACKET!
WAIT. WHAT?
HOW LONG DO YOU THINK YOU CAN DODGE THE LAST KUMIHO, WOMAN?
I...
WHAT THE HELL'S A KUMIHO?

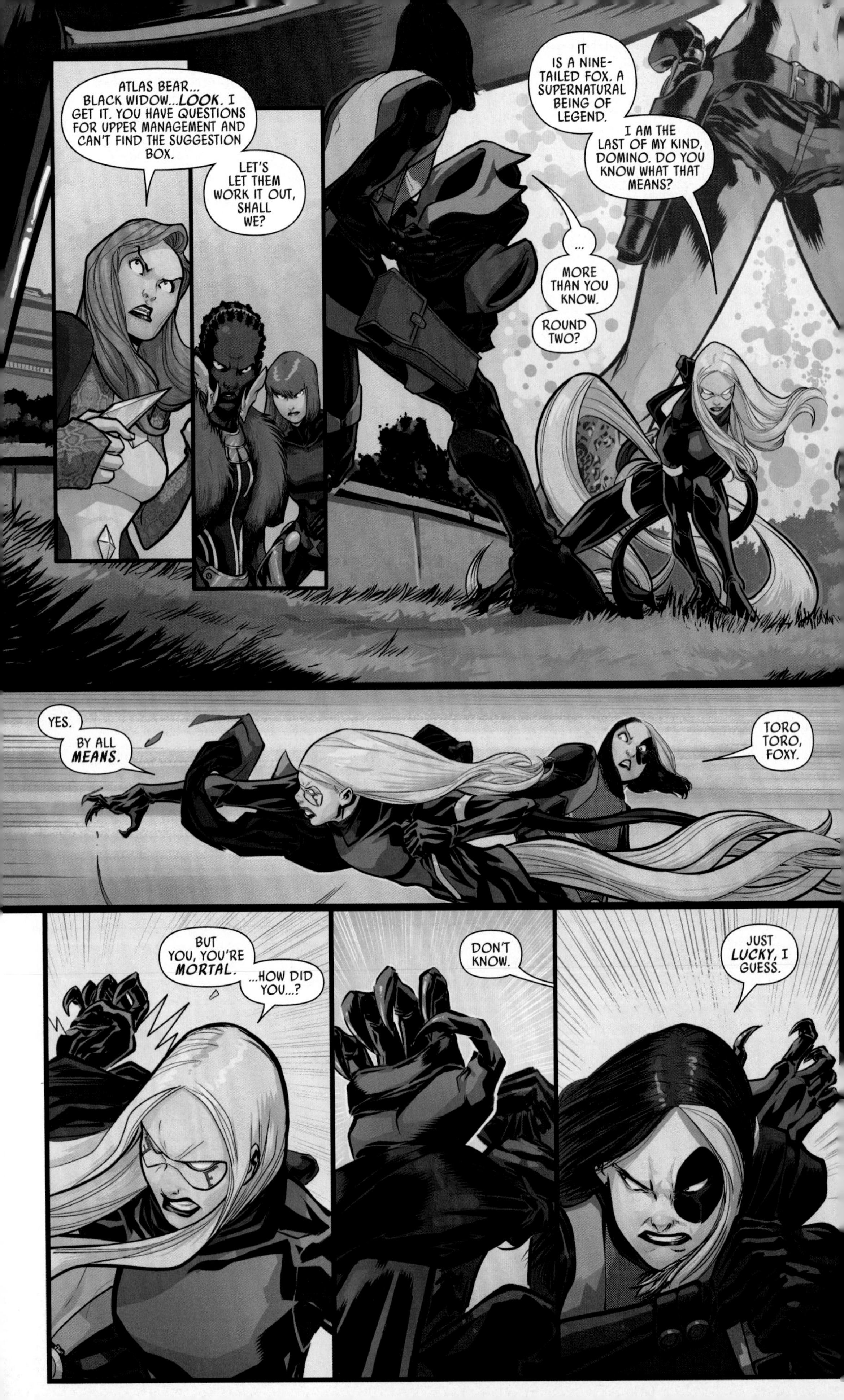
ATLAS BEAR... BLACK WIDOW...LOOK. I GET IT. YOU HAVE QUESTIONS FOR UPPER MANAGEMENT AND CAN'T FIND THE SUGGESTION BOX.
LET'S LET THEM WORK IT OUT, SHALL WE?
IT IS A NINE-TAILED FOX. A SUPERNATURAL BEING OF LEGEND.
I AM THE LAST OF MY KIND, DOMINO. DO YOU KNOW WHAT THAT MEANS?
...
MORE THAN YOU KNOW.
ROUND TWO?
YES.
BY ALL MEANS.
TORO TORO, FOXY.
BUT YOU, YOU'RE MORTAL.
...HOW DID YOU...?
DON'T KNOW.
JUST LUCKY, I GUESS.

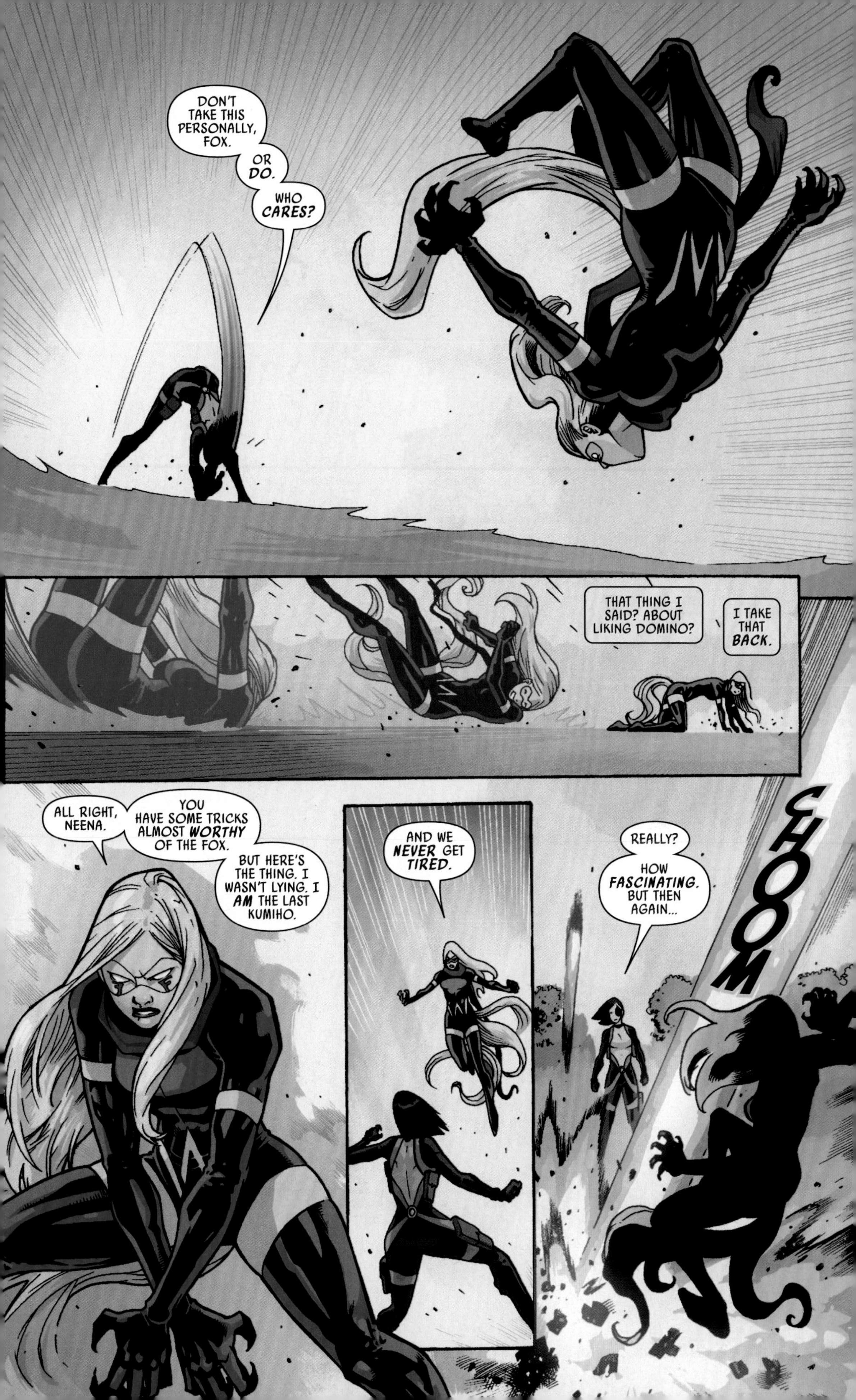
DON'T TAKE THIS PERSONALLY, FOX.
OR DO.
WHO CARES?
THAT THING I SAID? ABOUT LIKING DOMINO?
I TAKE THAT BACK.
ALL RIGHT, NEENA.
YOU HAVE SOME TRICKS ALMOST WORTHY OF THE FOX.
BUT HERE'S THE THING. I WASN'T LYING. I AM THE LAST KUMIHO.
AND WE NEVER GET TIRED.
REALLY?
HOW FASCINATING. BUT THEN AGAIN...
CHOOOM

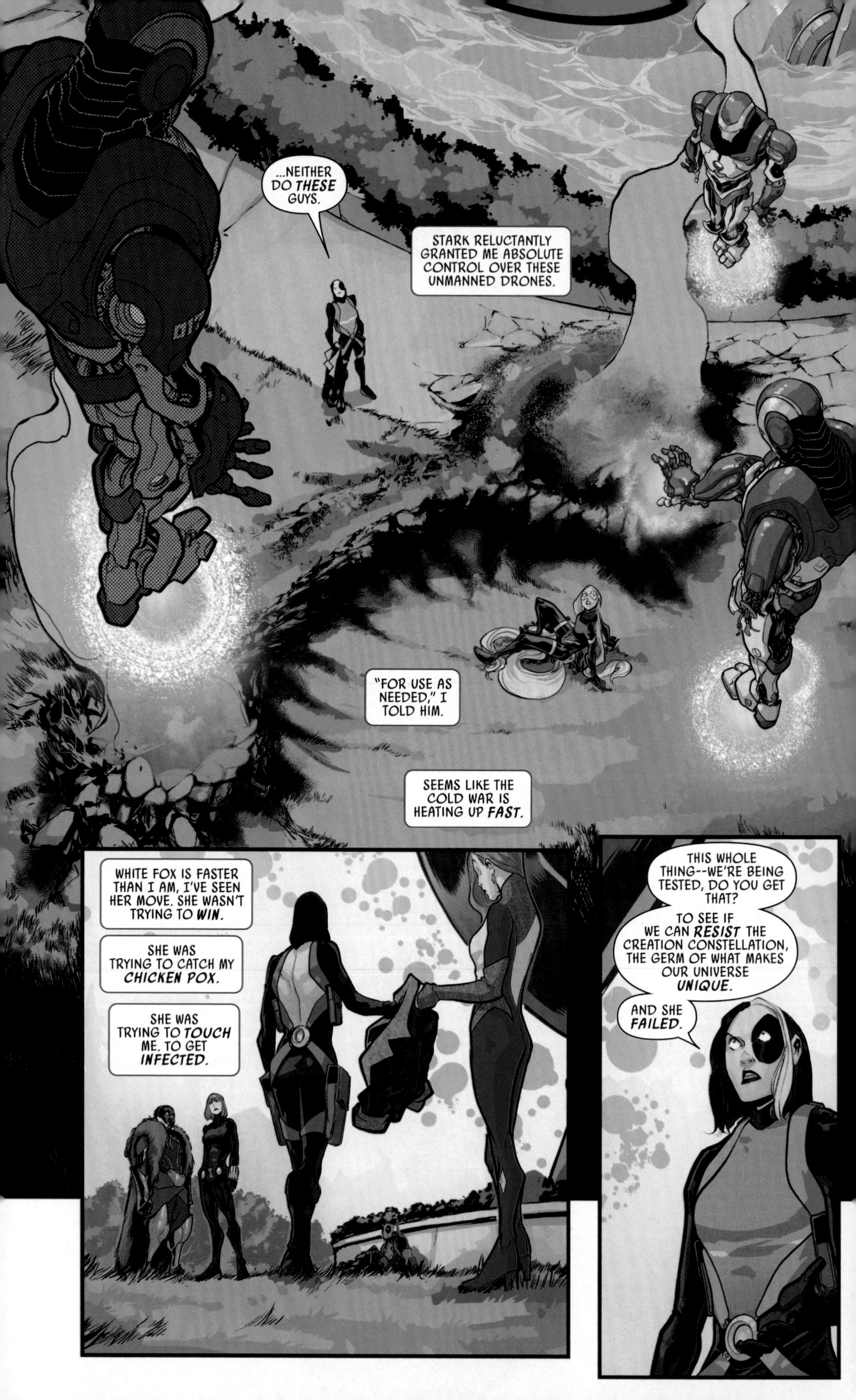
...NEITHER DO THESE GUYS.
STARK RELUCTANTLY GRANTED ME ABSOLUTE CONTROL OVER THESE UNMANNED DRONES.
"FOR USE AS NEEDED," I TOLD HIM.
SEEMS LIKE THE COLD WAR IS HEATING UP FAST.
WHITE FOX IS FASTER THAN I AM, I'VE SEEN HER MOVE. SHE WASN'T TRYING TO WIN.
SHE WAS TRYING TO CATCH MY CHICKEN POX.
SHE WAS TRYING TO TOUCH ME. TO GET INFECTED.
THIS WHOLE THING--WE'RE BEING TESTED, DO YOU GET THAT?
TO SEE IF WE CAN RESIST THE CREATION CONSTELLATION, THE GERM OF WHAT MAKES OUR UNIVERSE UNIQUE.
AND SHE FAILED.

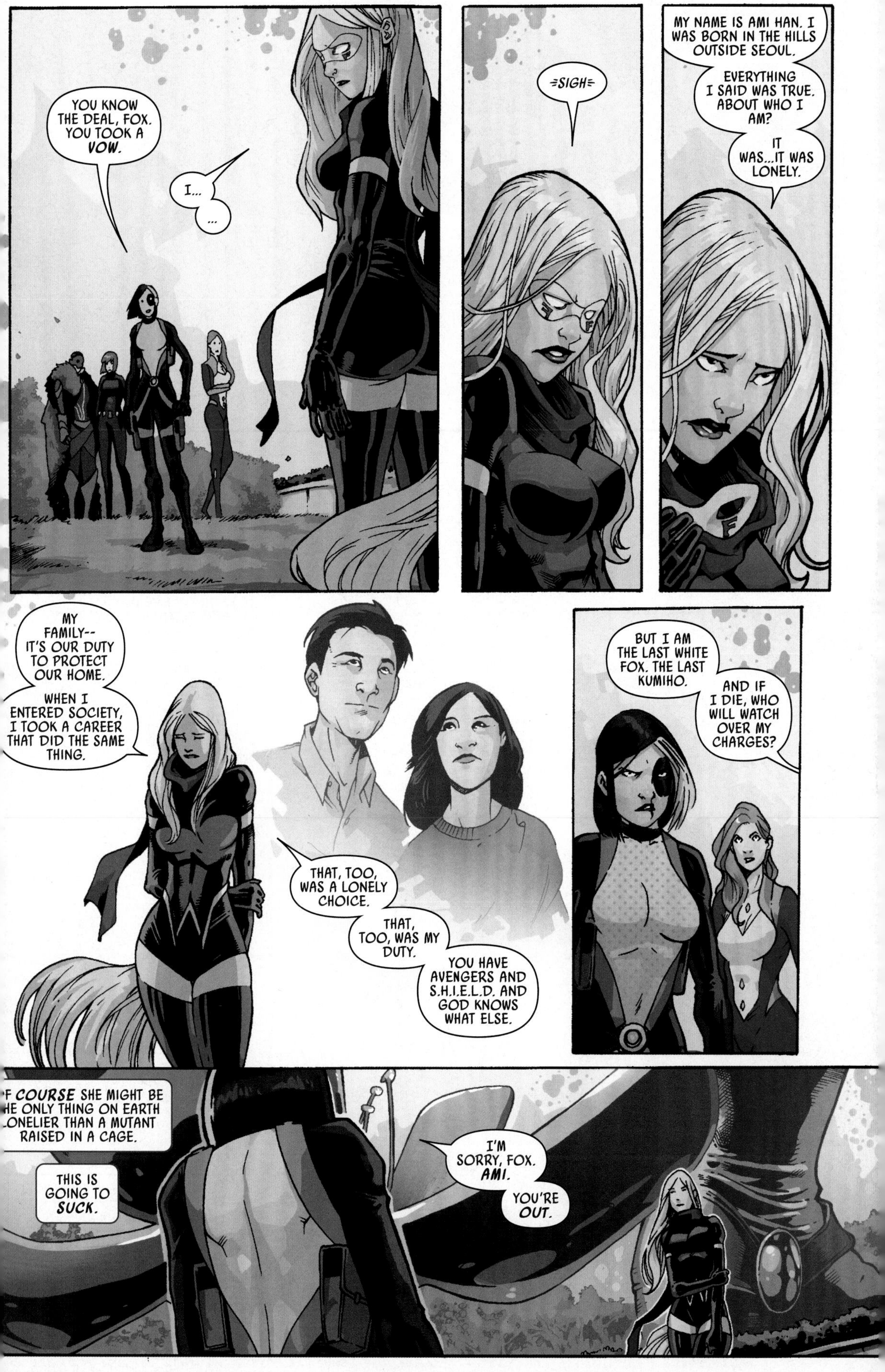
YOU KNOW THE DEAL, FOX. YOU TOOK A VOW.
I...
...
=SIGH=
MY NAME IS AMI HAN. I WAS BORN IN THE HILLS OUTSIDE SEOUL.
EVERYTHING I SAID WAS TRUE. ABOUT WHO I AM?
IT WAS...IT WAS LONELY.
MY FAMILY-- IT'S OUR DUTY TO PROTECT OUR HOME.
WHEN I ENTERED SOCIETY, I TOOK A CAREER THAT DID THE SAME THING.
THAT, TOO, WAS A LONELY CHOICE.
THAT, TOO, WAS MY DUTY.
YOU HAVE AVENGERS AND S.H.I.E.L.D. AND GOD KNOWS WHAT ELSE.
BUT I AM THE LAST WHITE FOX. THE LAST KUMIHO.
AND IF I DIE, WHO WILL WATCH OVER MY CHARGES?
F COURSE SHE MIGHT BE HE ONLY THING ON EARTH LONELIER THAN A MUTANT RAISED IN A CAGE.
THIS IS GOING TO SUCK.
I'M SORRY, FOX. AMI.
YOU'RE OUT.

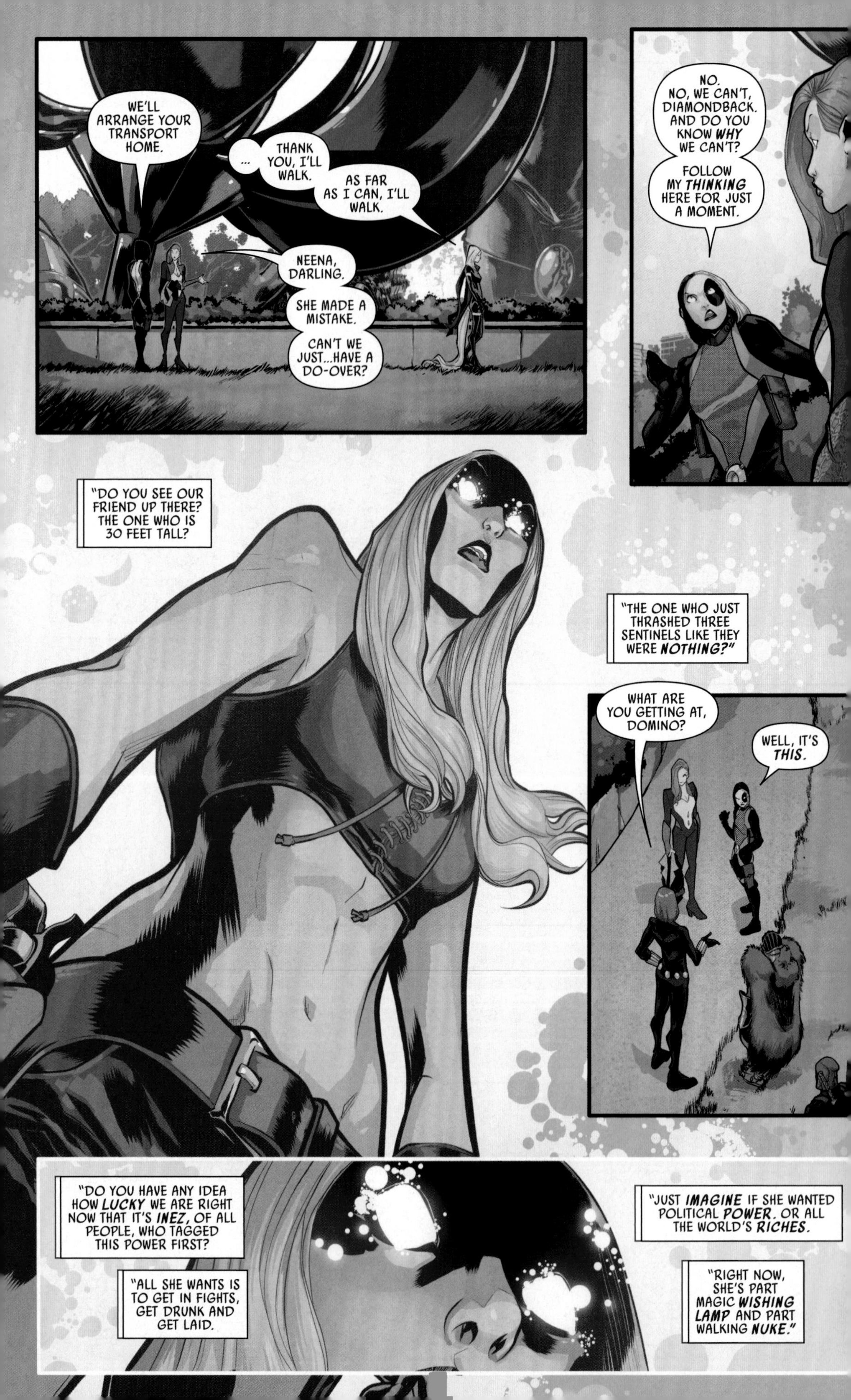
WE'LL ARRANGE YOUR TRANSPORT HOME.
... THANK YOU, I'LL WALK.
AS FAR AS I CAN, I'LL WALK.
NEENA, DARLING.
SHE MADE A MISTAKE.
CAN'T WE JUST...HAVE A DO-OVER?
NO. NO, WE CAN'T, DIAMONDBACK. AND DO YOU KNOW WHY WE CAN'T?
FOLLOW MY THINKING HERE FOR JUST A MOMENT.
"DO YOU SEE OUR FRIEND UP THERE? THE ONE WHO IS 30 FEET TALL?
"THE ONE WHO JUST THRASHED THREE SENTINELS LIKE THEY WERE NOTHING?"
WHAT ARE YOU GETTING AT, DOMINO?
WELL, IT'S THIS.
"DO YOU HAVE ANY IDEA HOW LUCKY WE ARE RIGHT NOW THAT IT'S INEZ, OF ALL PEOPLE, WHO TAGGED THIS POWER FIRST?
"ALL SHE WANTS IS TO GET IN FIGHTS, GET DRUNK AND GET LAID.
"JUST IMAGINE IF SHE WANTED POLITICAL POWER. OR ALL THE WORLD'S RICHES.
"RIGHT NOW, SHE'S PART MAGIC WISHING LAMP AND PART WALKING NUKE."

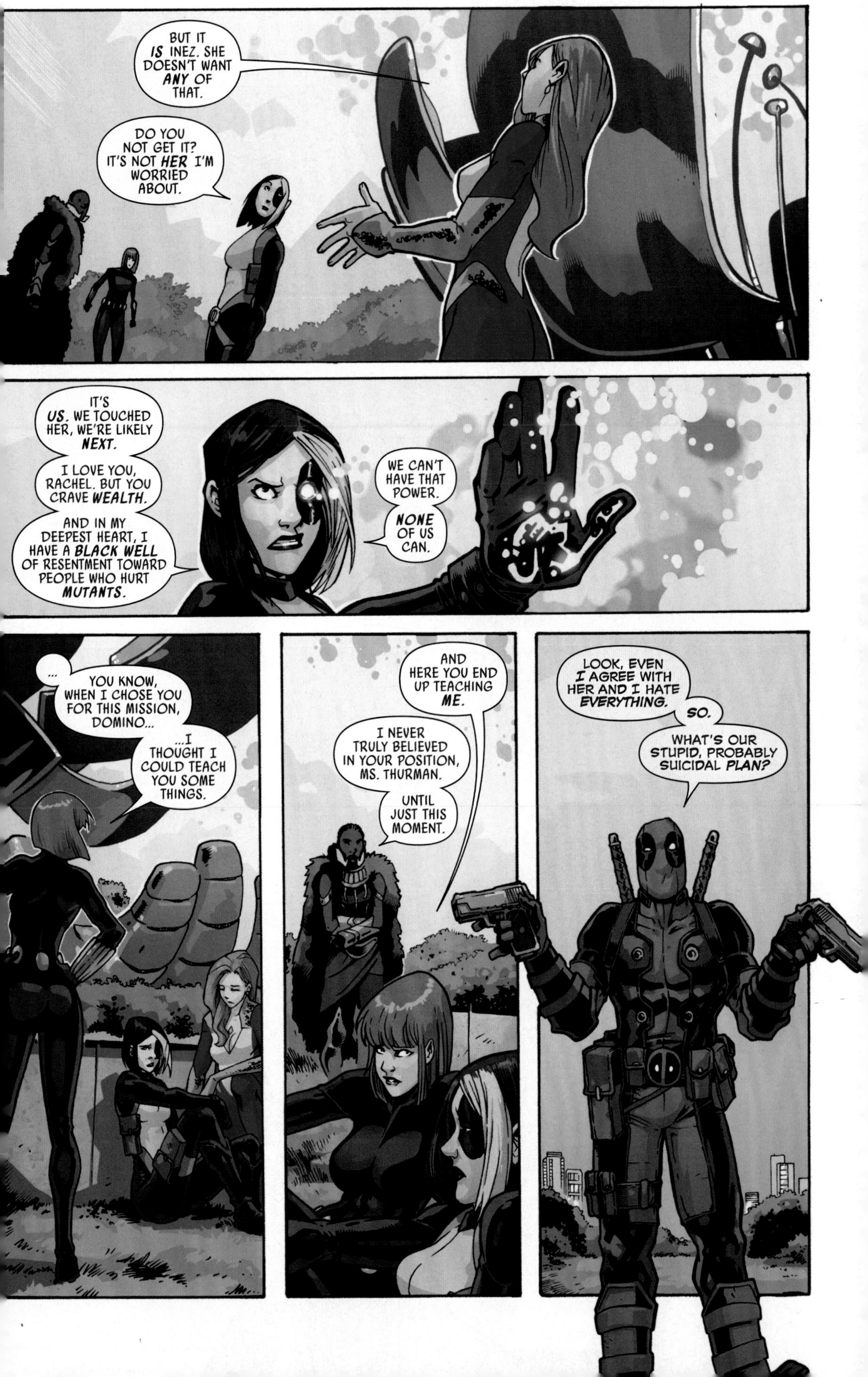

BUT IT IS INEZ. SHE DOESN'T WANT ANY OF THAT.
DO YOU NOT GET IT? IT'S NOT HER I'M WORRIED ABOUT.
IT'S US. WE TOUCHED HER, WE'RE LIKELY NEXT.
I LOVE YOU, RACHEL. BUT YOU CRAVE WEALTH.
AND IN MY DEEPEST HEART, I HAVE A BLACK WELL OF RESENTMENT TOWARD PEOPLE WHO HURT MUTANTS.
WE CAN'T HAVE THAT POWER.
NONE OF US CAN.
...
YOU KNOW, WHEN I CHOSE YOU FOR THIS MISSION, DOMINO...
...I THOUGHT I COULD TEACH YOU SOME THINGS.
AND HERE YOU END UP TEACHING ME.
I NEVER TRULY BELIEVED IN YOUR POSITION, MS. THURMAN.
UNTIL JUST THIS MOMENT.
LOOK, EVEN I AGREE WITH HER AND I HATE EVERYTHING.
SO.
WHAT'S OUR STUPID, PROBABLY SUICIDAL PLAN?

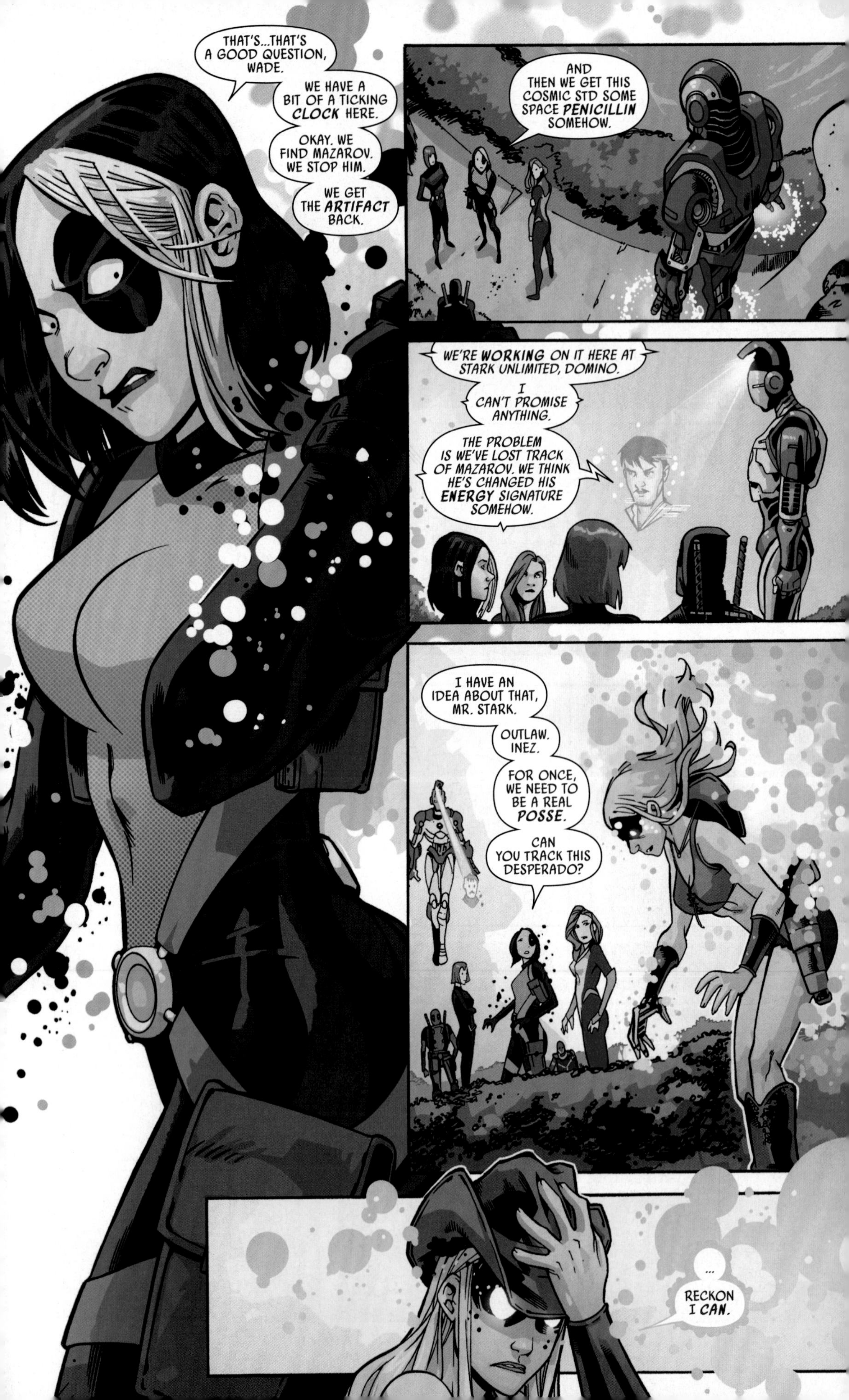
THAT'S...THAT'S A GOOD QUESTION, WADE.
WE HAVE A BIT OF A TICKING CLOCK HERE.
OKAY. WE FIND MAZAROV. WE STOP HIM.
WE GET THE ARTIFACT BACK.
AND THEN WE GET THIS COSMIC STD SOME SPACE PENICILLIN SOMEHOW.
WE'RE WORKING ON IT HERE AT STARK UNLIMITED, DOMINO.
I CAN'T PROMISE ANYTHING.
THE PROBLEM IS WE'VE LOST TRACK OF MAZAROV. WE THINK HE'S CHANGED HIS ENERGY SIGNATURE SOMEHOW.
I HAVE AN IDEA ABOUT THAT, MR. STARK.
OUTLAW. INEZ.
FOR ONCE, WE NEED TO BE A REAL POSSE.
CAN YOU TRACK THIS DESPERADO?
...
RECKON I CAN.

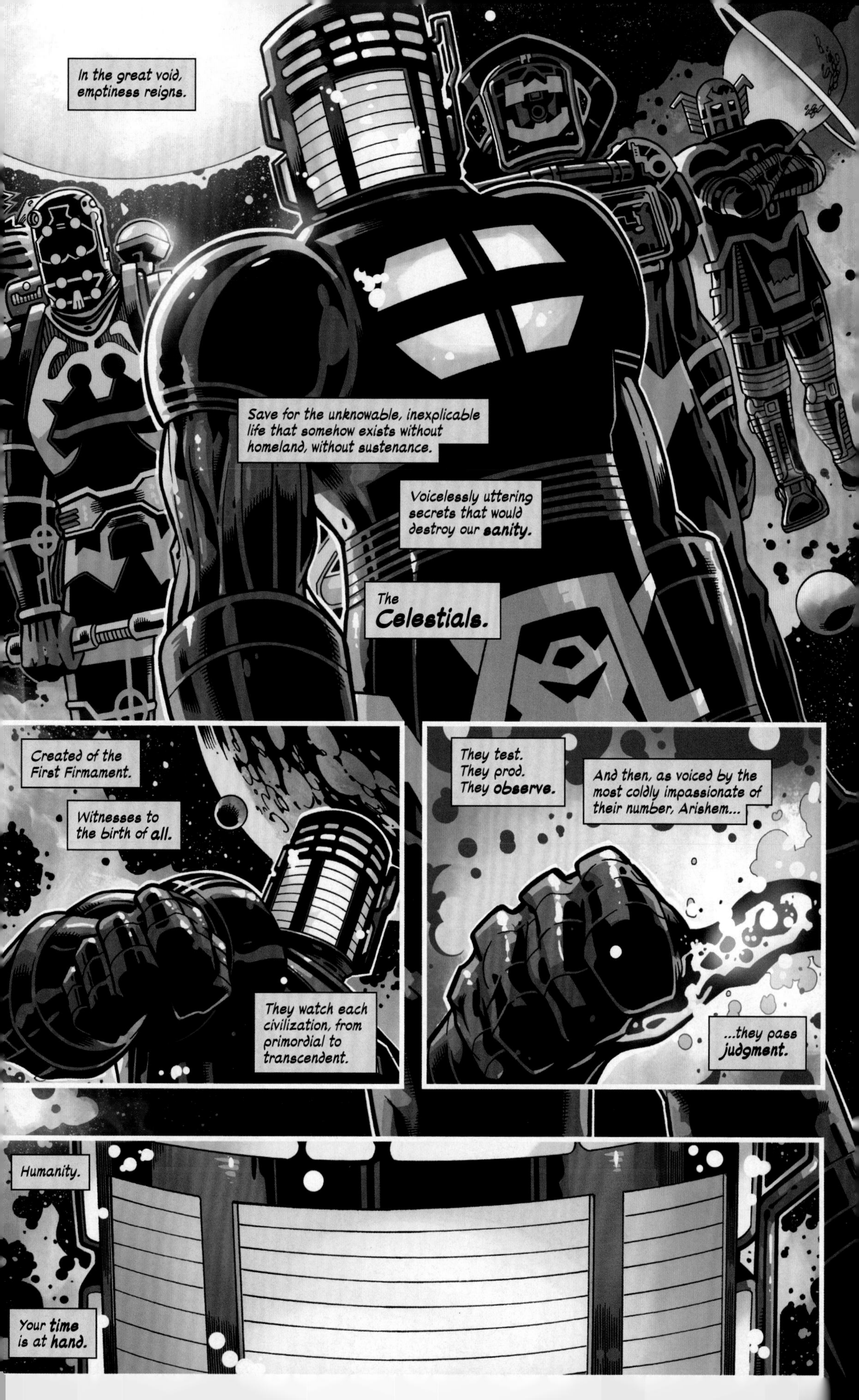
In the great void, emptiness reigns.
Save for the unknowable, inexplicable life that somehow exists without homeland, without sustenance.
Voicelessly uttering secrets that would destroy our sanity.
The Celestials.
Created of the First Firmament.
Witnesses to the birth of all.
They watch each civilization, from primordial to transcendent.
They test. They prod. They observe.
And then, as voiced by the most coldly impassionate of their number, Arishem...
...they pass judgment.
Humanity.
Your time is at hand.

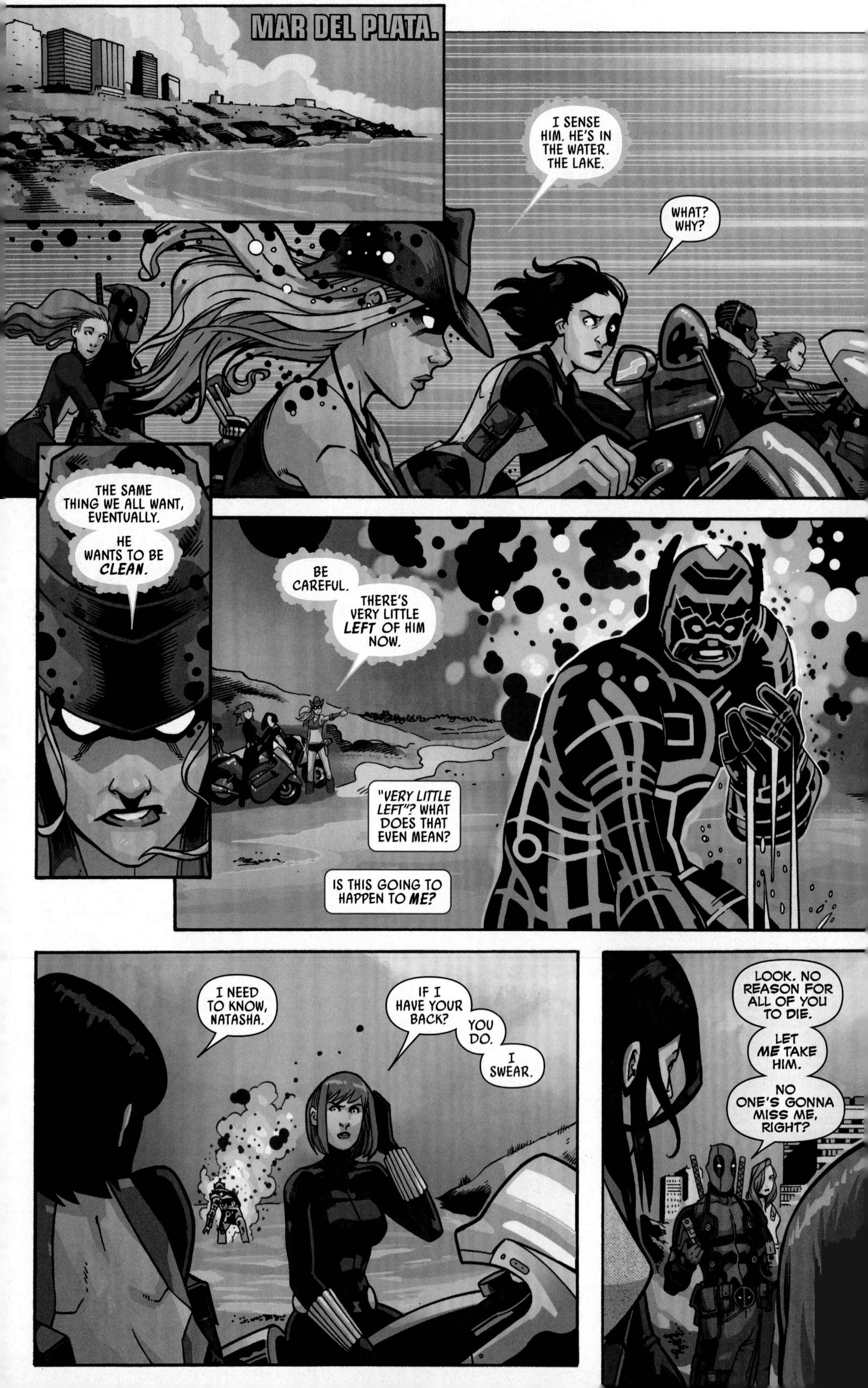
MAR DEL PLATA.
I SENSE HIM. HE'S IN THE WATER. THE LAKE.
WHAT? WHY?
THE SAME THING WE ALL WANT, EVENTUALLY.
HE WANTS TO BE CLEAN.
BE CAREFUL.
THERE'S VERY LITTLE LEFT OF HIM NOW.
"VERY LITTLE LEFT"? WHAT DOES THAT EVEN MEAN?
IS THIS GOING TO HAPPEN TO ME?
I NEED TO KNOW, NATASHA.
IF I HAVE YOUR BACK?
YOU DO.
I SWEAR.
LOOK. NO REASON FOR ALL OF YOU TO DIE.
LET ME TAKE HIM.
NO ONE'S GONNA MISS ME, RIGHT?

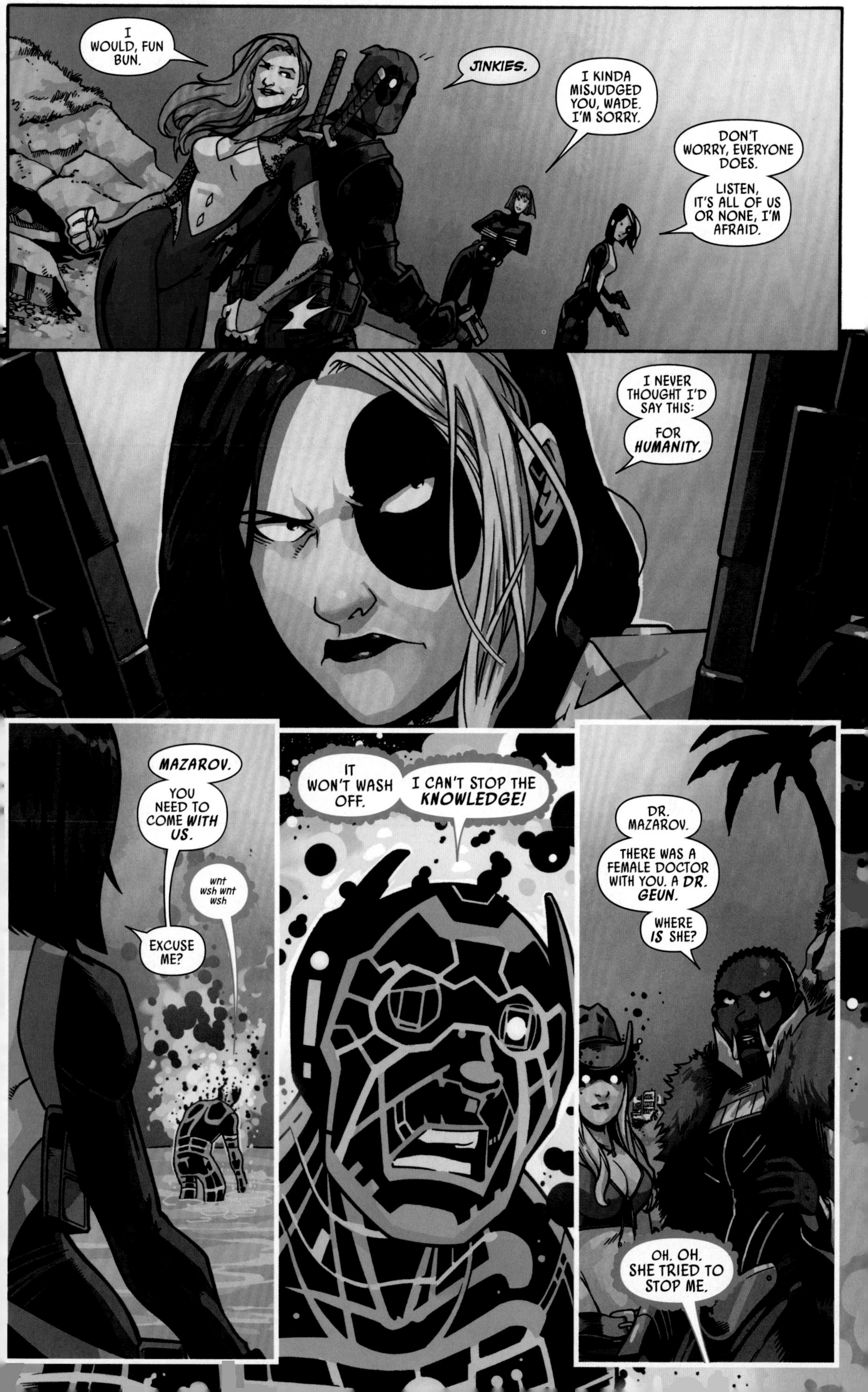
I WOULD, FUN BUN.
JINKIES.
I KINDA MISJUDGED YOU, WADE. I'M SORRY.
DON'T WORRY, EVERYONE DOES.
LISTEN, IT'S ALL OF US OR NONE, I'M AFRAID.
I NEVER THOUGHT I'D SAY THIS:
FOR HUMANITY.
MAZAROV.
YOU NEED TO COME WITH US.
wnt wsh wnt wsh
EXCUSE ME?
IT WON'T WASH OFF.
I CAN'T STOP THE KNOWLEDGE!
DR. MAZAROV.
THERE WAS A FEMALE DOCTOR WITH YOU. A DR. GEUN.
WHERE IS SHE?
OH. OH. SHE TRIED TO STOP ME.

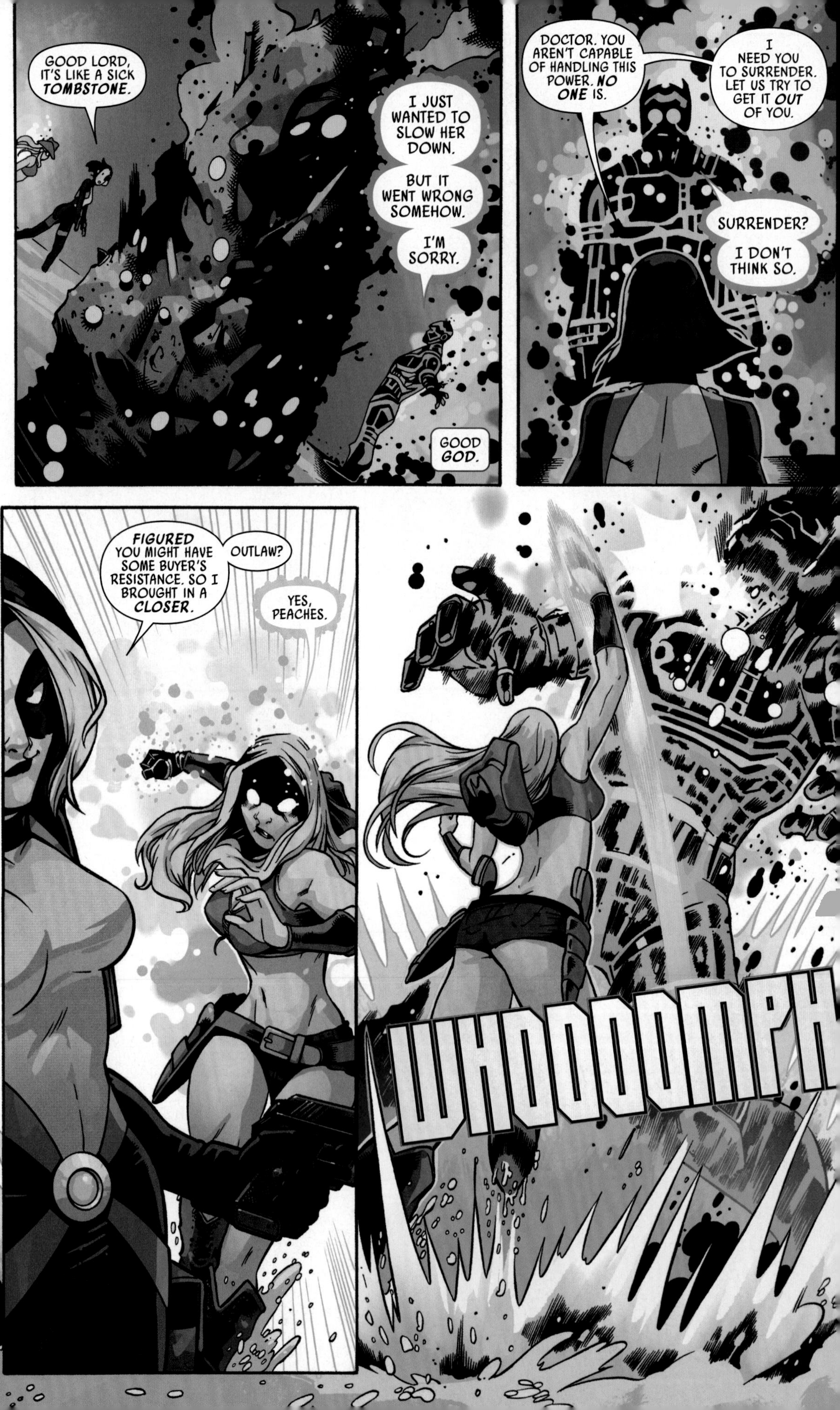
GOOD LORD, IT'S LIKE A SICK TOMBSTONE.
I JUST WANTED TO SLOW HER DOWN.
BUT IT WENT WRONG SOMEHOW.
I'M SORRY.
GOOD GOD.
DOCTOR. YOU AREN'T CAPABLE OF HANDLING THIS POWER. NO ONE IS.
I NEED YOU TO SURRENDER. LET US TRY TO GET IT OUT OF YOU.
SURRENDER?
I DON'T THINK SO.
FIGURED YOU MIGHT HAVE SOME BUYER'S RESISTANCE. SO I BROUGHT IN A CLOSER.
OUTLAW?
YES, PEACHES.
WHOOOOMPH

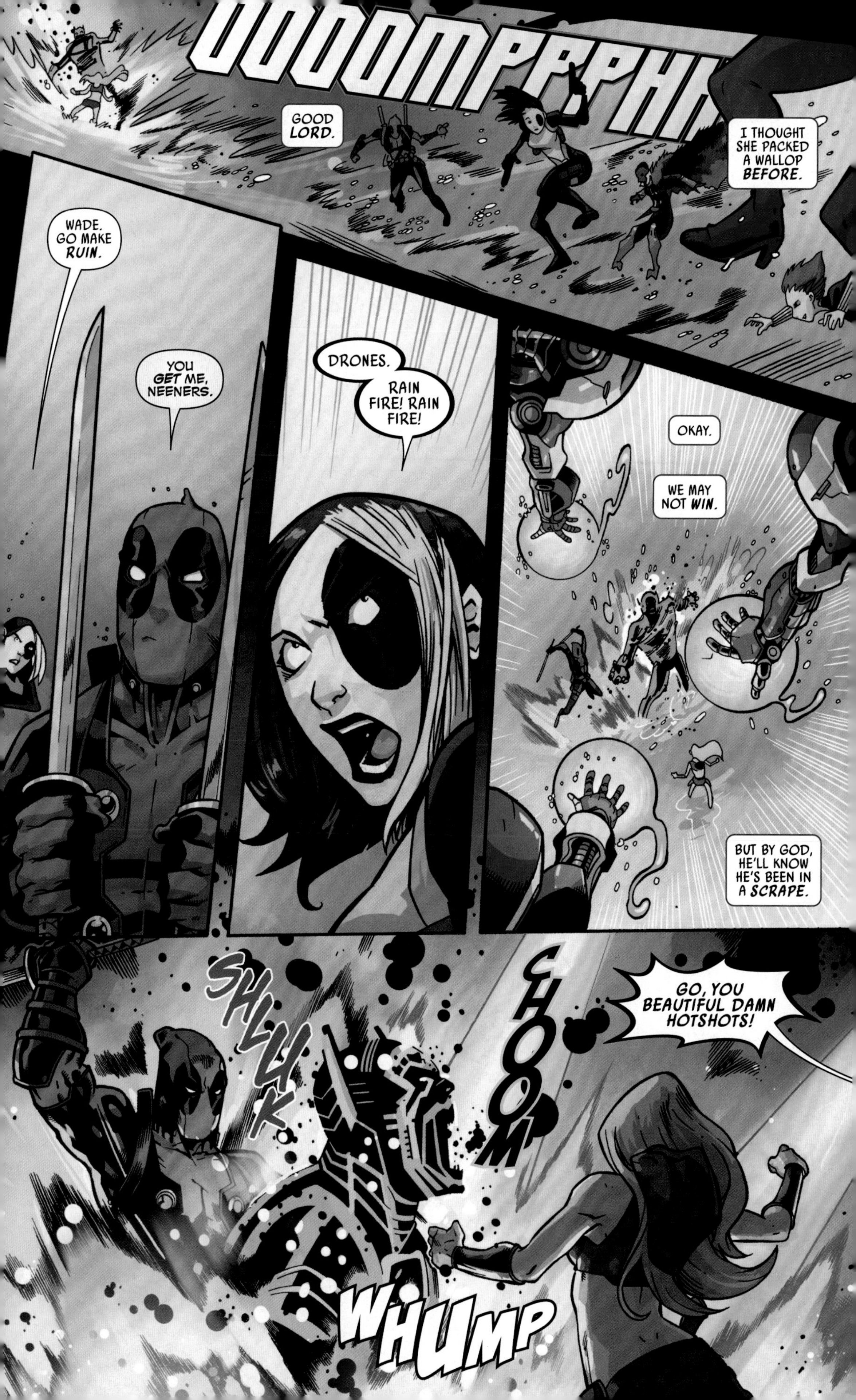
UUOOOMPPPHH
GOOD LORD.
I THOUGHT SHE PACKED A WALLOP BEFORE.
WADE. GO MAKE RUIN.
YOU GET ME, NEENERS.
DRONES.
RAIN FIRE! RAIN FIRE!
OKAY.
WE MAY NOT WIN.
BUT BY GOD, HE'LL KNOW HE'S BEEN IN A SCRAPE.
SHLUUK
CHOOOM
GO, YOU BEAUTIFUL DAMN HOTSHOTS!
WHUMP

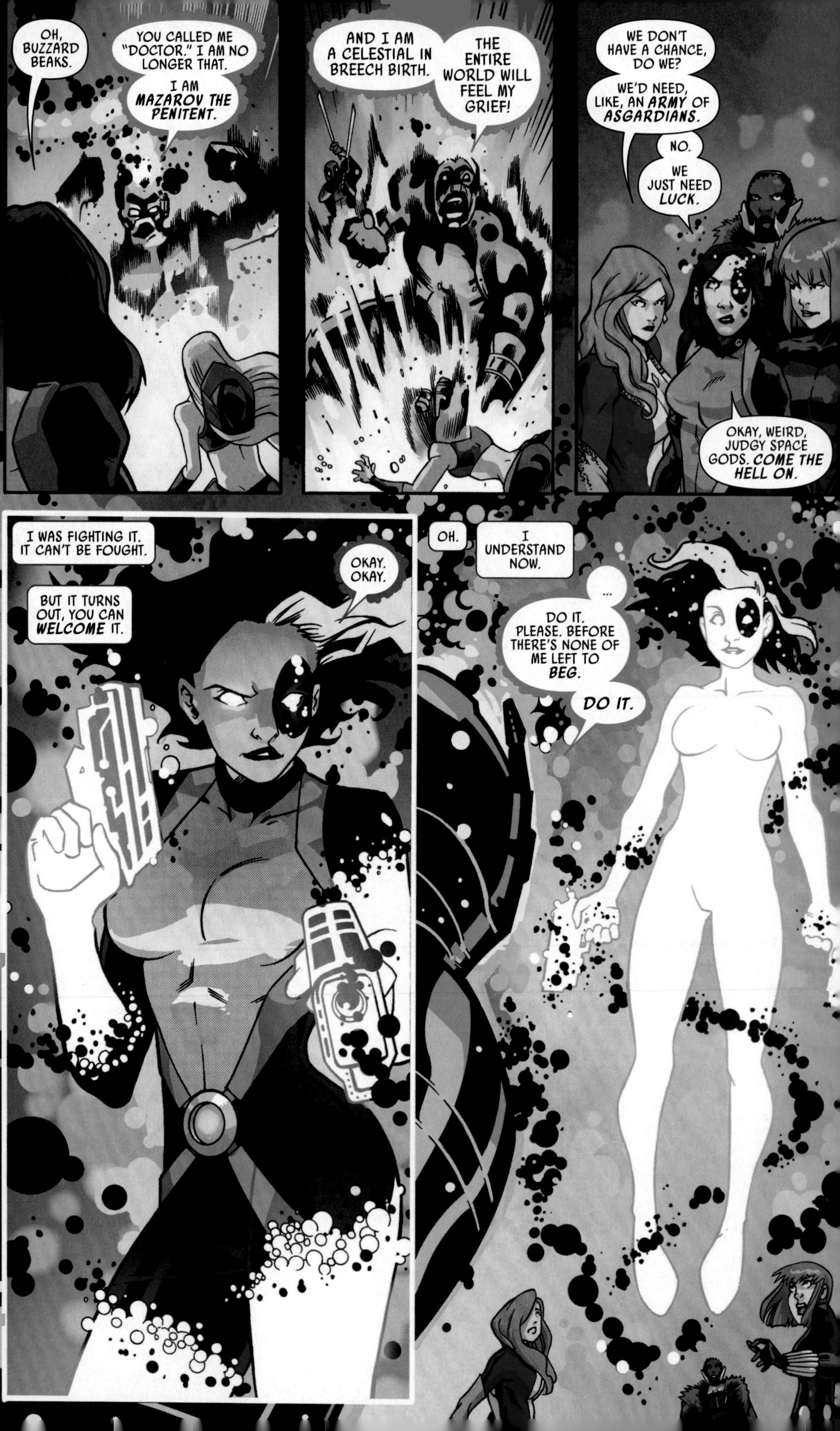
OH, BUZZARD BEAKS.
YOU CALLED ME "DOCTOR." I AM NO LONGER THAT.
I AM MAZAROV THE PENITENT.
AND I AM A CELESTIAL IN BREECH BIRTH.
THE ENTIRE WORLD WILL FEEL MY GRIEF!
WE DON'T HAVE A CHANCE, DO WE?
WE'D NEED, LIKE, AN ARMY OF ASGARDIANS.
NO.
WE JUST NEED LUCK.
OKAY, WEIRD, JUDGY SPACE GODS. COME THE HELL ON.
I WAS FIGHTING IT. IT CAN'T BE FOUGHT.
BUT IT TURNS OUT, YOU CAN WELCOME IT.
OKAY. OKAY.
OH.
I UNDERSTAND NOW.
...
DO IT. PLEASE. BEFORE THERE'S NONE OF ME LEFT TO BEG.
DO IT.

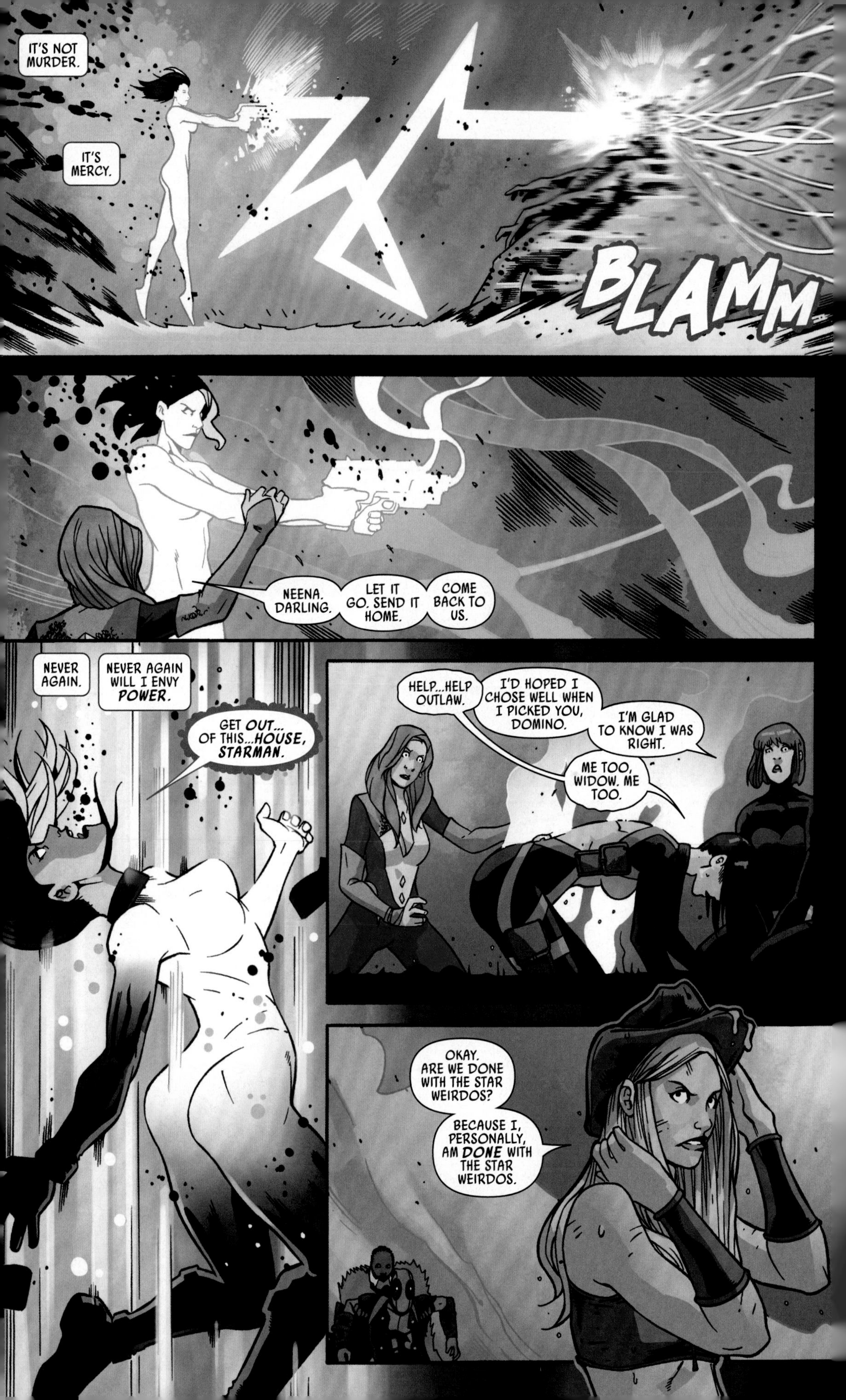
IT'S NOT MURDER.
IT'S MERCY.
BLAMM
NEENA. DARLING.
LET IT GO. SEND IT HOME.
COME BACK TO US.
NEVER AGAIN.
NEVER AGAIN WILL I ENVY POWER.
GET OUT... OF THIS...HOUSE, STARMAN.
HELP...HELP OUTLAW.
I'D HOPED I CHOSE WELL WHEN I PICKED YOU, DOMINO.
I'M GLAD TO KNOW I WAS RIGHT.
ME TOO, WIDOW. ME TOO.
OKAY. ARE WE DONE WITH THE STAR WEIRDOS?
BECAUSE I, PERSONALLY, AM DONE WITH THE STAR WEIRDOS.

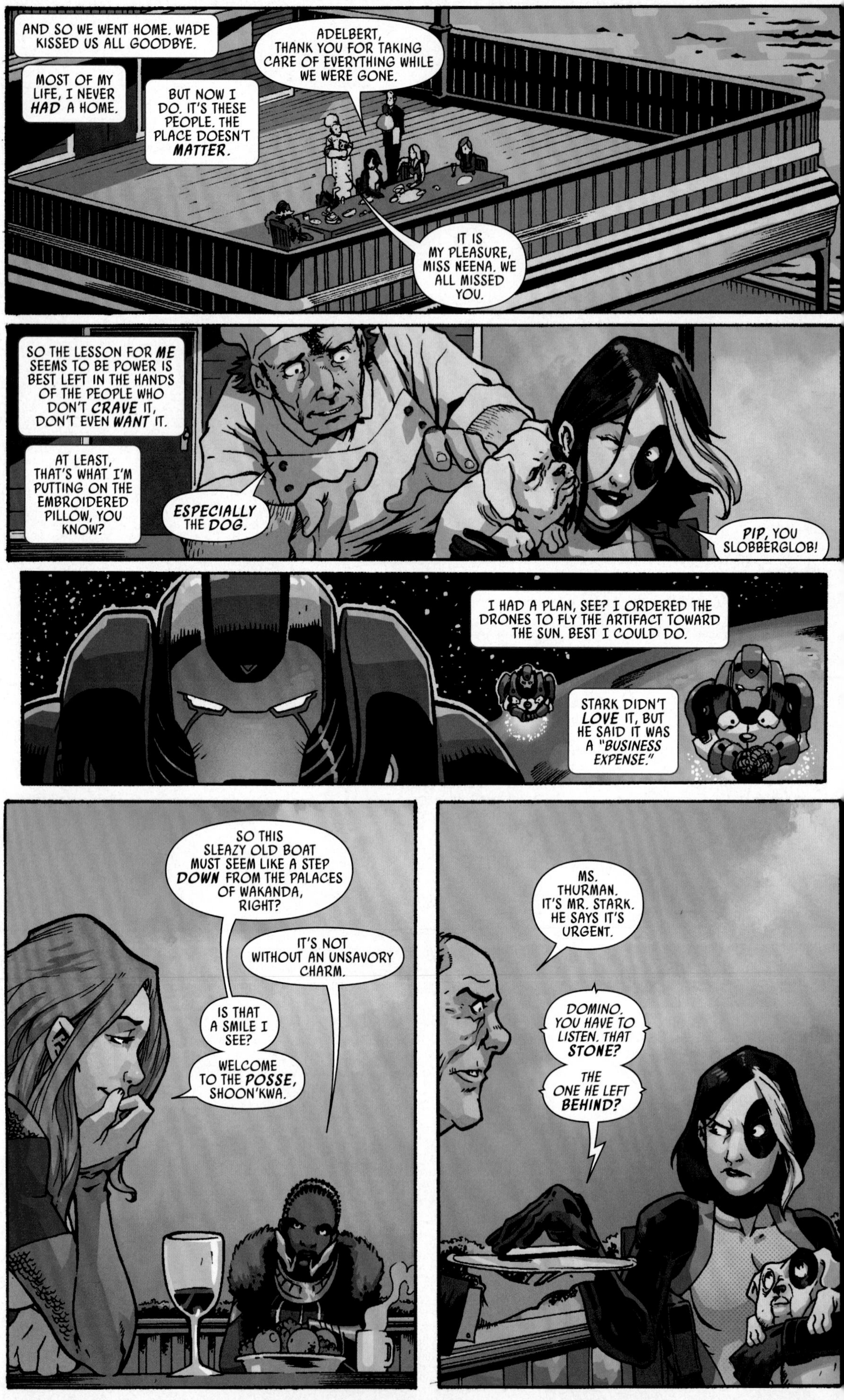
AND SO WE WENT HOME. WADE KISSED US ALL GOODBYE.
MOST OF MY LIFE, I NEVER HAD A HOME.
BUT NOW I DO. IT'S THESE PEOPLE. THE PLACE DOESN'T MATTER.
ADELBERT, THANK YOU FOR TAKING CARE OF EVERYTHING WHILE WE WERE GONE.
IT IS MY PLEASURE, MISS NEENA. WE ALL MISSED YOU.
SO THE LESSON FOR ME SEEMS TO BE POWER IS BEST LEFT IN THE HANDS OF THE PEOPLE WHO DON'T CRAVE IT, DON'T EVEN WANT IT.
AT LEAST, THAT'S WHAT I'M PUTTING ON THE EMBROIDERED PILLOW, YOU KNOW?
ESPECIALLY THE DOG.
PIP, YOU SLOBBERGLOB!
I HAD A PLAN, SEE? I ORDERED THE DRONES TO FLY THE ARTIFACT TOWARD THE SUN. BEST I COULD DO.
STARK DIDN'T LOVE IT, BUT HE SAID IT WAS A "BUSINESS EXPENSE."
SO THIS SLEAZY OLD BOAT MUST SEEM LIKE A STEP DOWN FROM THE PALACES OF WAKANDA, RIGHT?
IT'S NOT WITHOUT AN UNSAVORY CHARM.
IS THAT A SMILE I SEE?
WELCOME TO THE POSSE, SHOON'KWA.
MS. THURMAN. IT'S MR. STARK. HE SAYS IT'S URGENT.
DOMINO. YOU HAVE TO LISTEN. THAT STONE?
THE ONE HE LEFT BEHIND?

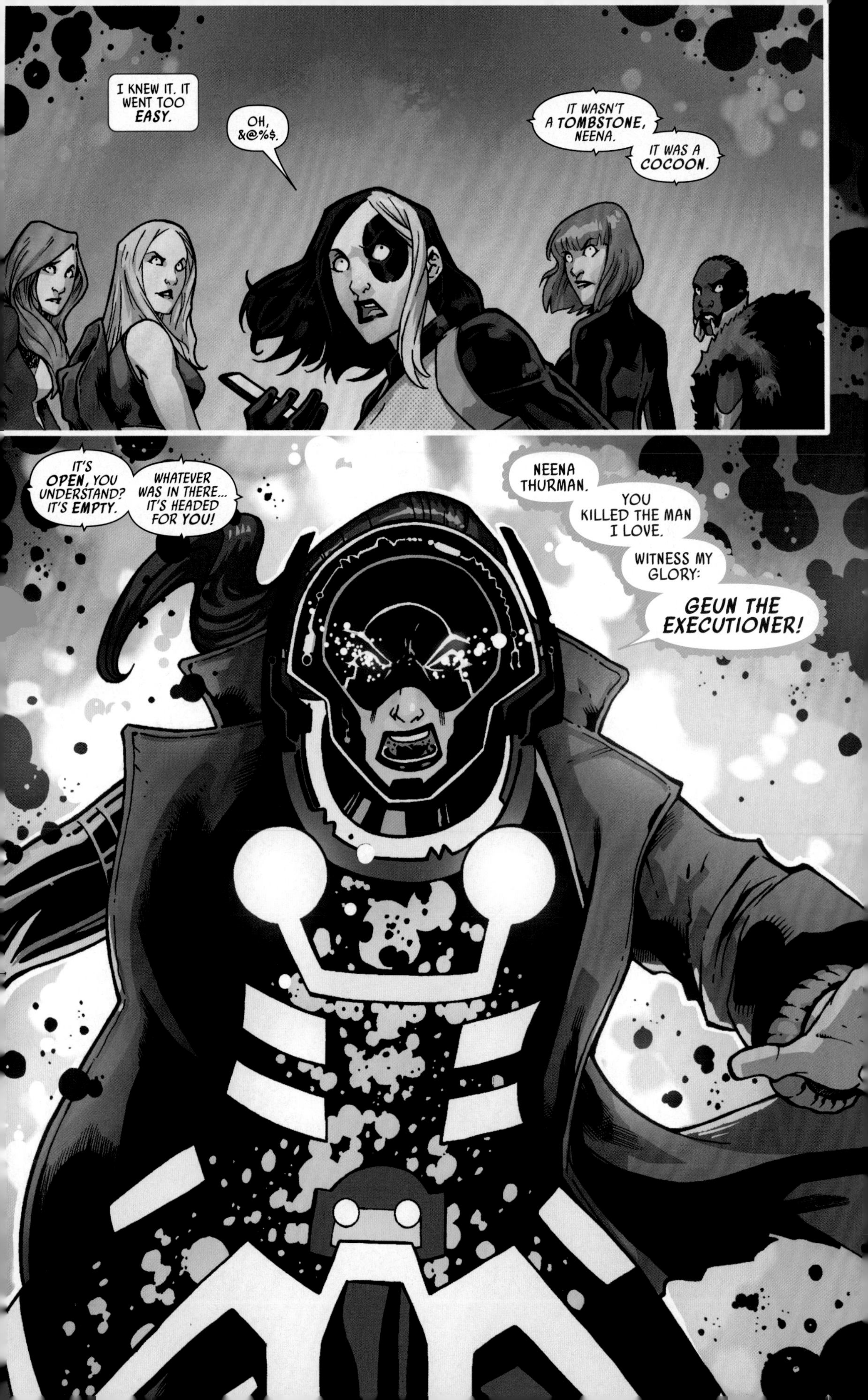
I KNEW IT. IT WENT TOO EASY.
OH, &@%$.
IT WASN'T A TOMBSTONE, NEENA.
IT WAS A COCOON.
IT'S OPEN, YOU UNDERSTAND? IT'S EMPTY.
WHATEVER WAS IN THERE... IT'S HEADED FOR YOU!
NEENA THURMAN.
YOU KILLED THE MAN I LOVE.
WITNESS MY GLORY:
GEUN THE EXECUTIONER!

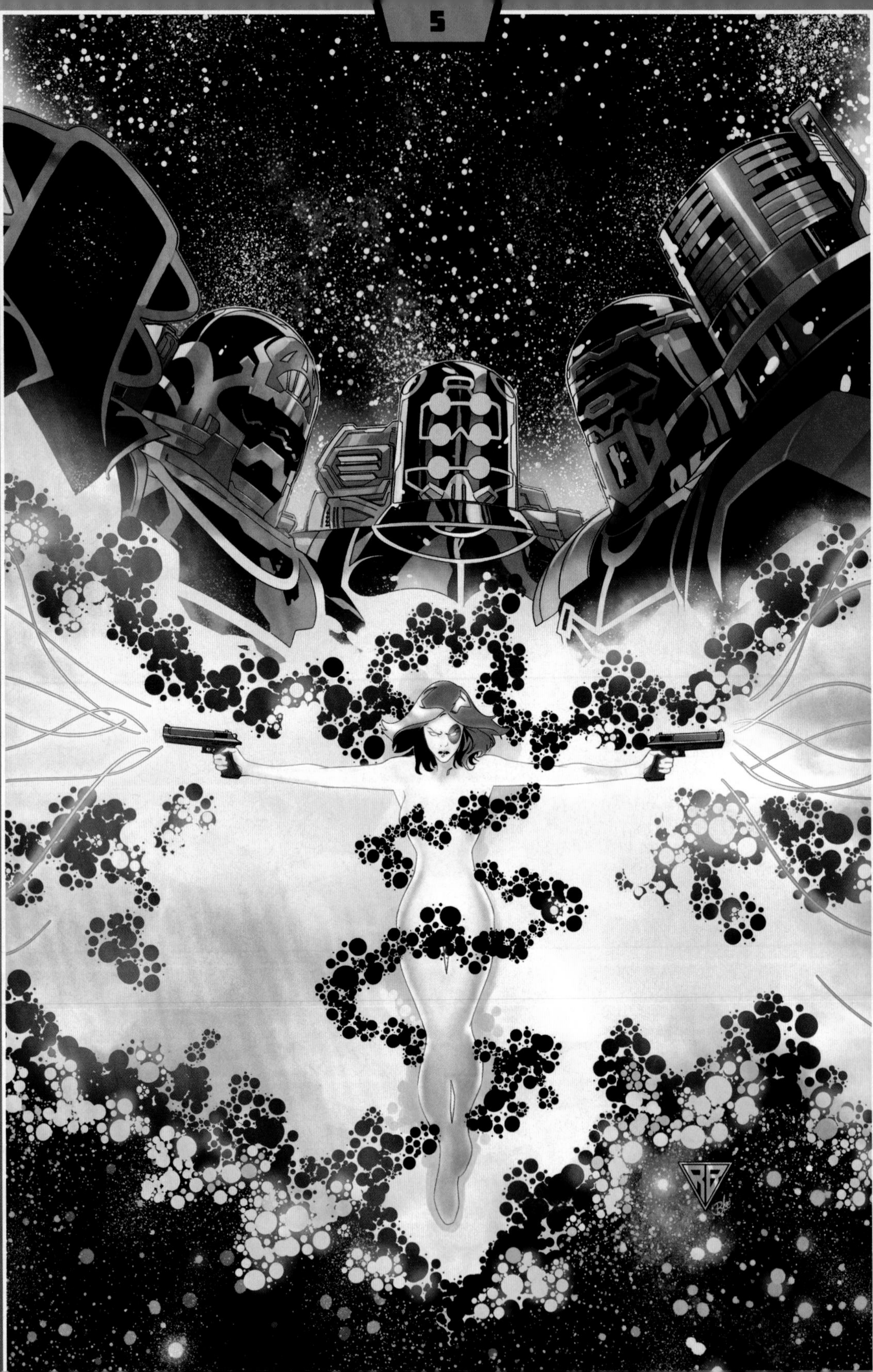
5

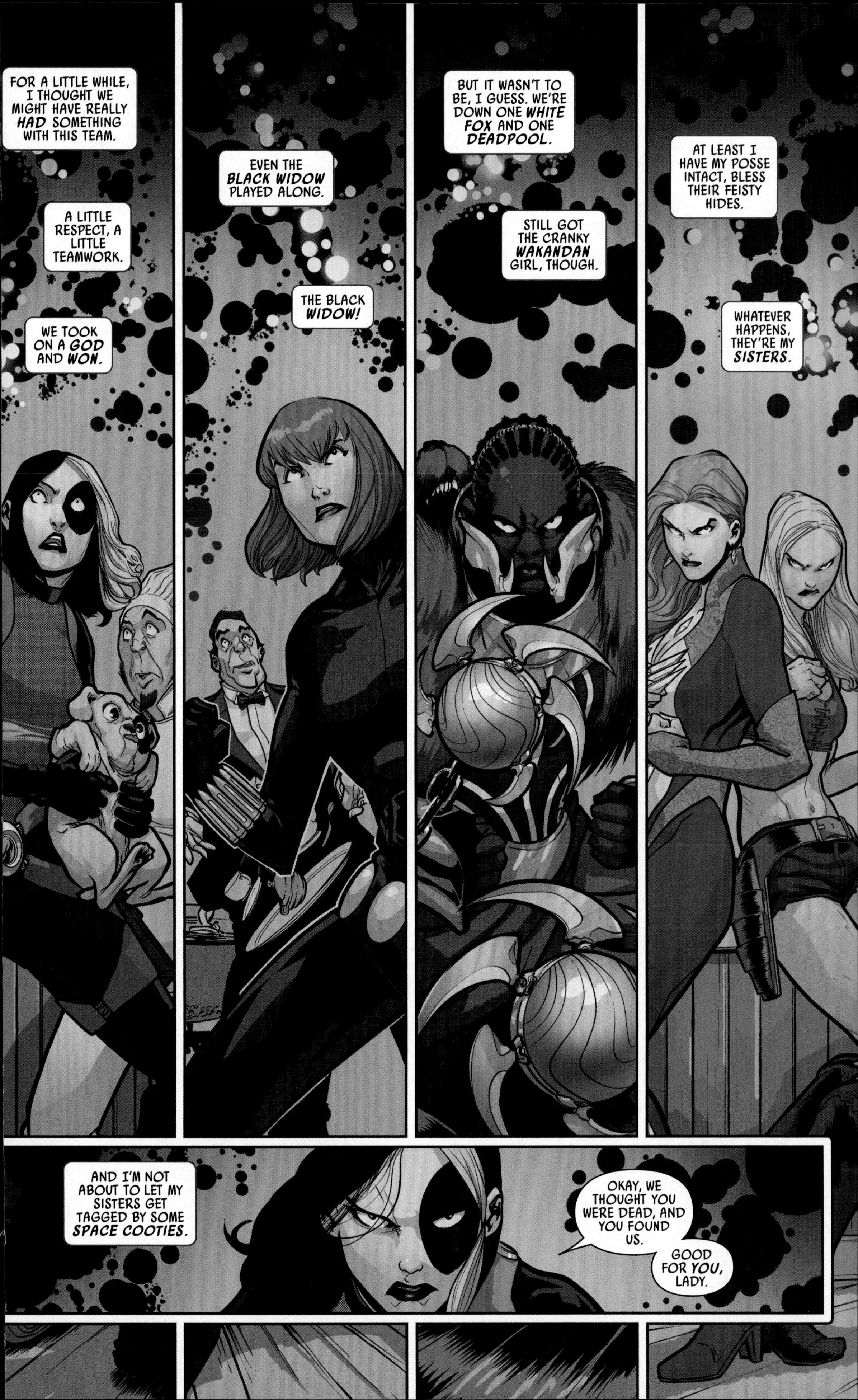
FOR A LITTLE WHILE, I THOUGHT WE MIGHT HAVE REALLY HAD SOMETHING WITH THIS TEAM.
A LITTLE RESPECT, A LITTLE TEAMWORK.
WE TOOK ON A GOD AND WON.
EVEN THE BLACK WIDOW PLAYED ALONG.
THE BLACK WIDOW!
BUT IT WASN'T TO BE, I GUESS. WE'RE DOWN ONE WHITE FOX AND ONE DEADPOOL.
STILL GOT THE CRANKY WAKANDAN GIRL, THOUGH.
AT LEAST I HAVE MY POSSE INTACT, BLESS THEIR FEISTY HIDES.
WHATEVER HAPPENS, THEY'RE MY SISTERS.
AND I'M NOT ABOUT TO LET MY SISTERS GET TAGGED BY SOME SPACE COOTIES.
OKAY, WE THOUGHT YOU WERE DEAD, AND YOU FOUND US.
GOOD FOR YOU, LADY.

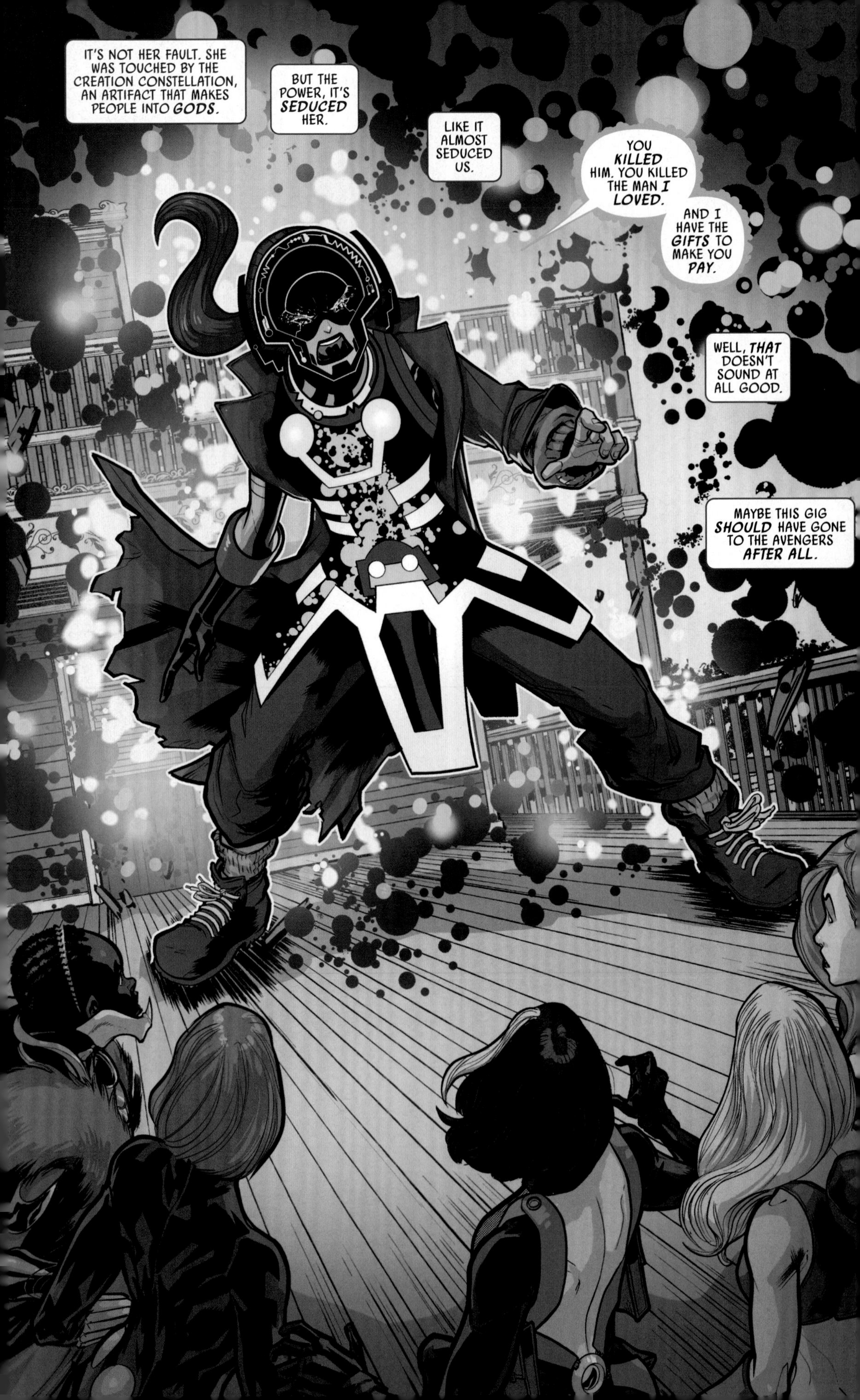
IT'S NOT HER FAULT. SHE WAS TOUCHED BY THE CREATION CONSTELLATION, AN ARTIFACT THAT MAKES PEOPLE INTO GODS.
BUT THE POWER, IT'S SEDUCED HER.
LIKE IT ALMOST SEDUCED US.
YOU KILLED HIM. YOU KILLED THE MAN I LOVED.
AND I HAVE THE GIFTS TO MAKE YOU PAY.
WELL, THAT DOESN'T SOUND AT ALL GOOD.
MAYBE THIS GIG SHOULD HAVE GONE TO THE AVENGERS AFTER ALL.

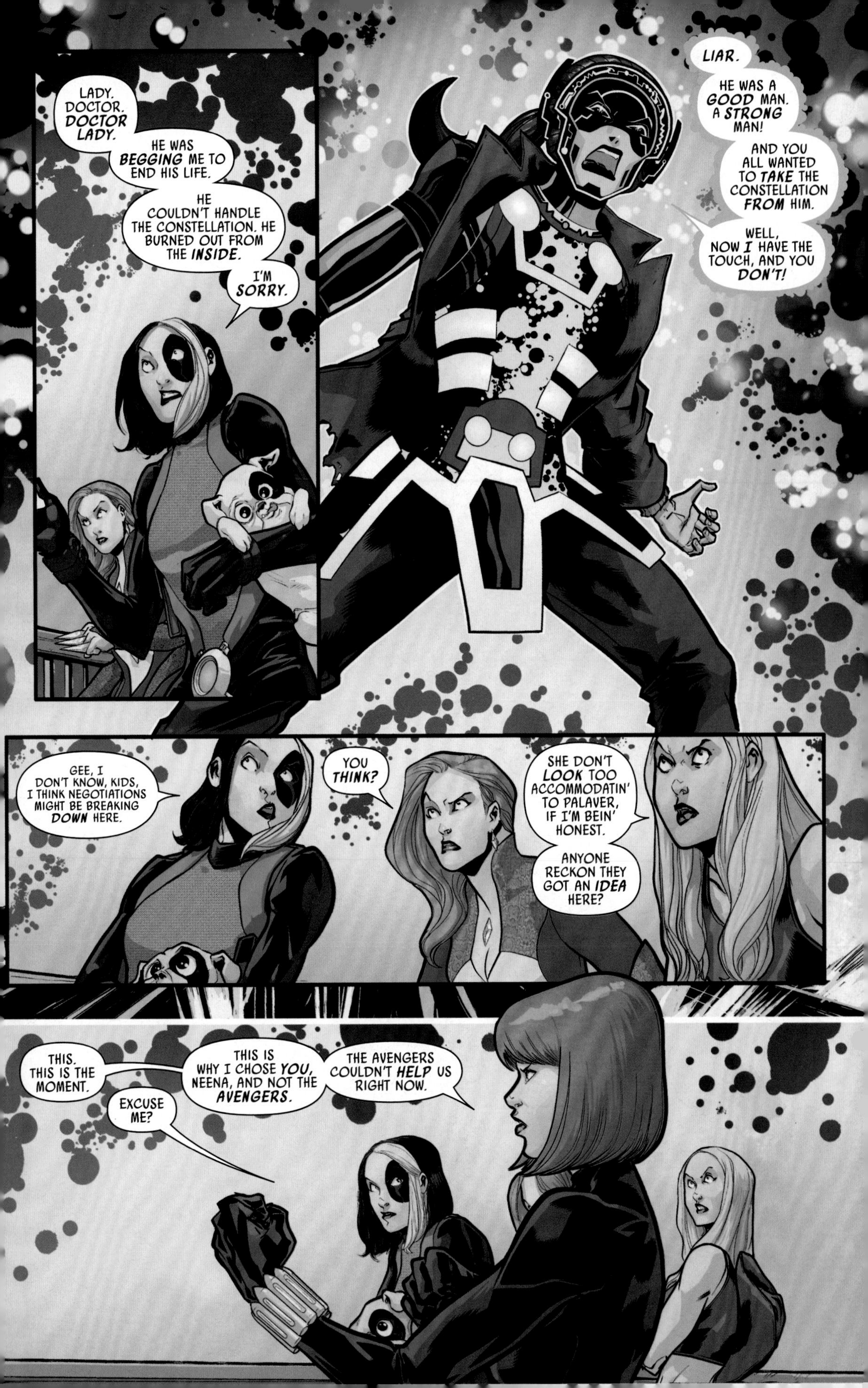
LADY. DOCTOR. DOCTOR LADY.
HE WAS BEGGING ME TO END HIS LIFE.
HE COULDN'T HANDLE THE CONSTELLATION. HE BURNED OUT FROM THE INSIDE.
I'M SORRY.
LIAR.
HE WAS A GOOD MAN. A STRONG MAN!
AND YOU ALL WANTED TO TAKE THE CONSTELLATION FROM HIM.
WELL, NOW I HAVE THE TOUCH, AND YOU DON'T!
GEE, I DON'T KNOW, KIDS, I THINK NEGOTIATIONS MIGHT BE BREAKING DOWN HERE.
YOU THINK?
SHE DON'T LOOK TOO ACCOMMODATIN' TO PALAVER, IF I'M BEIN' HONEST.
ANYONE RECKON THEY GOT AN IDEA HERE?
THIS. THIS IS THE MOMENT.
EXCUSE ME?
THIS IS WHY I CHOSE YOU, NEENA, AND NOT THE AVENGERS.
THE AVENGERS COULDN'T HELP US RIGHT NOW.

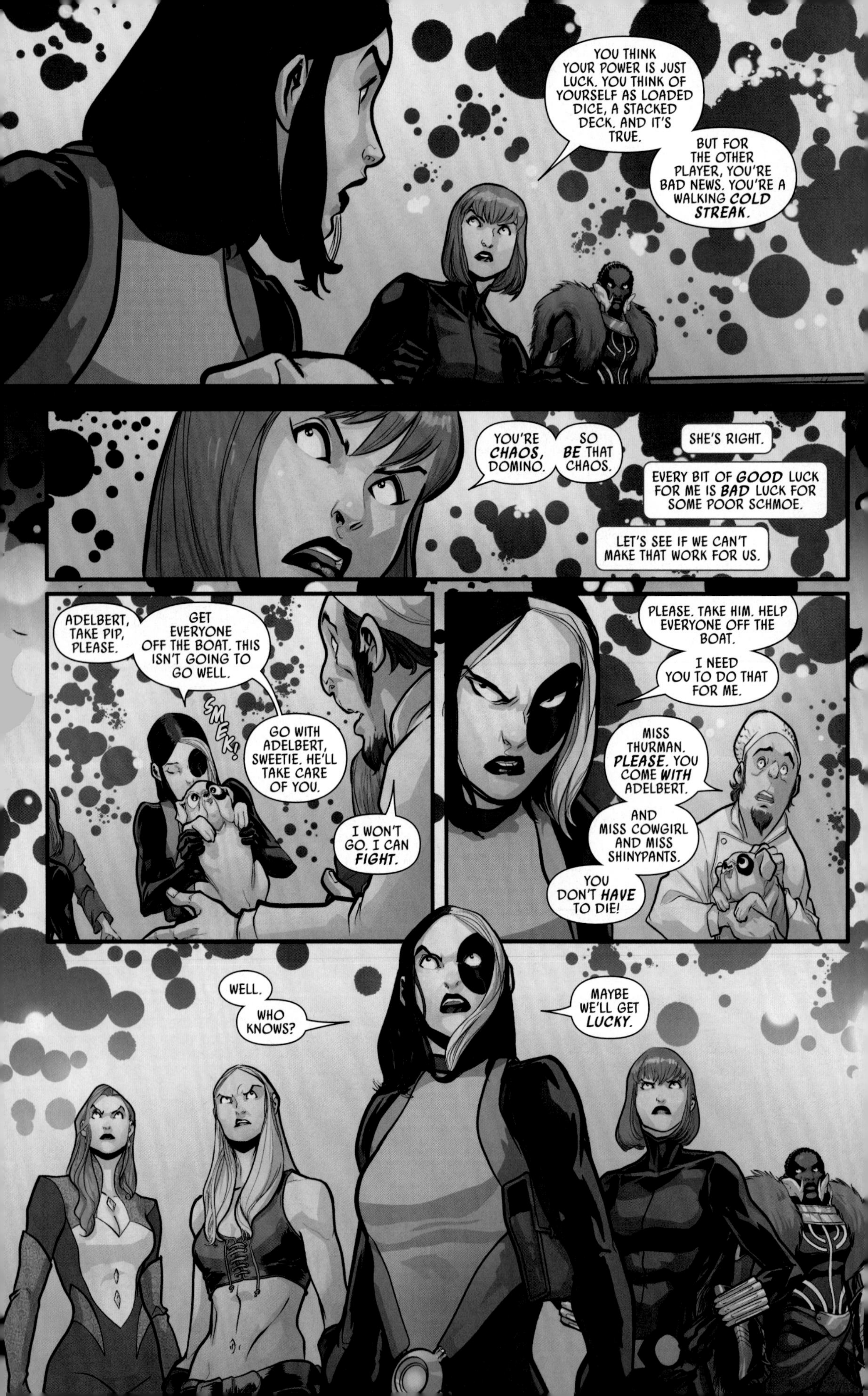

YOU THINK YOUR POWER IS JUST LUCK. YOU THINK OF YOURSELF AS LOADED DICE, A STACKED DECK. AND IT'S TRUE.
BUT FOR THE OTHER PLAYER, YOU'RE BAD NEWS. YOU'RE A WALKING COLD STREAK.
YOU'RE CHAOS, DOMINO.
SO BE THAT CHAOS.
SHE'S RIGHT.
EVERY BIT OF GOOD LUCK FOR ME IS BAD LUCK FOR SOME POOR SCHMOE.
LET'S SEE IF WE CAN'T MAKE THAT WORK FOR US.
ADELBERT, TAKE PIP, PLEASE.
GET EVERYONE OFF THE BOAT. THIS ISN'T GOING TO GO WELL.
SMEK!
GO WITH ADELBERT, SWEETIE. HE'LL TAKE CARE OF YOU.
I WON'T GO. I CAN FIGHT.
PLEASE. TAKE HIM. HELP EVERYONE OFF THE BOAT.
I NEED YOU TO DO THAT FOR ME.
MISS THURMAN. PLEASE. YOU COME WITH ADELBERT.
AND MISS COWGIRL AND MISS SHINYPANTS.
YOU DON'T HAVE TO DIE!
WELL.
WHO KNOWS?
MAYBE WE'LL GET LUCKY.

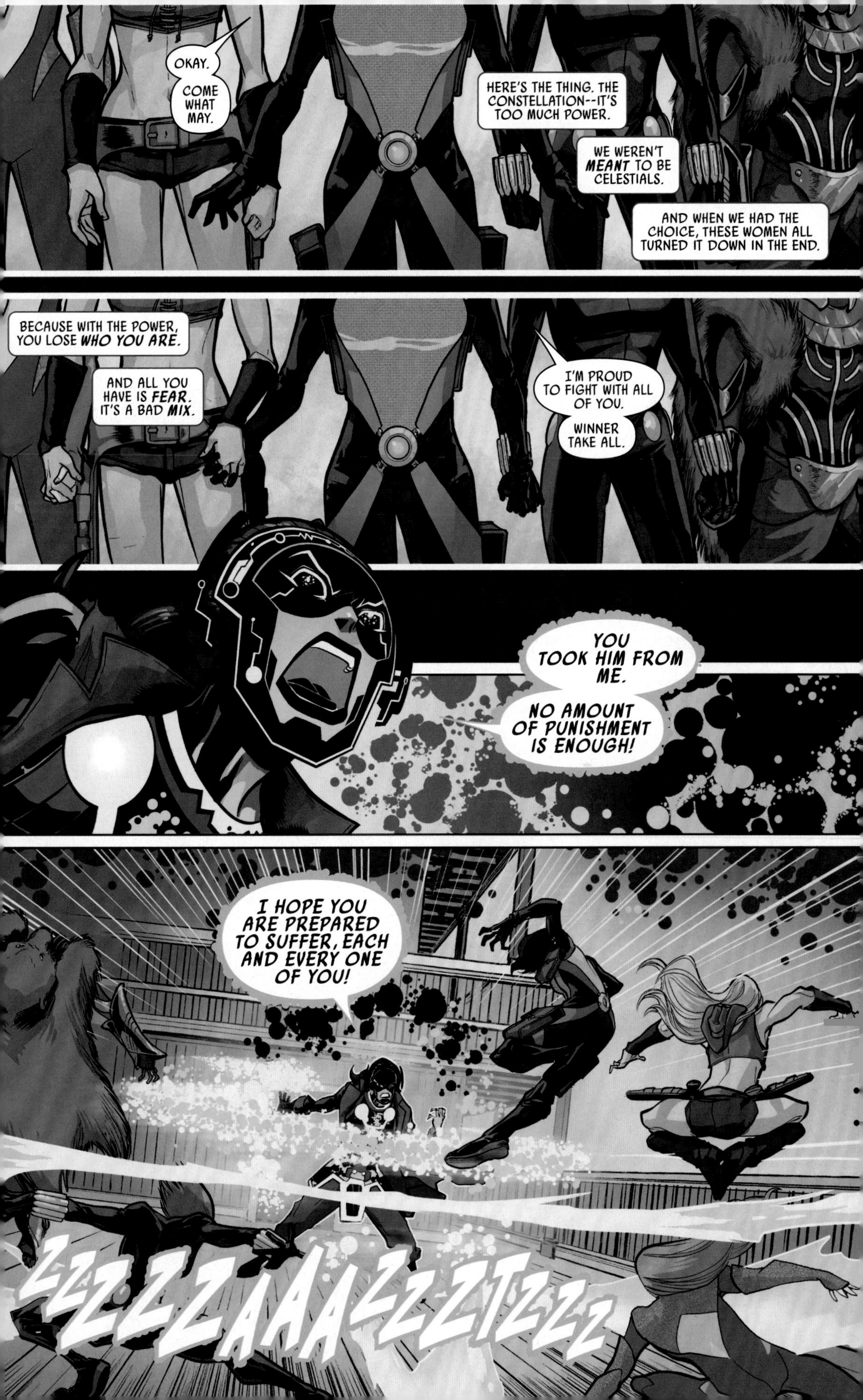
OKAY.
COME WHAT MAY.
HERE'S THE THING. THE CONSTELLATION--IT'S TOO MUCH POWER.
WE WEREN'T MEANT TO BE CELESTIALS.
AND WHEN WE HAD THE CHOICE, THESE WOMEN ALL TURNED IT DOWN IN THE END.
BECAUSE WITH THE POWER, YOU LOSE WHO YOU ARE.
AND ALL YOU HAVE IS FEAR. IT'S A BAD MIX.
I'M PROUD TO FIGHT WITH ALL OF YOU.
WINNER TAKE ALL.
YOU TOOK HIM FROM ME.
NO AMOUNT OF PUNISHMENT IS ENOUGH!
I HOPE YOU ARE PREPARED TO SUFFER, EACH AND EVERY ONE OF YOU!
ZZZZZAAAZZZTZZZ

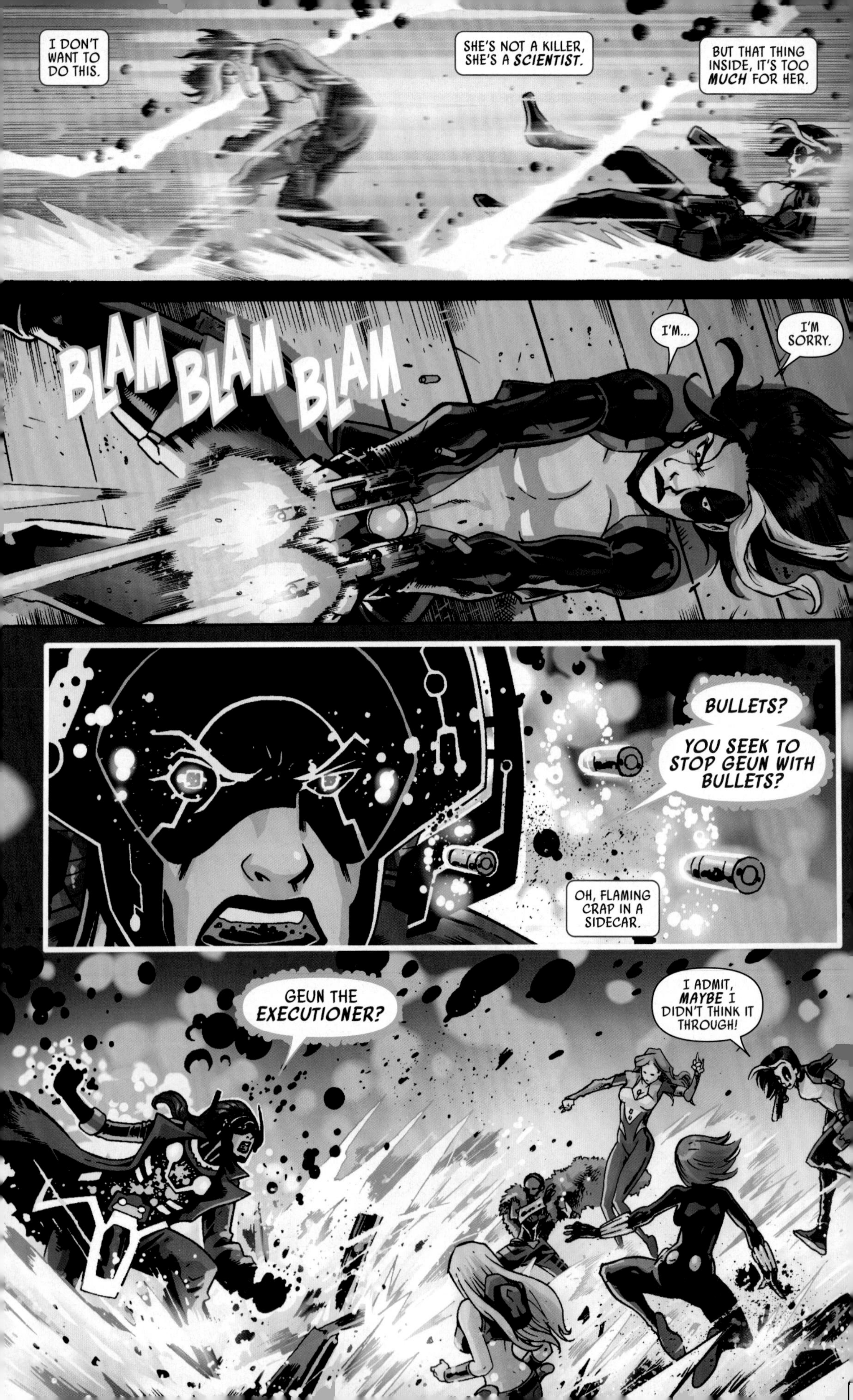
I DON'T WANT TO DO THIS.
SHE'S NOT A KILLER, SHE'S A SCIENTIST.
BUT THAT THING INSIDE, IT'S TOO MUCH FOR HER.
BLAM BLAM BLAM
I'M...
I'M SORRY.
BULLETS?
YOU SEEK TO STOP GEUN WITH BULLETS?
OH, FLAMING CRAP IN A SIDECAR.
GEUN THE EXECUTIONER?
I ADMIT, MAYBE I DIDN'T THINK IT THROUGH!

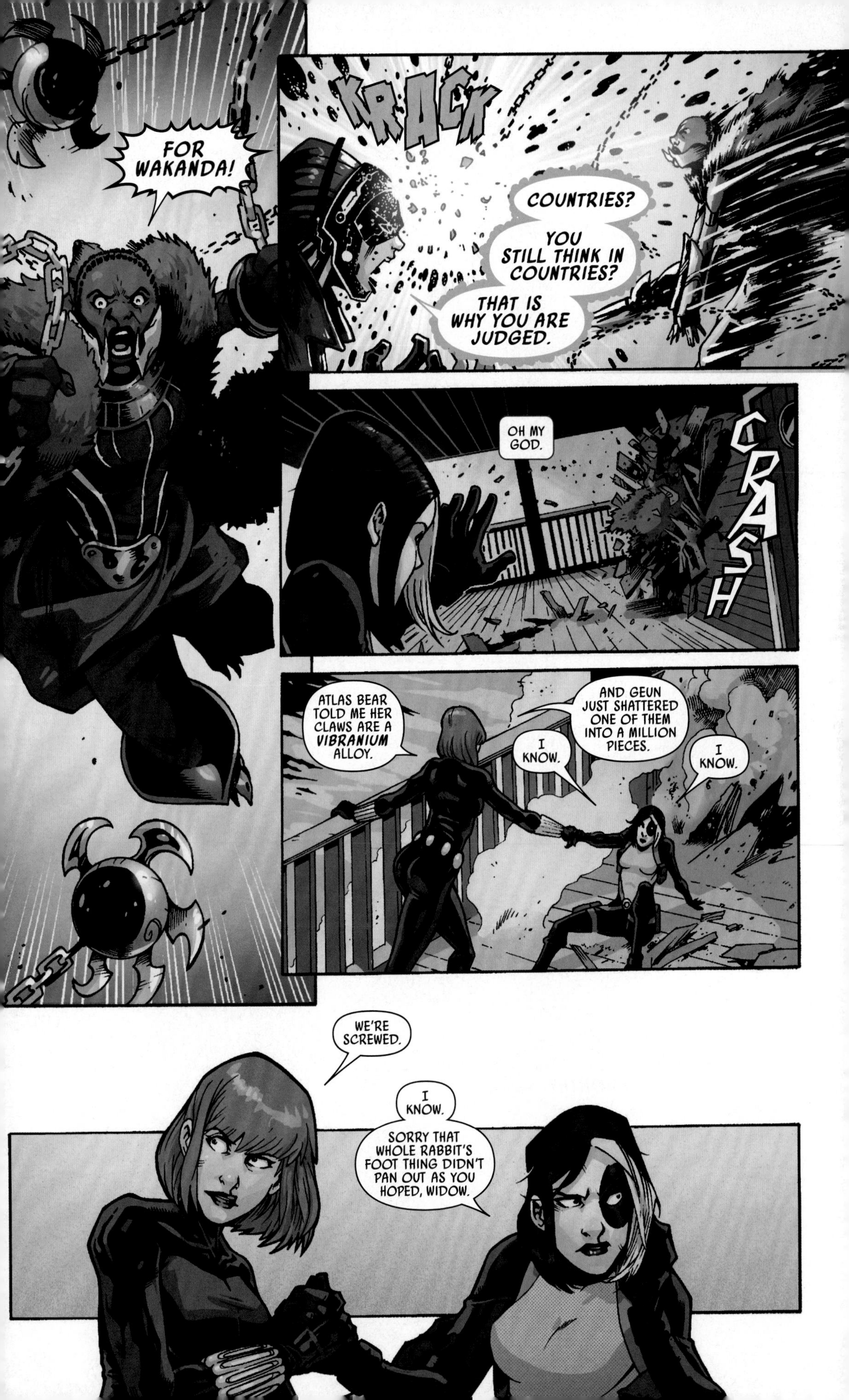
FOR WAKANDA!
KRACK
COUNTRIES?
YOU STILL THINK IN COUNTRIES?
THAT IS WHY YOU ARE JUDGED.
OH MY GOD.
CRASH
ATLAS BEAR TOLD ME HER CLAWS ARE A VIBRANIUM ALLOY.
I KNOW.
AND GEUN JUST SHATTERED ONE OF THEM INTO A MILLION PIECES.
I KNOW.
WE'RE SCREWED.
I KNOW.
SORRY THAT WHOLE RABBIT'S FOOT THING DIDN'T PAN OUT AS YOU HOPED, WIDOW.

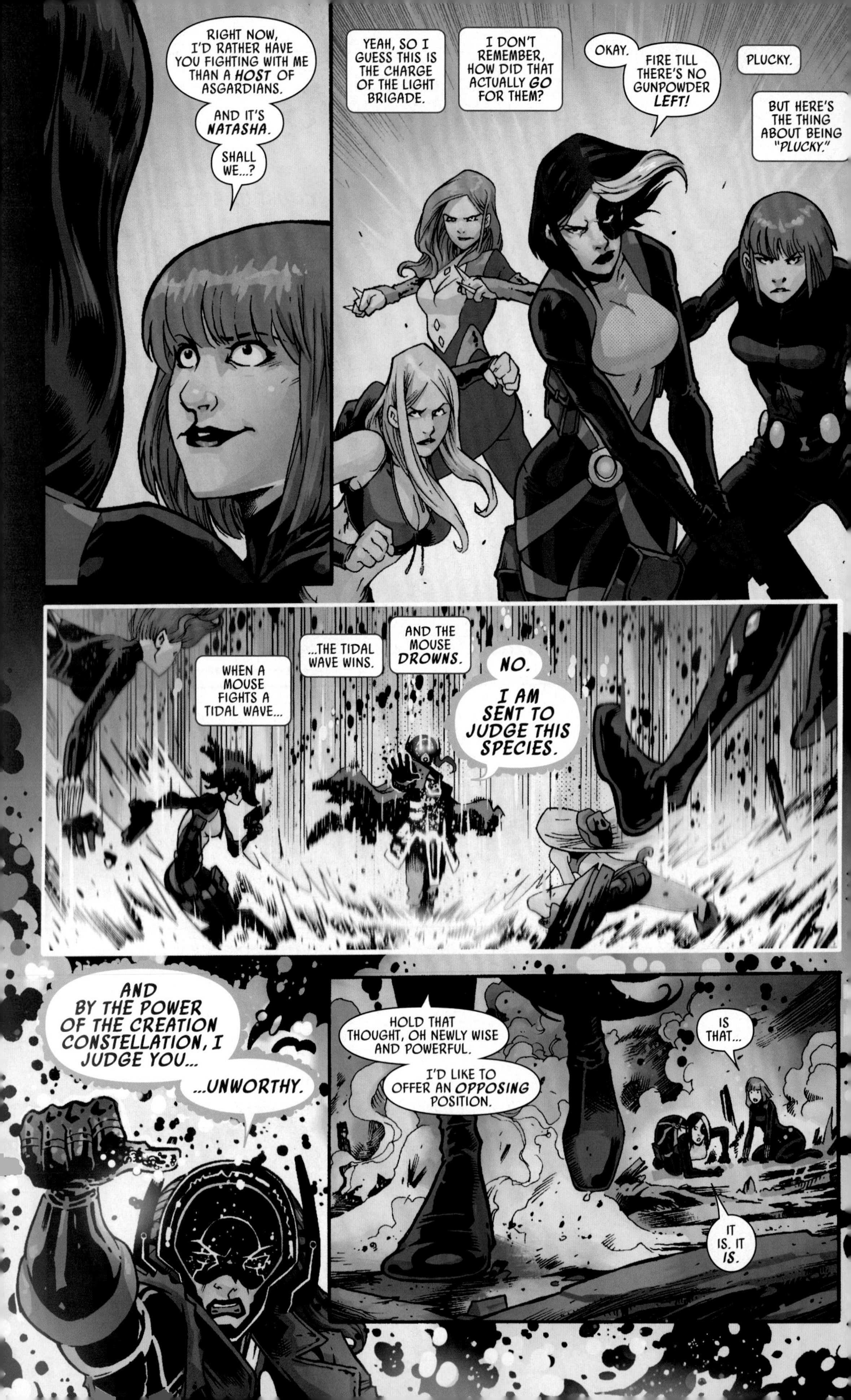
RIGHT NOW, I'D RATHER HAVE YOU FIGHTING WITH ME THAN A HOST OF ASGARDIANS.
AND IT'S NATASHA.
SHALL WE...?
YEAH, SO I GUESS THIS IS THE CHARGE OF THE LIGHT BRIGADE.
I DON'T REMEMBER, HOW DID THAT ACTUALLY GO FOR THEM?
OKAY.
FIRE TILL THERE'S NO GUNPOWDER LEFT!
PLUCKY.
BUT HERE'S THE THING ABOUT BEING "PLUCKY."
WHEN A MOUSE FIGHTS A TIDAL WAVE...
...THE TIDAL WAVE WINS.
AND THE MOUSE DROWNS.
NO.
I AM SENT TO JUDGE THIS SPECIES.
AND BY THE POWER OF THE CREATION CONSTELLATION, I JUDGE YOU...
...UNWORTHY.
HOLD THAT THOUGHT, OH NEWLY WISE AND POWERFUL.
I'D LIKE TO OFFER AN OPPOSING POSITION.
IS THAT...
IT IS. IT IS.

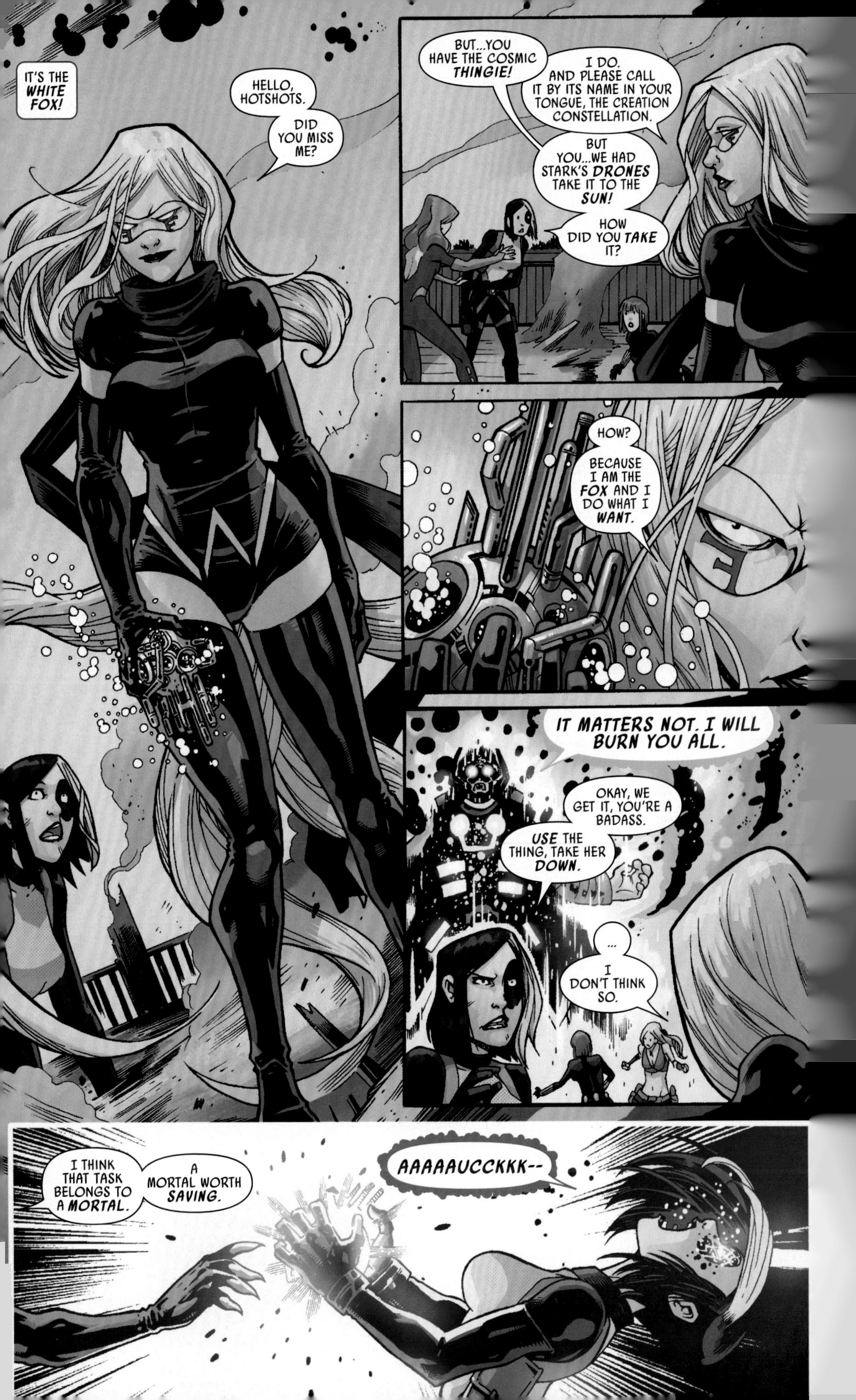
IT'S THE WHITE FOX!
HELLO, HOTSHOTS.
DID YOU MISS ME?
BUT...YOU HAVE THE COSMIC THINGIE!
I DO. AND PLEASE CALL IT BY ITS NAME IN YOUR TONGUE, THE CREATION CONSTELLATION.
BUT YOU...WE HAD STARK'S DRONES TAKE IT TO THE SUN!
HOW DID YOU TAKE IT?
HOW?
BECAUSE I AM THE FOX AND I DO WHAT I WANT.
IT MATTERS NOT. I WILL BURN YOU ALL.
OKAY, WE GET IT, YOU'RE A BADASS.
USE THE THING, TAKE HER DOWN.
...
I DON'T THINK SO.
I THINK THAT TASK BELONGS TO A MORTAL.
A MORTAL WORTH SAVING.
AAAAAUCCKKK--

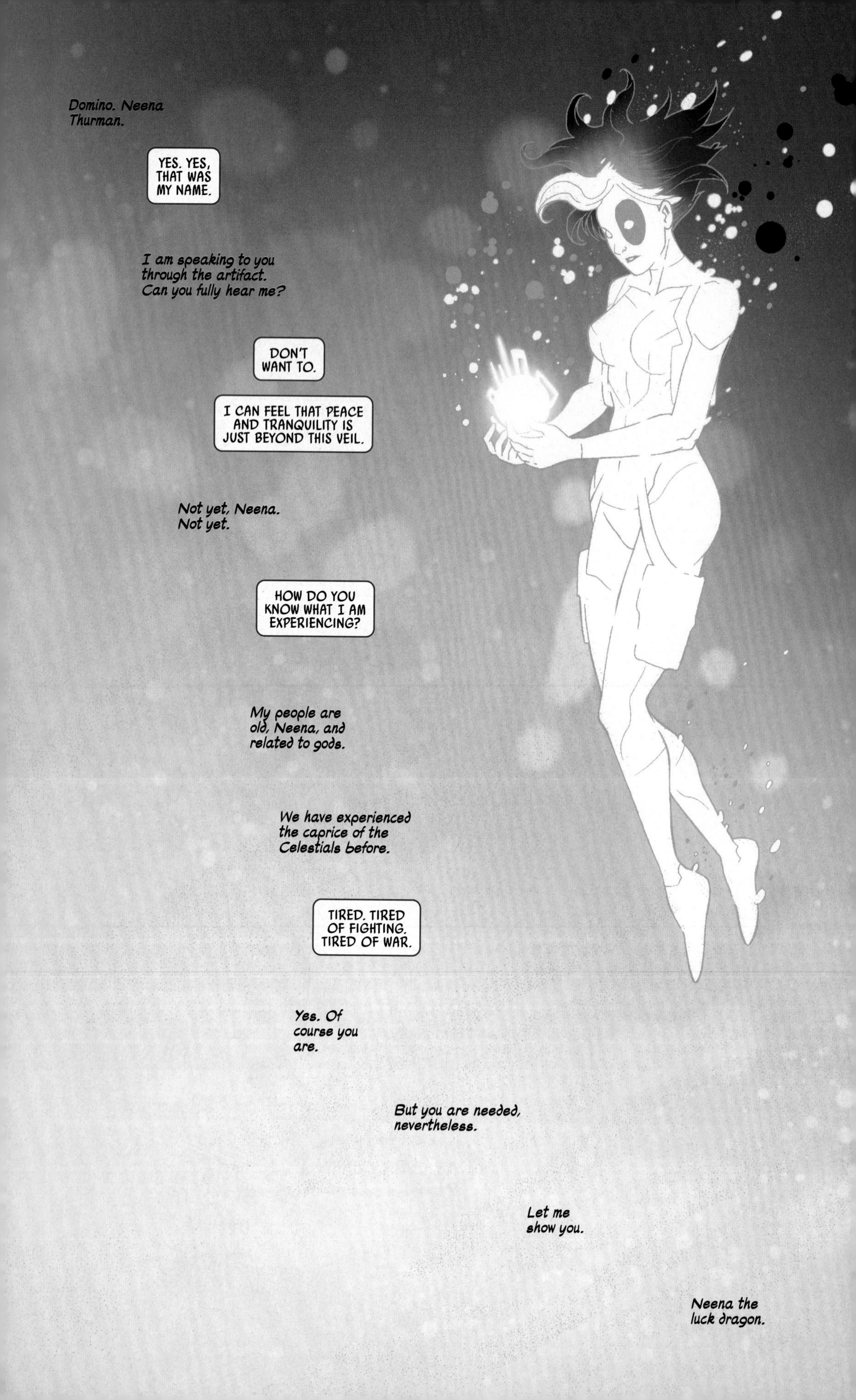
Domino. Neena Thurman.
YES. YES, THAT WAS MY NAME.
I am speaking to you through the artifact. Can you fully hear me?
DON'T WANT TO.
I CAN FEEL THAT PEACE AND TRANQUILITY IS JUST BEYOND THIS VEIL.
Not yet, Neena. Not yet.
HOW DO YOU KNOW WHAT I AM EXPERIENCING?
My people are old, Neena, and related to gods.
We have experienced the caprice of the Celestials before.
TIRED. TIRED OF FIGHTING. TIRED OF WAR.
Yes. Of course you are.
But you are needed, nevertheless.
Let me show you.
Neena the luck dragon.

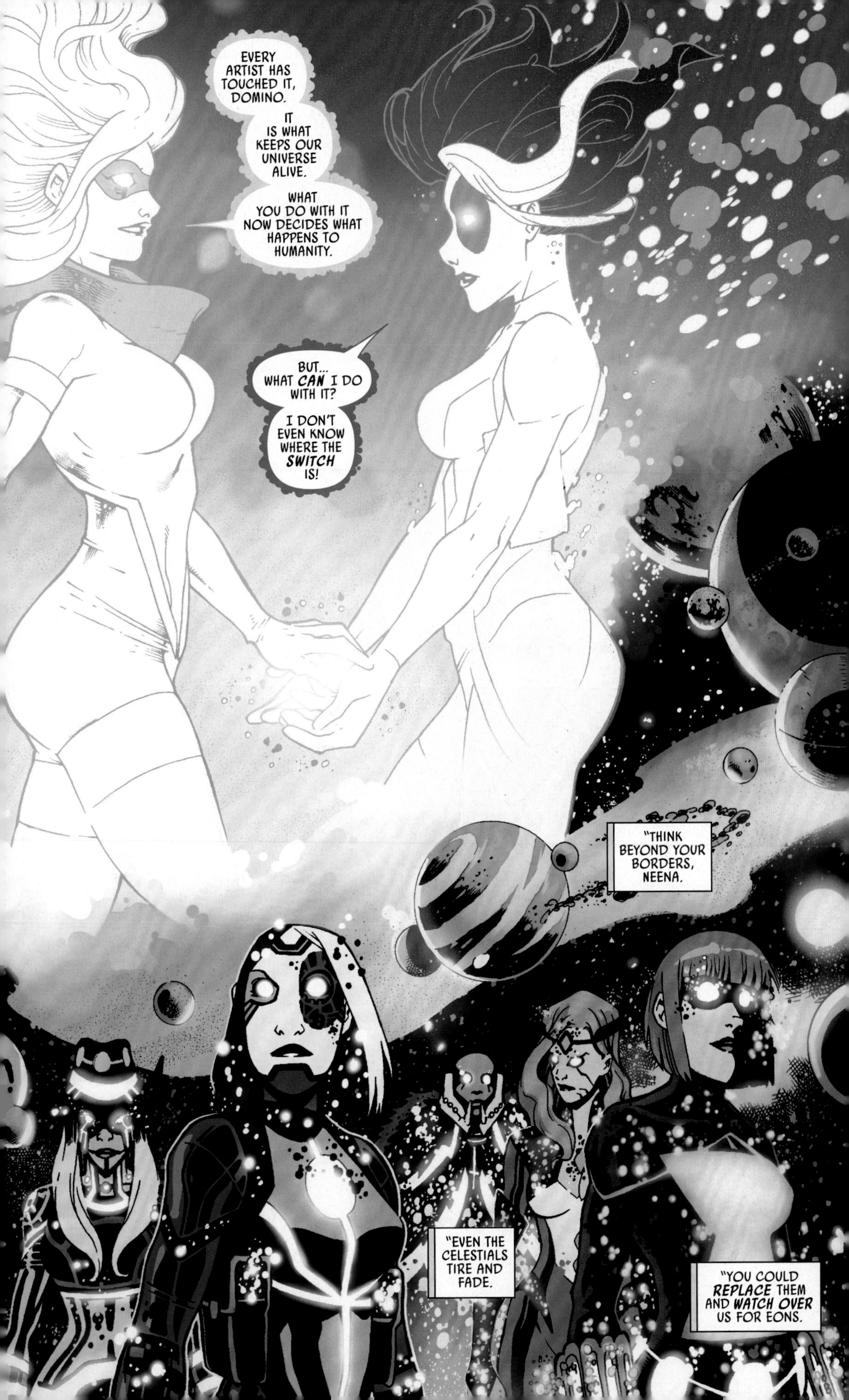
EVERY ARTIST HAS TOUCHED IT, DOMINO.
IT IS WHAT KEEPS OUR UNIVERSE ALIVE.
WHAT YOU DO WITH IT NOW DECIDES WHAT HAPPENS TO HUMANITY.
BUT... WHAT CAN I DO WITH IT?
I DON'T EVEN KNOW WHERE THE SWITCH IS!
"THINK BEYOND YOUR BORDERS, NEENA.
"EVEN THE CELESTIALS TIRE AND FADE.
"YOU COULD REPLACE THEM AND WATCH OVER US FOR EONS.

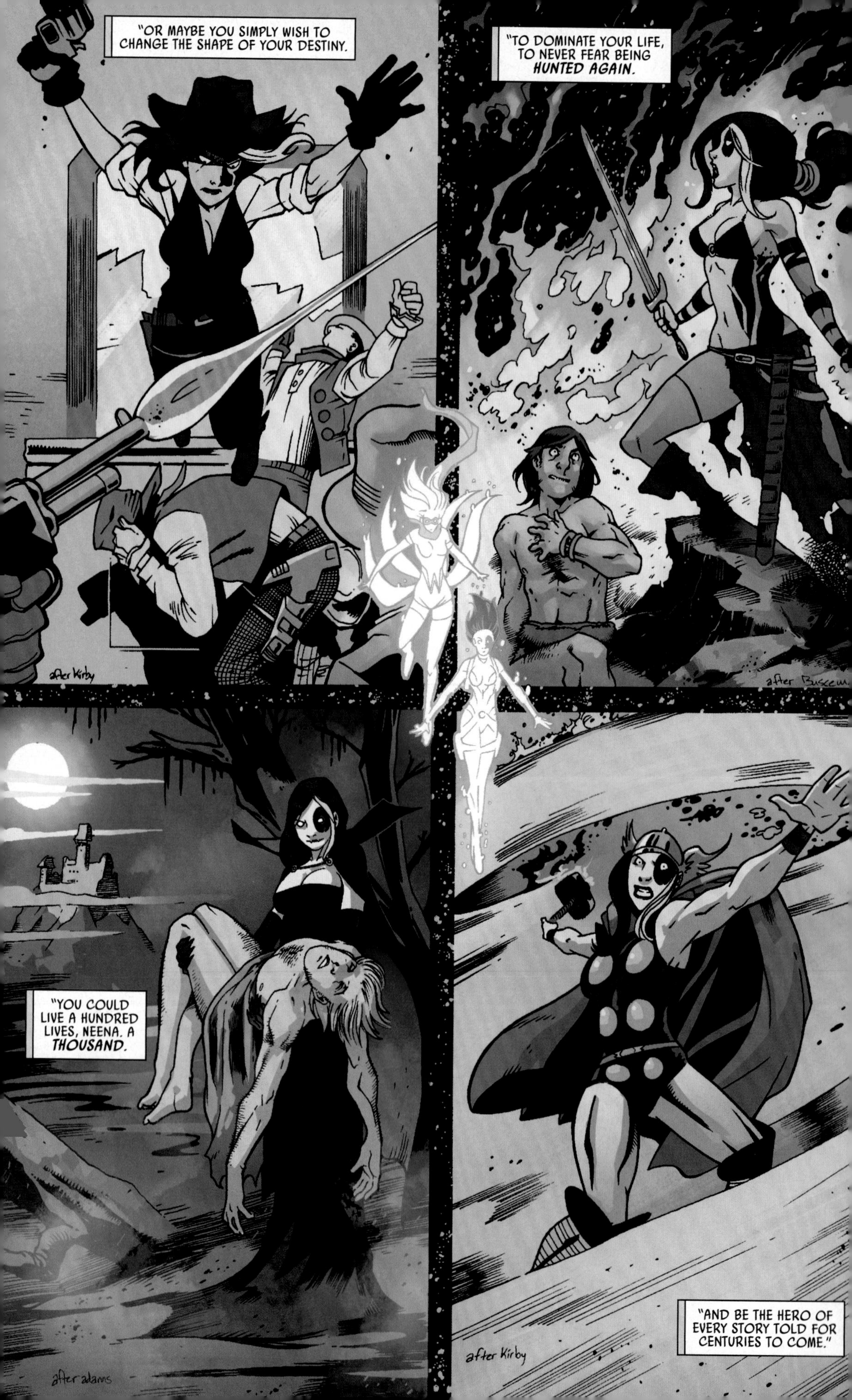
"OR MAYBE YOU SIMPLY WISH TO CHANGE THE SHAPE OF YOUR DESTINY.
after Kirby
"TO DOMINATE YOUR LIFE, TO NEVER FEAR BEING HUNTED AGAIN.
"YOU COULD LIVE A HUNDRED LIVES, NEENA. A THOUSAND.
after adams
"AND BE THE HERO OF EVERY STORY TOLD FOR CENTURIES TO COME."
after Kirby

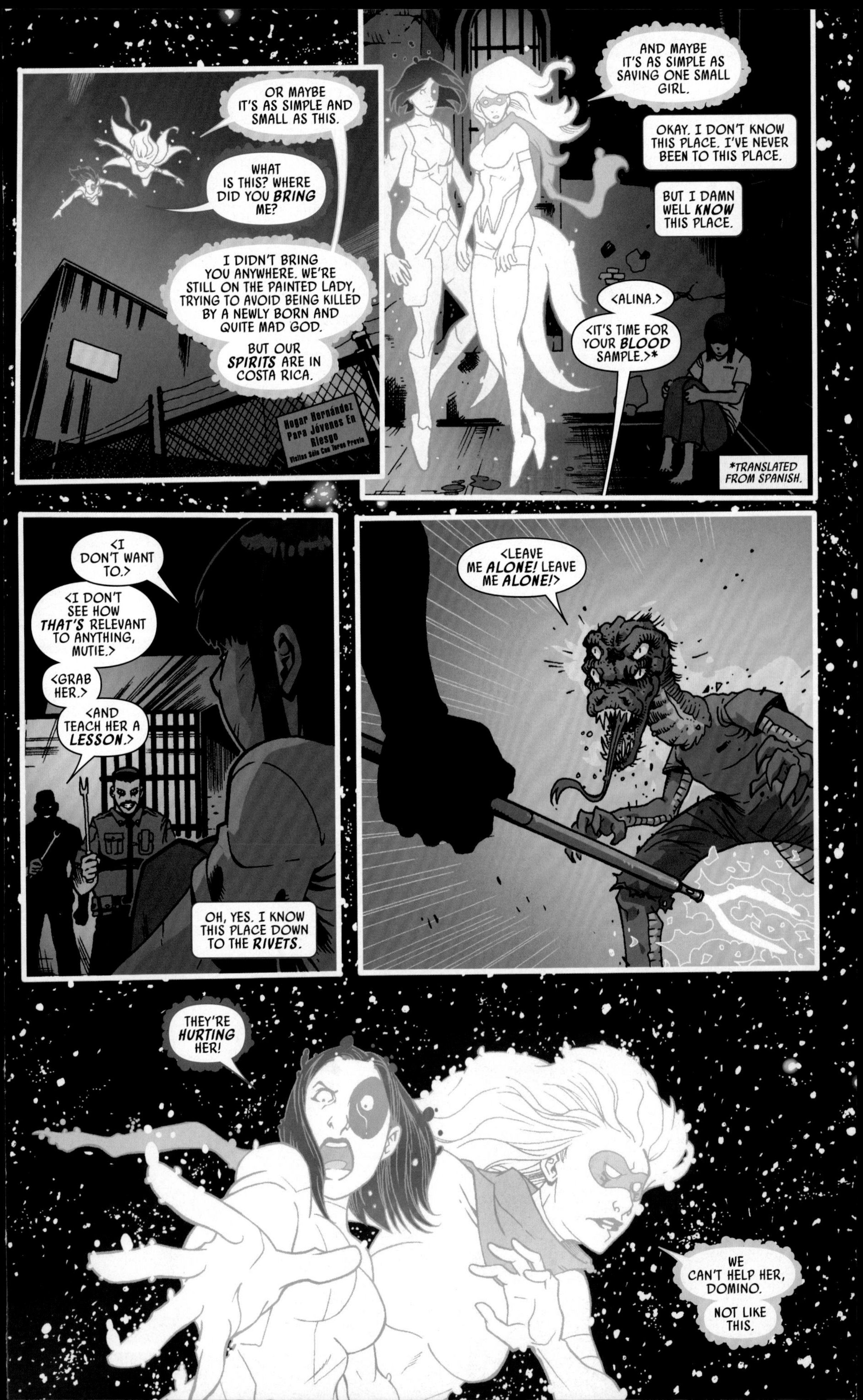

OR MAYBE IT'S AS SIMPLE AND SMALL AS THIS.
WHAT IS THIS? WHERE DID YOU BRING ME?
I DIDN'T BRING YOU ANYWHERE. WE'RE STILL ON THE PAINTED LADY, TRYING TO AVOID BEING KILLED BY A NEWLY BORN AND QUITE MAD GOD.
BUT OUR SPIRITS ARE IN COSTA RICA.
Hogar Hernández Para Jóvenes En Riesgo Visitas Sólo Con Turno Previo
AND MAYBE IT'S AS SIMPLE AS SAVING ONE SMALL GIRL.
OKAY. I DON'T KNOW THIS PLACE. I'VE NEVER BEEN TO THIS PLACE.
BUT I DAMN WELL KNOW THIS PLACE.
<ALINA.>
<IT'S TIME FOR YOUR BLOOD SAMPLE.>*
*TRANSLATED FROM SPANISH.
<I DON'T WANT TO.>
<I DON'T SEE HOW THAT'S RELEVANT TO ANYTHING, MUTIE.>
<GRAB HER.>
<AND TEACH HER A LESSON.>
OH, YES. I KNOW THIS PLACE DOWN TO THE RIVETS.
<LEAVE ME ALONE! LEAVE ME ALONE!>
THEY'RE HURTING HER!
WE CAN'T HELP HER, DOMINO.
NOT LIKE THIS.

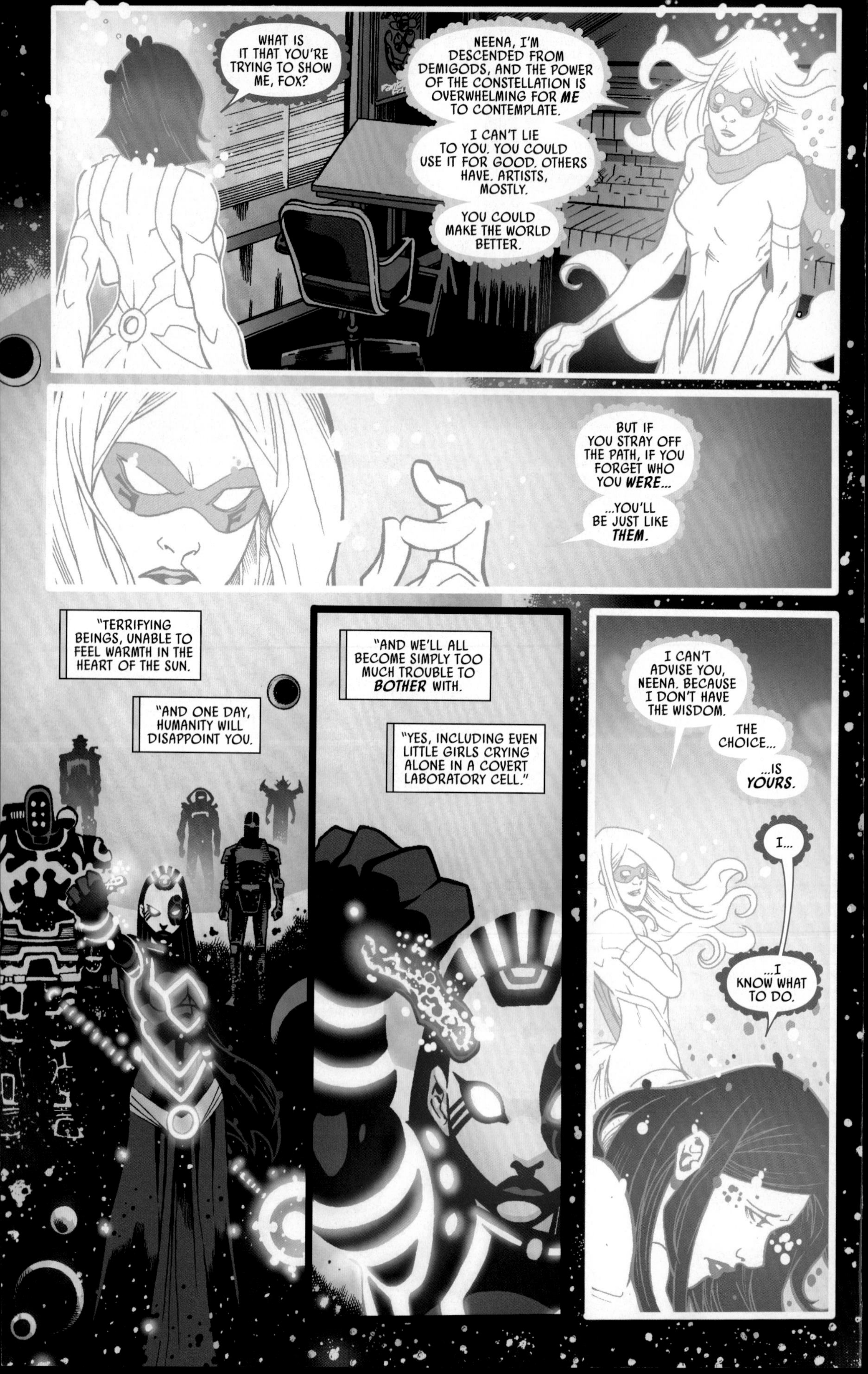
WHAT IS IT THAT YOU'RE TRYING TO SHOW ME, FOX?
NEENA, I'M DESCENDED FROM DEMIGODS, AND THE POWER OF THE CONSTELLATION IS OVERWHELMING FOR ME TO CONTEMPLATE.
I CAN'T LIE TO YOU. YOU COULD USE IT FOR GOOD. OTHERS HAVE. ARTISTS, MOSTLY.
YOU COULD MAKE THE WORLD BETTER.
BUT IF YOU STRAY OFF THE PATH, IF YOU FORGET WHO YOU WERE...
...YOU'LL BE JUST LIKE THEM.
"TERRIFYING BEINGS, UNABLE TO FEEL WARMTH IN THE HEART OF THE SUN.
"AND ONE DAY, HUMANITY WILL DISAPPOINT YOU.
"AND WE'LL ALL BECOME SIMPLY TOO MUCH TROUBLE TO BOTHER WITH.
"YES, INCLUDING EVEN LITTLE GIRLS CRYING ALONE IN A COVERT LABORATORY CELL."
I CAN'T ADVISE YOU, NEENA. BECAUSE I DON'T HAVE THE WISDOM.
THE CHOICE...
...IS YOURS.
I...
...I KNOW WHAT TO DO.

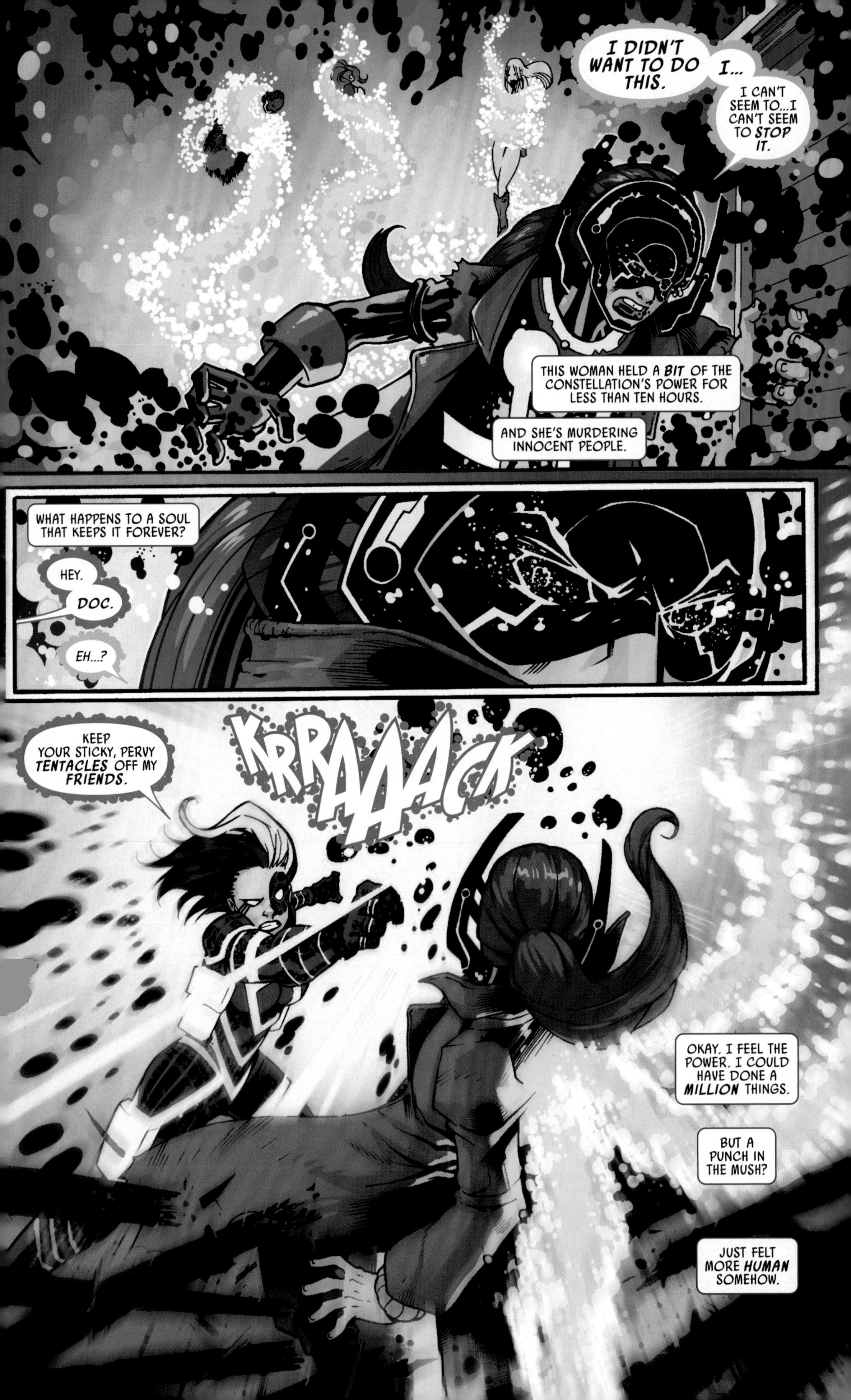

I DIDN'T WANT TO DO THIS.
I...
I CAN'T SEEM TO...I CAN'T SEEM TO STOP IT.
THIS WOMAN HELD A BIT OF THE CONSTELLATION'S POWER FOR LESS THAN TEN HOURS.
AND SHE'S MURDERING INNOCENT PEOPLE.
WHAT HAPPENS TO A SOUL THAT KEEPS IT FOREVER?
HEY.
DOC.
EH...?
KEEP YOUR STICKY, PERVY TENTACLES OFF MY FRIENDS.
KRRAAAACK
OKAY. I FEEL THE POWER. I COULD HAVE DONE A MILLION THINGS.
BUT A PUNCH IN THE MUSH?
JUST FELT MORE HUMAN SOMEHOW.

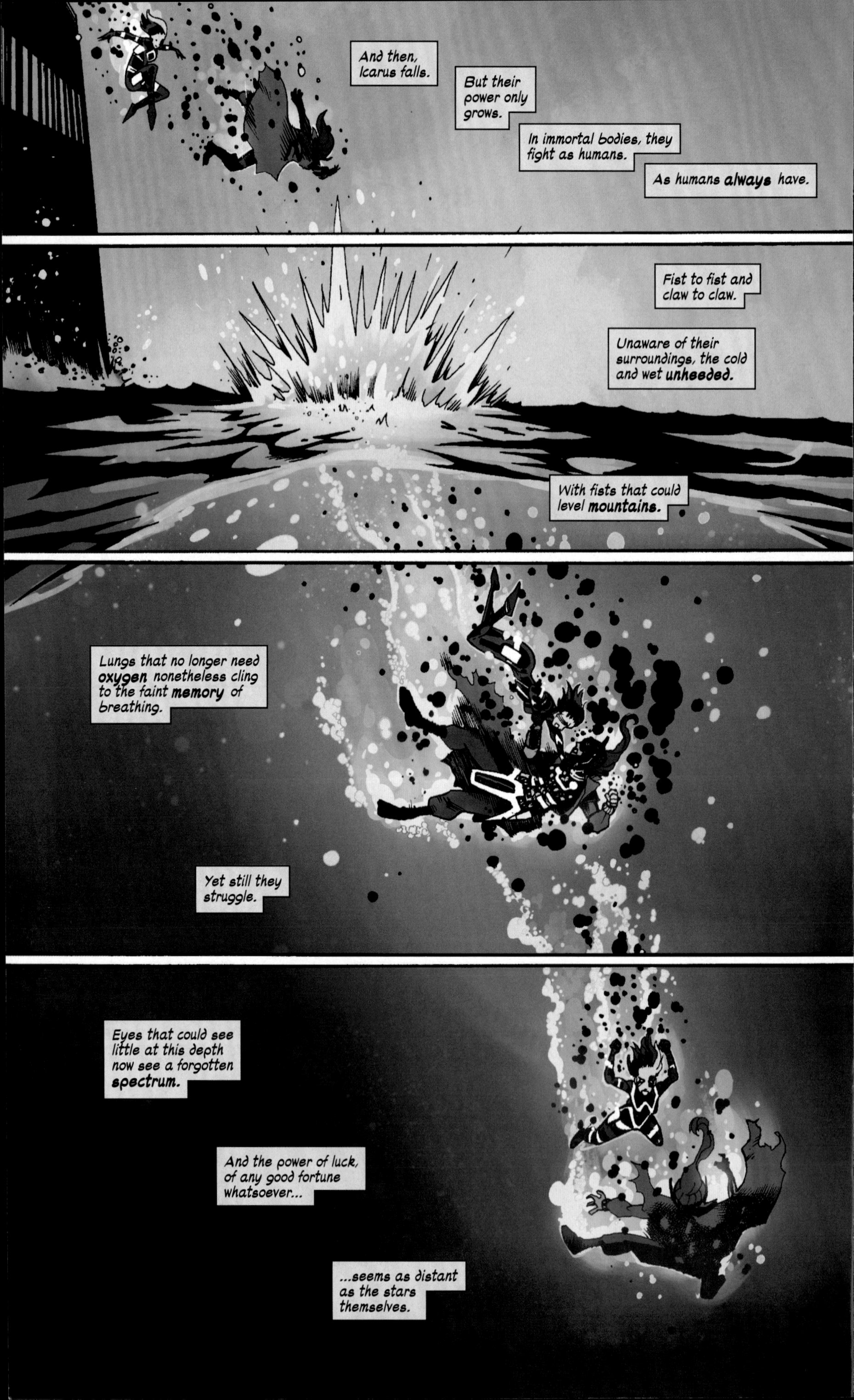
And then, Icarus falls.
But their power only grows.
In immortal bodies, they fight as humans.
As humans **always** have.
Fist to fist and claw to claw.
Unaware of their surroundings, the cold and wet **unheeded.**
With fists that could level **mountains.**
Lungs that no longer need **oxygen** nonetheless cling to the faint **memory** of breathing.
Yet still they struggle.
Eyes that could see little at this depth now see a forgotten **spectrum.**
And the power of luck, of any good fortune whatsoever...
...seems as distant as the stars themselves.

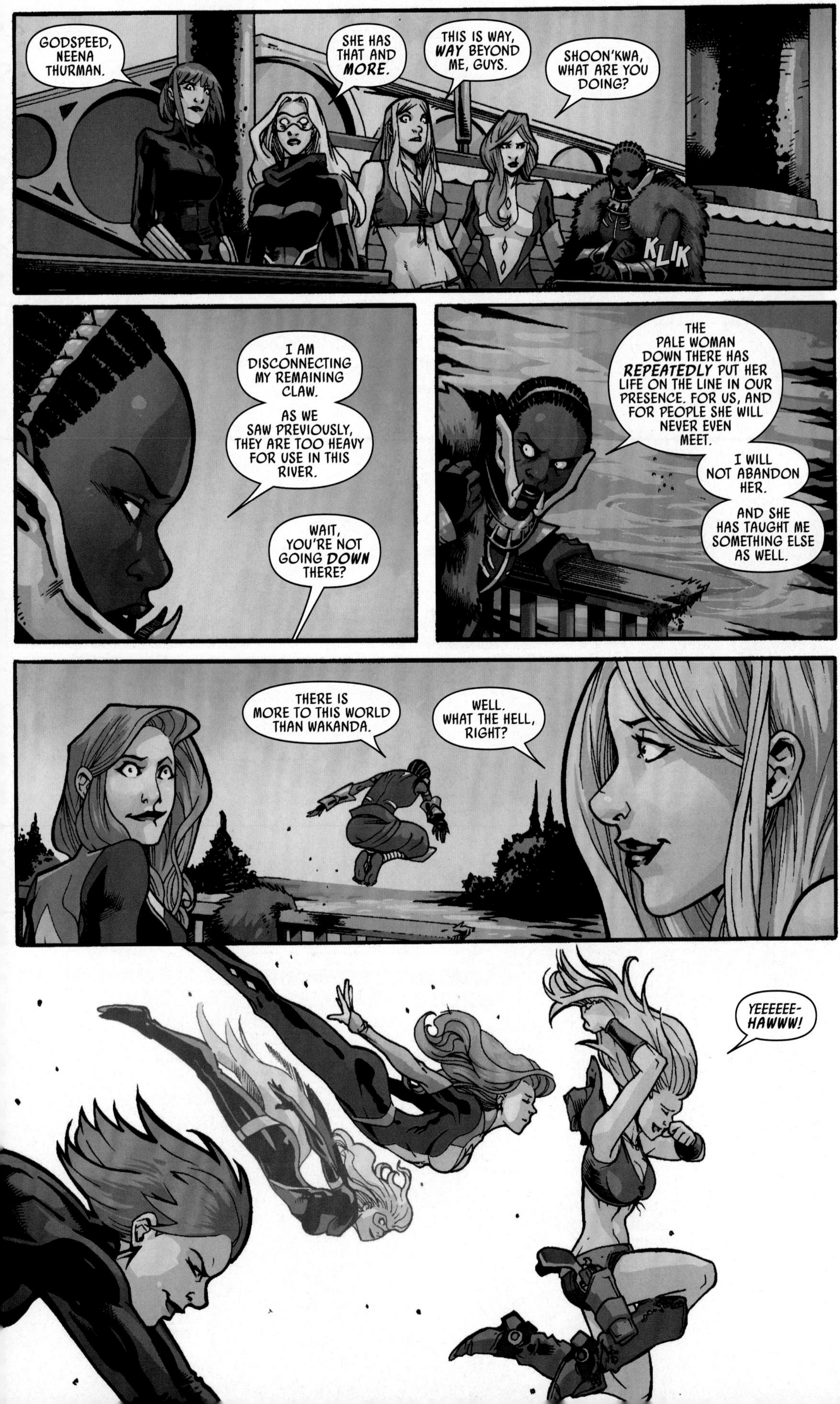
GODSPEED, NEENA THURMAN.
SHE HAS THAT AND MORE.
THIS IS WAY, WAY BEYOND ME, GUYS.
SHOON'KWA, WHAT ARE YOU DOING?
KLIK
I AM DISCONNECTING MY REMAINING CLAW.
AS WE SAW PREVIOUSLY, THEY ARE TOO HEAVY FOR USE IN THIS RIVER.
WAIT, YOU'RE NOT GOING DOWN THERE?
THE PALE WOMAN DOWN THERE HAS REPEATEDLY PUT HER LIFE ON THE LINE IN OUR PRESENCE. FOR US, AND FOR PEOPLE SHE WILL NEVER EVEN MEET.
I WILL NOT ABANDON HER.
AND SHE HAS TAUGHT ME SOMETHING ELSE AS WELL.
THERE IS MORE TO THIS WORLD THAN WAKANDA.
WELL. WHAT THE HELL, RIGHT?
YEEEEEE-HAWWW!

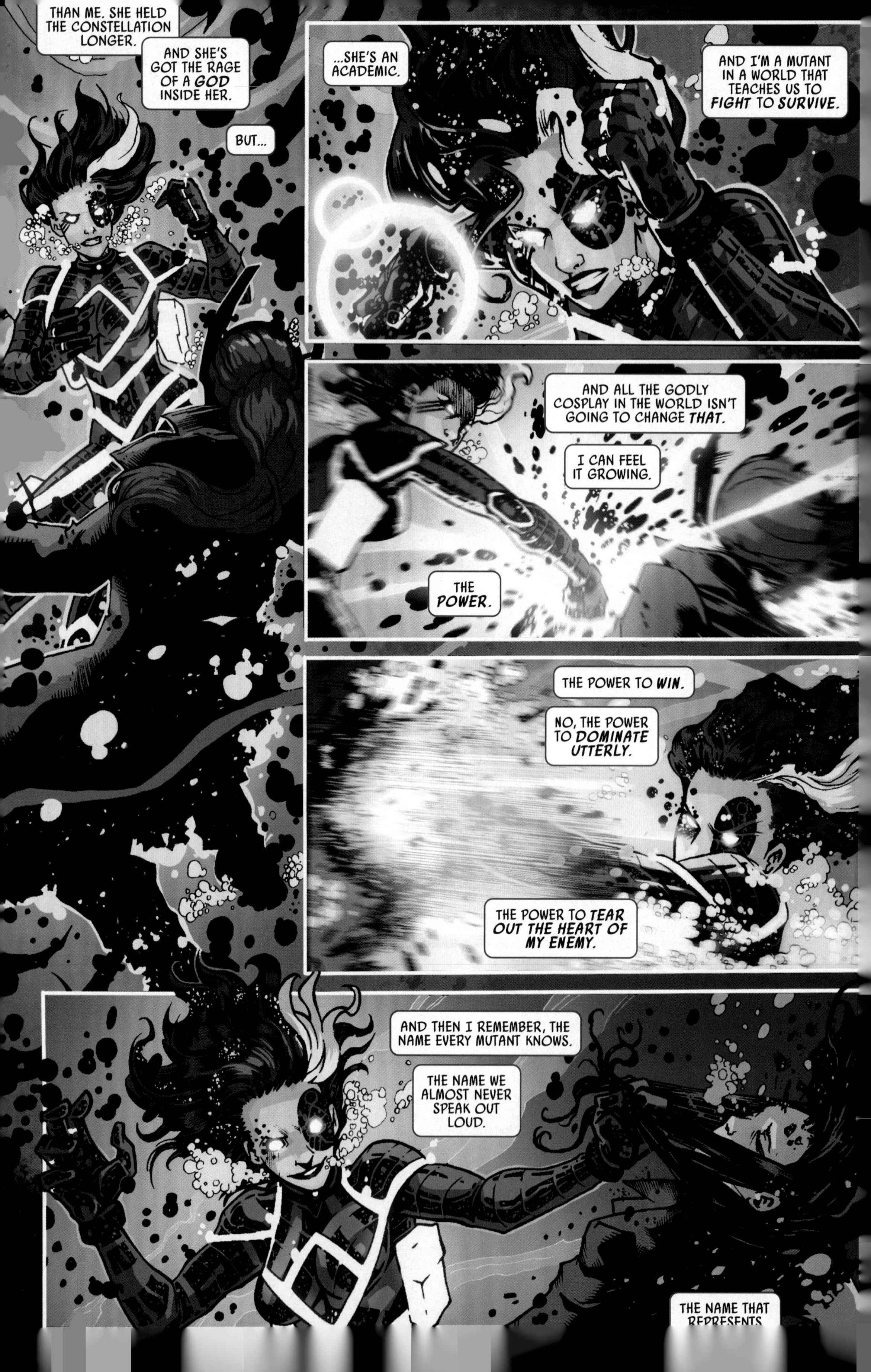
THAN ME. SHE HELD THE CONSTELLATION LONGER.
AND SHE'S GOT THE RAGE OF A GOD INSIDE HER.
BUT...
...SHE'S AN ACADEMIC.
AND I'M A MUTANT IN A WORLD THAT TEACHES US TO FIGHT TO SURVIVE.
AND ALL THE GODLY COSPLAY IN THE WORLD ISN'T GOING TO CHANGE THAT.
I CAN FEEL IT GROWING.
THE POWER.
THE POWER TO WIN.
NO, THE POWER TO DOMINATE UTTERLY.
THE POWER TO TEAR OUT THE HEART OF MY ENEMY.
AND THEN I REMEMBER, THE NAME EVERY MUTANT KNOWS.
THE NAME WE ALMOST NEVER SPEAK OUT LOUD.
THE NAME THAT REPRESENTS

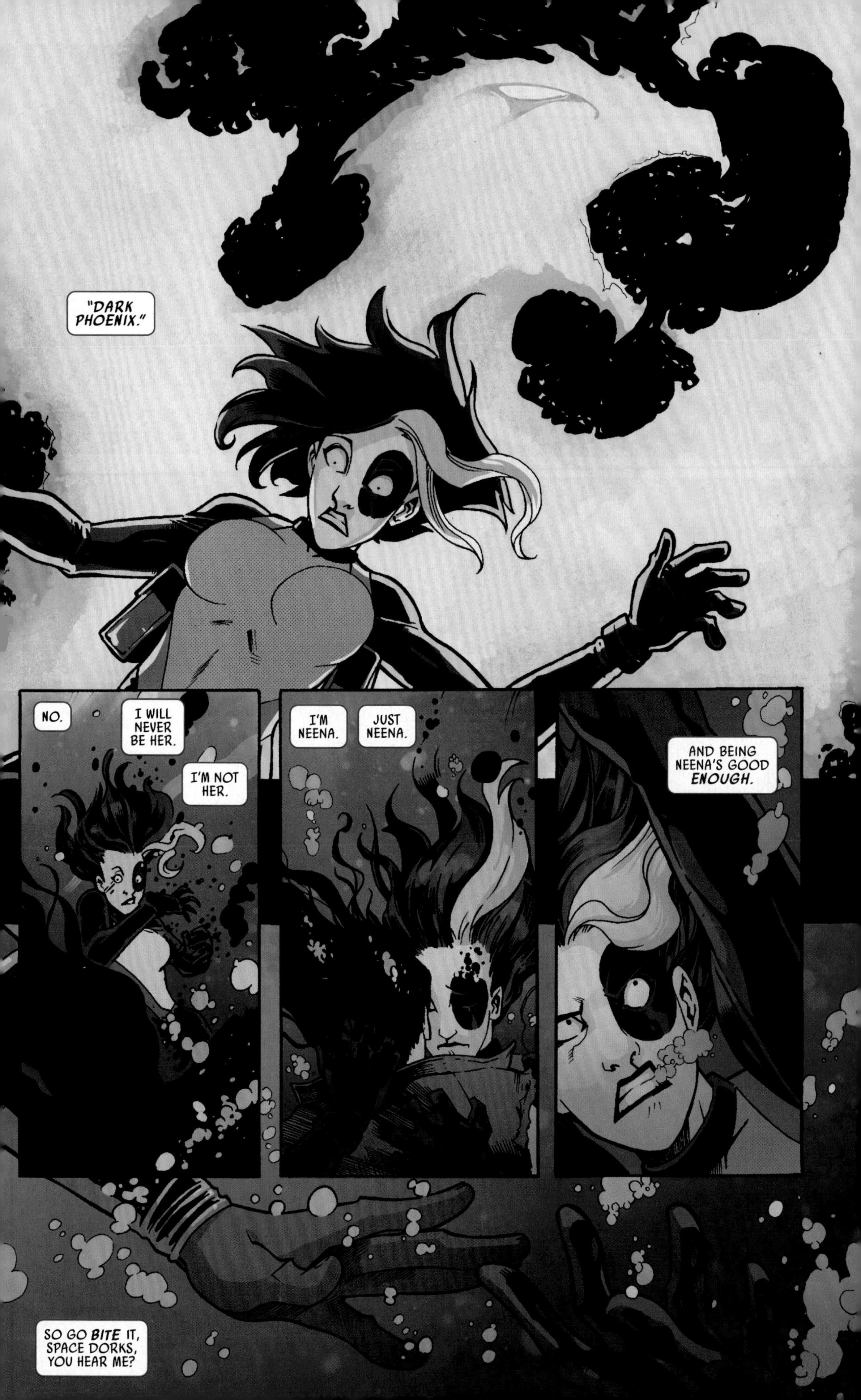
"DARK PHOENIX."
NO.
I WILL NEVER BE HER.
I'M NOT HER.
I'M NEENA.
JUST NEENA.
AND BEING NEENA'S GOOD ENOUGH.
SO GO BITE IT, SPACE DORKS, YOU HEAR ME?

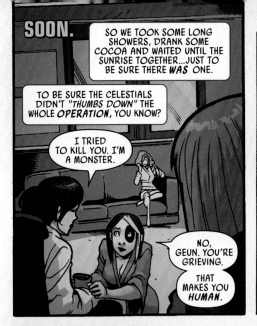

SOON.

SO WE TOOK SOME LONG SHOWERS, DRANK SOME COCOA AND WAITED UNTIL THE SUNRISE TOGETHER...JUST TO BE SURE THERE *WAS* ONE.

TO BE SURE THE CELESTIALS DIDN'T "THUMBS DOWN" THE WHOLE *OPERATION*, YOU KNOW?

I TRIED TO KILL YOU. I'M A MONSTER.

NO, GEUN. YOU'RE GRIEVING.

THAT MAKES YOU *HUMAN*.

YOU DID GOOD, DOMINO. WE WON.

CALL ME IF YOU EVER, YOU KNOW...NEED SOME *AVENGERS* OR ANYTHING.

STRICTLY AS *BACKUP*, I MEAN.

I NEVER MEANT TO LEAD TROOPS INTO BATTLE.

I JUST WANTED TO HAVE A TEAM I BELIEVED IN, I GUESS.

TURNS OUT I GOT *BOTH*.

ATLAS BEAR, THINK YOU CAN ARRANGE FOR THE CONSTELLATION TO BE BURIED IN *VIBRANIUM*, MAYBE?

... IT SHALL BE DONE.

AND *THEN* WHAT, MY CAPTAIN?

THEN?

THEN WE GO TO COSTA RICA AND TEAR A CROOKED ORPHANAGE TO THE *GROUND*.

I NEVER WANTED TO BE A GENERAL *OR* A GOD.

I'M JUST *NEENA*.

AND THAT'S GOOD *ENOUGH*.

END.

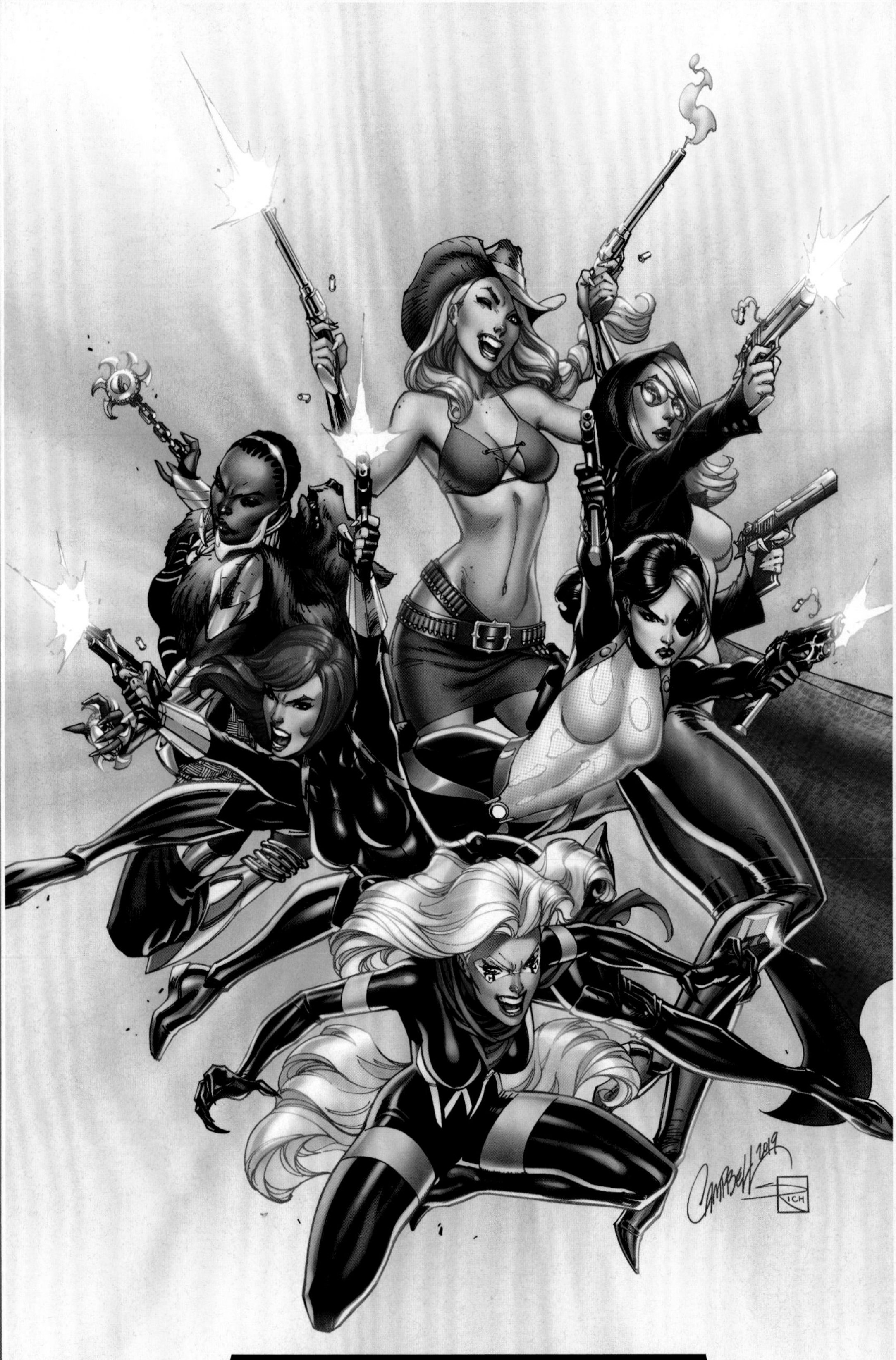

#1 VARIANT BY J. SCOTT CAMPBELL & SABINE RICH

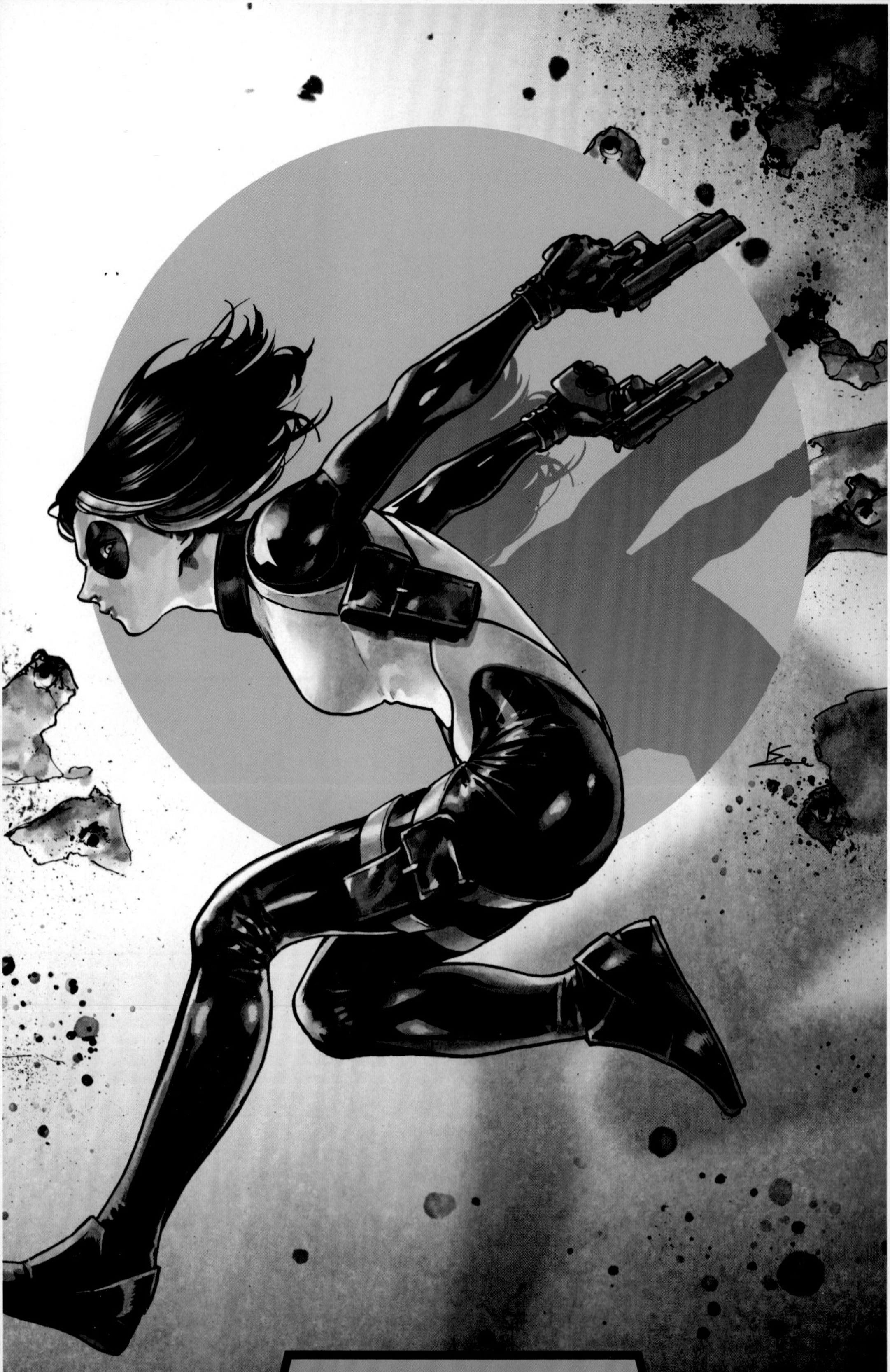

#2 VARIANT BY KAMOME SHIRAHAMA